Assessing Student Learning Outcomes for Information Literacy Instruction in Academic Institutions

edited by
Elizabeth Fuseler Avery

Association of College and Research Libraries
A Division of the American Library Association
Chicago 2003

The paper used in this publication meets the minimum requirements of American National Standard for Information Sciences-Permanence of Paper for Printed Library Materials, ANSI Z39.48-1992.

Library of Congress Cataloging-in-Publication Data
Assessing student learning outcomes for information literacy instruction in academic institutions / edited by Elizabeth Fuseler Avery.
p. cm.
Includes bibliographical references.
ISBN 0-8389-8261-1 (alk. paper)
1. Information literacy—Study and teaching (Higher)—Evaluation. 2. Information literacy—Ability testing. I. Avery, Elizabeth Fuseler.

ZA3075.A85 2003
028.7'071'173—dc22

2003021498

Printed on recycled paper.

Printed in the United States of America.

07 06 05 04 03 5 4 3 2 1

TABLE OF CONTENTS

Introduction

Shortly after the adoption of the *Information Literacy Competency Standards for Higher Education* in January 2000, ACRL applied for and received a National Leadership Grant from the Institute of Museum and Library Services to put these standards to work. The grant focused on training academic librarians in assessment techniques. It supported librarian/faculty teams in designing, implementing and evaluating tools for assessing student learning outcomes resulting from information literacy taught by librarians and faculty.

The grant activity was divided into three phases, a planning phase, an implementation phase and an evaluation phase. During each phase we had meetings at conferences where we were able to meet, discuss progress and get training from the assessment experts. A WebCT space provided a forum for sharing readings, posting and critiquing reports and discussions. Three web-based chat sessions also provided an opportunity to connect and discuss progress. A capstone experience, in the form of a full-day pre-conference workshop, allowed the participants to share their learning and distribute initial results of their assessments.

I cannot overstate the crucial role of Dr. Nana Lowell, Associate Director, Office of Educational Assessment, University of Washington, and her colleague, Dr. Laurie Collins. These two experts provided support for a WebCT-based training program of readings and discussions. More importantly they developed and delivered two workshops: one on the assessment process, and a second one on analyzing and reporting the results. Additionally they were tireless in reading reports and providing feedback and helping steer the grant down a successful path. I am most grateful for having worked with them.

I am very pleased to see that ACRL has agreed to publish and distribute the notable accomplishments of the 24 very hard working librarians. These pages represent two years of hard work on the part of numerous librarians and faculty at campuses across the country. To disseminate widely the results of their rich and varied learning experiences accomplished two of our goals, to share what we have done and all that we have learned, and to provide examples for others to use as they begin to craft plans for assessing information literacy in their institutions.

It has been a great pleasure for me to work with all the grant participants, a group of extraordinary professionals. Working with them has been one of the highlights of my career.

Gabriela Sonntag

Chapter 1: Assessing Information Literacy Instruction

Elizabeth Fuseler Avery

The ALA Presidential Committee on Information Literacy has called information literacy "a survival skill in the Information Age."[1] At a time when the amount of information available is exploding, a focus has developed on the information-literate individual in society. People need to be able to deal with information overload and constant changes in format and retrieval techniques. Colleges are placing increased emphasis on the ability to be a lifelong learner as an outcome of a college education so that their students can continue to grow in their careers and be productive citizens. At the same time, driven by demands for accountability from students and their parents, accrediting agencies, legislators, and governing boards, concentration on assessment has become pervasive in higher education. Often the first attempts at assessing learning outcomes are the result of an impending accreditation visit.

What Defines an Information-literate Individual?

The information-literate person can "recognize when information is needed and have the ability to locate, evaluate, and use effectively the needed information."[2] INFOLIT defines information literacy as "the ability of learners to access, use and evaluate information from different sources, in order to enhance learning, solve problems, and generate new knowledge.[3] The ACRL *Information Literacy Competency Standards for Higher Education* not only defines an information-literate student in its five standards, but it also includes performance objectives and specific outcome statements, as follows:

• *Standard One:* The information literate student determines the nature and extent of the information needed.

• *Standard Two:* The information-literate student accesses needed information effectively and efficiently.

• *Standard Three:* The information-literate student evaluates information and its sources critically and incorporates selected information into his or her knowledge base and value system.

• *Standard Four:* The information-literate student, individually or as a member of a group, uses information effectively to accomplish a specific purpose.

• *Standard Five:* The information-literate student understands many of the economic, legal, and social issues surrounding the use of information and accesses and uses information ethically and legally.[4]

All of these definitions focus on what the student should be able to know and do, not on specific knowledge of tools. As a result, there has been a shift in focus from teaching specific information resources to a set of critical thinking skills involving the use of information.[5]

What about Assessment Is Changing?

Traditional methods of assessment, such as standardized tests, multiple choice, matching questions, and fill-in-the-blank, are designed to test concrete knowledge and not the ability to use search skills in real life. The number of tested assessment tools available to measure student information literacy abilities was few. Early groups, such as California State University and UCLA, worked on developing assessment measures for their institutions. As early as 1995, The Middle States Association of Colleges and Schools was looking at institutionalizing information literacy.[6]

Outcomes assessment of information literacy is different from the traditional assessment of a course or an instructor. It is now the means for learning, not just the method of evaluation. It is designed to inform about the acquisition of skills and thought processes by students. Assessment should be student centered and proactive. The results should be used to implement positive changes in the teaching of information literacy. Assessment is a means of learning, not just a method of evaluation.[7]

According to Lorrie Evans and Diane Turner, assessment should help the educational process for students by (1) getting them actively engaged in the process, (2) encouraging them to think, (3) providing self-assessment, and (4) helping inform them about the purpose of library instruction. Assessment benefits instructors by (1) getting them actively engaged in the classroom and what they are doing, (2) giving them feedback as to the students' thinking and learning, (3) helping them focus on the goals and objectives of the session/course/etc.[8]

Why Should We Assess Information Literacy Instruction?

As librarians, we are accountable to our administrations and faculty, and we need to demonstrate a correlation between library instruction and research skill improvement as a result of undergraduate instruction. We also need to demonstrate the transferability of skills and thought processes learned in one class to other programs and courses.[9]

The ACRL Institute for Information Literacy's Best Practices Initiative emphasizes the importance of integrating information literacy instruction throughout a student's entire academic career and advises using multiple methods of assessment for evaluating programs.[10]

How Do We Make Assessment Work?

First, librarians need to be trained in assessment and data analysis. They need to know a variety of approaches that can be used to measure the institution's need. This will allow the librarian to make informed decisions on what information to collect, in addition to determining how to best analyze and present it.

Second, we need to decide what we want to learn from assessment. Do we want to establish a baseline? Measure improvement from the beginning to end, be it a semester or a college education? Measure retention and/or perceived usefulness of information literacy after graduation?

Third, we need to take into consideration the cost of assessment. Costs are not merely the cost of printing a test. The cost to have individuals, librarians, and faculty actively involved in assessment can be high in terms of work hours and personal investment of energy.

Fourth, we need to involve our faculty. Faculty and librarians working together can create a synergy to transform the traditional bibliographic instruction session(s) into meaningful and lasting experiences that go a long way toward creating lifelong learners.

Fifth, as a result of assessment activities we "encourage dialogue between librarians, faculty and administrators on significant academic issues, such as identifying learning outcomes for student success, finding ways to improve academic programs, and documenting change and improvement over time in student learning."[11]

With careful planning and buy-in from the faculty and administration, assessment should establish the process of ongoing planning/improvement of the program.

The Future

Project SAIL, a joint project of Kent State University Libraries and the Association of Research Libraries, "envisioned a tool to measure information literacy that:

- is standardized;
- contains items not specific to a particular institution or library;
- is easily administered;

- has been proven valid and reliable;
- assesses at institutional level;
- provides for both external and internal benchmarking.[12]

The Institute for Information Literacy, an initiative of the Association of College and Research Libraries, a division of the ALA, proposes to carry out a thirty-seven-month-long project to identify criteria for assessing information literacy programs in undergraduate education, and based on those criteria, to select benchmark programs.[13]

Conclusion

A well-done assessment is essential to documenting the effects of information literacy programs. Such an assessment will acknowledge differences in learning and teaching styles by using a variety of appropriate outcome measures, such as portfolio assessment, oral defense, quizzes, essays, direct observation, anecdotal, peer and self review, and experience. It will assume multiple methods and purposes for assessment/evaluation—formative and summative, and short term and longitudinal.[14]

Notes

1. American Library Association, Presidential Committee on Information Literacy, *Final Report.* Chicago: ALA, 1999. [Accessed 19 February 2003.] Available online from http://www.ala.org/acrl/nili/ilit1st.html.
2. Ibid.
3. Brenda Leibowitz, "INFOLIT: Annual Report July 1997–June 1998," unpublished.
4. American Library Association, Association of College and Research Libraries, *Information Literacy Competency Standards for Higher Education.* [Accessed 28 June 2003.] Available online form http://www.ala.org/Content/NavigationMenu/ACRL/Standards_and_Guidelines/Information_Literacy_Competency_Standards_for_Higher_Education.htm#f1.
5. Abby Kasowitz-Scheer and Michael Pasqualoni, "Information Literacy Instruction in Higher Education," *ERIC Digest,* 2002. ERIC #465 375.
6. Commission on Higher Education, Middle States Association of Colleges and Schools, *Information Literacy: Lifelong Learning in the Middle State Region: A Summary of Two Symposia,* ERIC #ED 386 157.
7. Mark Battersby, "So, What's a Learning Outcome Anyway? 1999. ERIC Document ED430611.
8. Lorrie Evans and Diane Turner, "Assessment on the Fly," presentation at the Colorado Association of Libraries Conference, Keystone, Colo., October 18, 2002.
9. ACRL, Instruction Section, Research and Scholarship Committee, "Research Agenda for Library Instruction and Information Literacy: The Updated Version," *C&RL News* 64 (2): 108–13.
10. ACRL Institute for Information Literacy, "Characteristics of Programs of Informa-

tion Literacy That Illustrate Best Practice: A Draft," *C&RL News* 64 (1): 32–35.

11. Kathleen Dunn, "Assessing Information Literacy Skills in California State University: A Progress Report," *Journal of Academic Librarianship* 28 (½): 26–35.

12. Project SAILS, *Project Description.* [Accessed 23 May 2003.] Available online from http://sails.lms.kent.edu/projdescription.html.

13. National Information Literacy Institute, *Best Practices and Assessment of Information Literacy Programs,* A Project Plan Prepared for the Association of College and Research Libraries, a division of the ALA. [Accessed 28 July 2003.] Available online from http://www.ala.org/Content/NavigationMenu/ACRL/Issues_and_Advocacy1/Information_Literacy1/ACRLs_Institute_for_Information_Literacy/Best_Practices_Description.htm.

14. ACRL Institute for Information Literacy, "Characteristics of Programs of Information Literacy That Illustrate Best Practice."

Also of Interest

ACRL Institute for Information Literacy's Best Practices Initiative. "Characteristics of Programs of Information Literacy that Illustrate Best Practices: A Guideline." [Accessed 15 July 2003.] Available online from http://www.ala.org/Content/NavigationMenu/ACRL/Standards_and_Guidelines/Characteristics_of_Programs_of_Information_Literacy_that_Illustrate_Best_Practices.htm.

Chapter 2: Planning for Assessment

Gabriela Sonntag and Yvonne Meulemans

Many of us have asked ourselves, "I'm teaching, but what, if anything, are students really learning?" Our desire to excel in what we do challenges us to begin to answer this hard question. We want to reframe our work and measure it in terms of student learning. Assessment, as defined by Dugan and Hernon, is to document "observed, reported, or otherwise quantified changes in attitudes or skills of students on an individual basis because of contact with library services, programs, or instruction."[1]

Outside pressures, including campus administration, governing bodies, accrediting organizations, a trend toward standards-based instruction and testing, and the budgeting process, among others, are providing additional incentives for us to initiate a plan for assessing student learning. Measuring student progress with predetermined standards and clear learning outcomes, such as the *Information Literacy Standards for Higher Education*, ensures accountability, quantifies effectiveness, allows for comparisons across institutions, and increases responsiveness to our constituents. It allows us, as educators, to refine and develop our pedagogy, communicate more effectively with others about what we do, and, ultimately, improve student learning.

Challenges

Making the decision to improve can be an easy one. However, moving beyond a desire and actually planning and implementing assessment can be a real challenge to librarians. Already familiar with the constraints placed on instruction, it is easy to identify and be overwhelmed by perceived barriers. Implementing an assessment program can seem too burdensome given regular job responsibilities. Some fear that the results of any assessment may reflect negatively on current programs and services and thus on job performance. Limited possibilities, such as few instructional opportunities or a perceived inability to change the general curriculum, also can lead to resistance. Moreover, librarians can be hesitant because they may lack knowledge about assessment theories or practice. Institutional barriers can include a lack of administrative support for a project that can appear time-consuming, superfluous, and perhaps outside the purview of the library. Despite these challenges, however, librarians already engage in some of the first steps of an assessment plan each time they plan an instruction session. These first, individual steps can eventually lead to a broader approach successfully surmounting these campus obstacles.

Among the early examples of information literacy assessment are those at the University of Northern Colorado and the University of California at Berkeley and Los Angeles. These libraries developed surveys to gather data on aspects of user satisfaction and user self-assessment of information literacy abilities as measured by correct answers on a test. Although these are not forms of "authentic assessment" where abilities are measured as students perform in real-life situations, some useful data can be collected. For example, the Berkeley survey showed that "students think they know more about accessing information and conducting library research than they are able to demonstrate when put to the test."[2] However, the authors of the UCLA test concluded that "sometimes... a testing instrument does not lend itself to measuring certain competencies."[3]

In each of these institutions it was the librarians who worked to develop, administer, and analyze the tests. These campuswide assessment efforts were ambitious and, while advancing our understanding of student information literacy, they also resulted in additional questions about student learning and about assessment of information literacy. The UCLA conclusion sums up the concerns many of us have:

> On the whole, the short multiple-choice test has its limits for assessing a large and complex set of knowledge and skill. Ideas for completely different types of testing should be considered, in which the student would actively demonstrate competence with research strategy concepts and tools rather than passively pick from given choices on a test. This might give a better, more comprehensive impression of information competence and where the weaknesses and misunderstandings lie. Such testing might take the form of live sessions where the tester watches the student search online or open-ended questions where students have to come up with their own research strategies for given topics.

Maughan also concludes that a true information literacy assessment is ambitious and "calls for comprehensive programs of assessment to be carried out . . . not just by librarians but by faculty and other academic personnel on the campus as well."[4]

Patricia Iannuzzi agrees that this challenge of measuring student information literacy must be a collaborative effort involving not just a librarian or the library but, rather, the entire institution.[5] She identifies four levels of assessment (library, classroom, department or program, and institutional level) and recognizes that "[T]here is an increased need for collaboration at each level and the logistics of assessment become more complex. The measure of student learning also becomes more meaningful at each level." She also describes student learning outcomes, names key people to involve, and suggests tools for assessment at each of these levels. Ralph Catts agrees that assessment of information literacy may be difficult but insists that it is a "valid outcome of higher education" that should be assessed in the classroom, across programs, and on an institutional level much the same way that other learning outcomes are assessed.[6]

One path toward achieving this campuswide assessment approach can be through assessment that already may be occurring on an individual level. Consider your own instructional activities. Each time an instruction session is constructed and delivered is an opportunity to measure student learning. Librarians engaged in instruction can implement some basic, yet highly informative, assessment techniques when devising a lesson plan, constructing assignments, and choosing classroom management approaches. Authentic assessment is, among other things, iterative. Librarians can evaluate student learning, implement changes, and continue this cycle so that improvement via assessment becomes an inherent part of the instructional process. Planning an assessment project in collaboration with classroom faculty, a department, or your institution may begin to seem less daunting when assessment becomes a regular part of your instruction. As familiarity and comfort with assessment increase, ideas for assessment with faculty collaboration may increase as well.

Classroom-level Assessment

Concerned about the need to promote student learning assessment at the classroom level, the Association of College and Research Libraries (ACRL) applied for and received a National Leadership Grant from the Institute of Museum and Library Services (IMLS). The purpose of this grant project was to give librarians the skills to create baseline data that supported the merits of information literacy programs. The grant provided training for twenty-four academic librarians to work with faculty to design, implement, and evaluate tools for assessing student learning outcomes generally with a specific course. Some of the experiences of these librarians are shared in this chapter.[7]

Classroom-level assessment can take relatively simple forms. Such approaches are legitimate and highly informative, and implementation and data analysis are still easily managed. In "Assessment for Library Instruction," Sharon Lee Stewart discusses assessment at the classroom level using the Cross/Angelo Classroom Assessment Techniques (CATs) model.[8] This model is described in full in Angelo and Cross's *Classroom Assessment Techniques: A Handbook for College Teachers*.[9] Using the short feedback methods they suggest, such as the minute paper or the muddiest point, we can gauge at any given time in the instruction what students are learning, how much they understand, and how well they have grasped the concepts we are teaching. The importance of this continuous feedback is that we can be confident students are learning. CATs also can be used to gather formative (as you conduct the instruction) or summative (at the conclusion of instruction) student learning information.

This assessment of student learning is very quick to administer and analyze and provides useful feedback for the instructor. But CATs are limited in many respects. Our ability to quantify how much has been learned may be better measured using a pre-/posttest. We may best be able to determine if students have developed critical thinking skills, the behaviors and the abilities to synthesize crucial concepts and ideas, by having them write a term paper or complete another term project. CATs also are limited in their ability to capture the bigger picture of student information literacy skills as a survey or questionnaire would. Dugan and Hernon identify direct and indirect assessment methods for gathering qualitative and quantitative data. Their chart (shown in table 2-1) allows us to quickly review the various methodologies for assessing individual students' information literacy skills.[10]

Iannuzzi also offers alternative techniques. Information literacy assessment within the classroom includes strategies that focus on the course syllabus, the

Table 2-1. Direct and Indirect Assessment Methods

	Direct Methods	Indirect Methods
Qualitative	developmental portfolios, think-aloud/think-after protocol, and directed conversations;	focus group interviews, curriculum and syllabus evaluation, exit interviews, external reviewers, observation, self-assessment;
Quantitative	content analysis, evaluation of theses/dissertations, tests (even ones administered as pre- and post-tests), videotape and audiotape evaluation, and nationally developed tests;	general surveys; satisfaction surveys

products for the course, and the process by which students create those products.[11] Methodologies might include evaluation of bibliographies, reviews of assignments that underscore the research process, and the use of portfolios or journals. Here, Iannuzzi discusses techniques that would be best implemented with the collaboration of the course instructor. These methodologies can provide a rich array of evidence of student learning as well as enrich the student's experience in the course. Student confusion regarding an assignment may be minimized or the types of acceptable information sources may be increased due to librarian and classroom faculty use of existing course materials in an assessment plan.

Ultimately, to make these assessment methods work, the goals and objectives of the instruction must be explicit and fully understood by the students as well as the instructor. Therefore, assessment always begins with thoughtful consideration of appropriate teaching approaches matched to learning outcomes. This is discussed later in more depth.

Collaboration with Faculty

These classroom assessment methods necessitate close collaboration with disciplinary faculty. Depending on campus culture, this may not be easy to do or even imagine. Even a casual review of current literature and job announcements reveals a continuous and growing emphasis on the faculty outreach and collaboration aspects of librarianship. As we work at promoting the library within the university and raising awareness of the teaching role of librarians, it is essential to cultivate strong liaison activities with a core of faculty who *do* recognize our value. Librarians often struggle to articulate to faculty that we complement and enrich their efforts to ensure student learning. Faculty and librarian collaboration can vibrantly illustrate to campus constituents how we contribute to students' educational experience.

Collaboration is based on shared goals, a shared vision, and a climate of trust and respect. Each partner brings different strengths and perspectives to the table. Instructors bring an understanding of the students, their strengths and weaknesses, and the course content to be taught. For example, they may discuss student overreliance on the Web and under utilization of scholarly resources but may not delve further into remedies for this problem. They recognize that student work is not meeting expectations but may not realize that the answer may be in the library. Course instructors also have a knowledge base of their discipline. Their understanding of the information needs of their field can be invaluable when working together to identify what and how to assess information literacy skills. The librarian has a thorough knowledge base of information literacy and a treasure chest of ideas for teaching these skills. In addition, the librarian is much more in tune with students' frustrations with the research process. Successful collaboration requires a dialogue that carefully outlines the roles of each partner, a plan of action, and shared leadership. Classroom faculty want their students to succeed. Communicate with your faculty partner that the assessment project does not serve as a critique of his or her abilities as an instructor but, rather, contributes to the shared goals for the students.

To show different stages of librarian–faculty collaboration and various levels of assessment, we can use the projects under way at the grant participant institutions. The following examples describe how the participants work with faculty, what courses had been selected for the project, and their initial plans for assessment.

> Librarian A: "I plan to work with a faculty member to integrate information literacy into a course and collaboratively design assessment methods. I hope to use this as a springboard for future collaborations. I have started a campus information literacy discussion group, and hope to promote our work through that."

In this first example, the librarian has not begun to work collaboratively with any faculty member. Establishing a discussion group can be a first step toward identifying faculty who might be interested in collaborating on assessment in their course. This group may review current practice and establish benchmarks to begin the assessment project.

> Librarian B: "I plan to work with an English instructor teaching a critical thinking class that includes collaborative research and writing assignments on controversial topics. We have begun discussing how to expand my involvement from a one-hour orientation to more substantial teaching. We will collaborate on revising the course syllabus and explore ways the instructor can take on a larger role in information skills instruction. I hope to be able to compare the information skills of these students (pre and post) to students in the same English course, but in sections that did not participate in the expanded curriculum."

This second example takes collaboration one step further. This librarian has worked with the English instructor in the past, has familiarized himself with the syllabus and assignments in the course, and has initiated a discussion hoping to deepen the collaboration. Initial ideas include revising the syllabus together and exploring ways that the instructor can teach the information literacy skills. The assessment method has been selected with hopes of comparing the course with others that did not receive the instruction.

> Librarian C: "I would like to continue my work with the sociology department here, to more thoroughly integrate information literacy into their

> curriculum, and develop ways to assess what they actually know already and are learning at different levels. I also hope to work with other librarians who are interested in incorporating more assessment into their instruction, as a sort of advisor, based on new things I learn from my participation in this grant project. We have already discussed this in a meeting, and several librarians have expressed interest in becoming involved in some way."

This sociology department has already benefited from close collaboration with this librarian. She has been actively promoting instruction in various courses. The next step is to broaden the collaboration to include a review of the sociology program with an eye toward integrating information literacy in a more systematic way. The assessment of sociology students could include entry and exit learning measures as well as longitudinal approaches. Including other librarians in the discussion allows for expansion into other departments and gives instructional librarians a forum for sharing ideas and experiences. Furthermore, this librarian can provide guidance to his or her colleagues that are embarking on the preliminary stages of an assessment plan.

> Librarian D: "This fall, I hope to do information literacy skills assessment of all the freshmen. I will also be working with twelve faculty members on developing assessment tools for their individual classes in the fall. Over the next two years, I will be doing the same with two other faculty groups. I also need to do an assessment of the entire information literacy program after three years."

This fourth example is the most ambitious as it focuses on all entering students as well as targets specific courses with a view to assessing the IL program in the near future. Mixing projects can lead to confusion unless much planning occurs. High-level collaboration among numerous participants in the project as well as administrative support is crucial. This is an example of a campuswide assessment project. Iannuzzi states:

> Strategies for campus wide assessment of information literacy extend far beyond coordination between the reference librarian and the individual faculty members, and beyond the library instruction coordinator talking to department chairs. Strategies at this level require a library culture for information literacy strong enough to influence a campus culture, and this begins with the senior administrators at our libraries and on our campuses.[12]

Campuswide assessment examples were discussed earlier. Other methods suggested by Iannuzzi include "a review of academic courses and programs for integration of information literacy components, evaluation of syllabi for integration of information literacy outcomes, and incorporation of assignments that promote information literacy. Assessment of faculty development programs could also be a part of campus wide assessment."

The sheer magnitude of a campus project, the necessary level of collaboration, and the cost and human resources needed all pose additional challenges not found in classroom assessments. We have already seen that classroom-level assessment can be more manageable and realistic for the librarian to attempt. The following discussion provides steps for initiating a collaborative assessment project.

First Steps

Much can be done prior to approaching a possible faculty partner. The best first step is to review current practice. This may include a look at feedback gathered from students or faculty after an instruction session or perhaps a campuswide student survey has been conducted that included questions on the library's instruction program. Take advantage of required program or department reviews. These required evaluations may provide a necessary impetus for faculty–librarian collaboration on an assessment project. All of these situations can be used to begin a discussion about student learning assessment with our faculty partners. Petrowski underscores this in saying, "Your assessment program is the richest source of 'perceived advantage' when you are talking to faculty. Find out what and how your program helps students improve their learning, deepen their engagement, and enhance their academic performance. Faculty want their students to succeed."[13] Statistics may already be gathered on how many students librarians have contact with as well as which faculty already work closely with librarians. Gathering existing data can be useful when approaching a possible faculty partner.

The typical fifty-minute session may appear to have limited flexibility to include assessment. Many times, we have marginal control over instructional content and varying degrees of collaboration with the course instructors. Not having faculty status may prove an additional barrier to communication and collaboration with instructors in moving the assessment agenda forward. However, none of these is insurmountable. Focusing on initiating a dialogue that can lead to a strategic partnership for assessment is most important at the onset. As seen in our first example above, starting a successful discussion group and working through issues and concerns may lead to a full-fledged project.

Should existing faculty collaboration be minimal or not occurring at all, consider that assessment can be integrated into your instructional design. As is discussed later in this chapter, clear and focused teaching objectives and learning outcomes can be an invaluable starting block for assessment ideas. Assessment begins with deciding what to teach. For example, in a fifty-minute session, your focus may be on ensuring that students understand the value of the thesaurus in *PsycInfo*. A pretest can simply be to ask students, before you begin the session, to write a brief explanation of why the thesaurus is valuable in *PsycInfo*. Most students will be unable to do so. The posttest can be the same question. Students can fill out a single blank note card for the pre- and posttest. As students leave, have them hand in the filled-out note card. With this process, a data set about student learning during your session has been acquired. This data set also can serve as a piece of evidence as you begin to speak with classroom faculty.

This type of simple CAT also illustrates that a larger assessment plan can begin with the individual librarian. Beginning to instill the habit of measuring student learning, as well as learning the value of assessment during your own instructional time, can serve as further motivation and experience as you embark on identifying faculty partners and implementing a more systematic assessment project.

Outside the classroom, review current assessment efforts on campus and look to the possibility of forming partnerships. List faculty collaborations that could be strengthened and courses where assessment could take place. Determine what data are being gathered on campus. What instruments are used to gather these data? Can this meet your needs, or is something new needed? Reviewing these carefully allows the librarian to become part of the current campus dialogue about assessment. This can prove very beneficial by making it easier to identify allies with similar interests and participants to develop a strategic collaboration for assessment.

One crucial outgrowth of having the *Information Literacy Standards* is that we now can more clearly plan an assessment project and work collaboratively with course instructors. The five standards delineate instructional goals and provide numerous outcomes for assessing student information literacy. These outcomes can become a framework for a dialogue with faculty. For example, the librarian can review a course syllabus and relevant assignments for evidence of information literacy outcomes. Doing so illustrates to the classroom faculty how they may already be integrating and assessing information literacy. The standards can be used to develop a checklist of these outcomes to share with the instructor and to discuss ways to enrich the course by developing the role of the librarian as a partner. Perhaps a fifty-minute library presentation can be expanded to include more time, a Web component, or a library-based assignment.

These examples from grant participants illustrate the role the standards can play in beginning faculty–librarian partnerships:

> "I have used the standards to talk about information literacy/intellectual competencies/developmental research skills. [Different departments use different language...]. This is my focus: use the standards to affirm and focus what is already happening. Also allow faculty to adapt the standards (i.e., within the revision of the political science major) they have identified the criteria for distinction in their department. These resonate with the

> standards although the wording is different. It is important to honor disciplinary discourse."

> "I used the standards in developing the current curriculum, in the areas of identifying a need, identifying the proper sources to meet the information needs, to establish a system for scanning the environment for ideas, to conduct research in company and industry, to evaluate the information, to synthesize the information, and to present it both in a multimedia presentation and in written format. This involved collaborating with faculty for the course development."

> "At this point, they are being used to help faculty determine what they are doing already in their classes and what could be added. We plan to use them in the assessment process as well."

> "I use them when collaborating with faculty... but without expressly saying, 'Let's teach such and such a standard.'"

> "I have not... used them in their entirety with faculty though I will probably use either the key 'performance indicators' or selected outcomes relevant to an assignment we're working on."

Notice in the examples above that although the standards were used, librarians and faculty tailored them to their disciplines and to particular situations. This will increase the standards' relevance to the classroom faculty as well as make them more manageable to use. Keep in mind that for classroom faculty the standards can seem imposing and irrelevant. Your familiarity with the standards is vital to conveying to faculty how they can be fully utilized.

In *Characteristics of Programs of Information Literacy That Illustrate Best Practices,* a result of the Best Practices Initiative of the Institute for Information Literacy, ten categories for developing, implementing, and assessing information literacy programs are defined.[14] The collaboration category (#6) is particularly important for assessing student learning outcomes and provides a thumbnail summary of our discussion of faculty–librarian collaboration. Specific characteristics of a successful information literacy program include:

1. centers around enhanced student learning and the development of lifelong learning skills;

2. engenders communication within the academic community to garner support for the program;

3. results in a fusion of information literacy concepts and disciplinary content;

4. identifies opportunities for achieving information literacy outcomes through course content and other learning experiences;

5. takes place at the planning stages, delivery, assessment of student learning, and evaluation and refinement of the program.

These characteristics may seem difficult to achieve. Begin with small assessment in your own instruction sessions, seek amenable faculty partnerships, and use these partnerships to create a plan to ultimately improve student learning. The shared goal of classroom faculty and librarians is to foster authentic student learning. A clear assessment plan is one step toward this shared goal.

The Assessment Plan

The collegial process, described above, involving meaningful conversations will greatly improve the assessment plan.[15] When you have selected a course or an instructor you are familiar with, reviewed the syllabus and assignments, and considered your own instructional approaches, you can begin a dialogue about assessment. Set up a meeting to explain your goals in terms of student learning and library support. Describe your instructional design process to the instructor. Explain the standards and perhaps provide a checklist tailored to their course or discipline. To facilitate the discussion, apply the standards to an instructor's existing assignments or syllabus and invite the instructor to critique your interpretation. Providing a forum for the instructor to react to can be a powerful discussion prompt and a guide for explaining what you propose to assess. Similarly, invite the instructor to share what he or she wants the students to learn, the teaching approaches he or she uses to achieve this, and how he or she sees a librarian complementing his or her efforts. Identify goals and learning outcomes that you both share. A discussion of what makes a student information literate in a particular discipline can greatly shape the assessment plan and implementation.

After the initial meeting, plan a series of meetings that can include a campus assessment officer to discuss assessment possibilities. Offer examples and ask for suggestions. As the project begins to form, you will want to clearly establish the boundaries of your project and develop this into a written assessment plan. This plan should include the purpose, content, audience, and results of the assessment.

Purpose

A first part of the plan is to define the scope of the assessment. Here you want to discuss and agree on the assessment's purpose or use. A decision is made as to what questions need to be answered in order to get appropriate data. Keep in mind that any current practices and data that already are being gathered. The scope of the assessment states specific goals and objectives, answering questions such as: Why are we conducting this assessment? What are we hoping to learn? Consult your instructional materials and consider pedagogical approaches you have used and are using. These may provide insight about what questions the assessment project aims to answer. Document a schedule for the project. A schedule will include information on reporting and disseminating the results of the assessment and answers the question: What will be done with the results? The process for communicating with the various participants and stakeholders also is a crucial part of this plan, as is establishing a process for monitoring the plan itself and making any needed changes. Focus on articulating all of this in concrete, yet simple, terms. Much in the same way learning objectives must be written to ensure they are measurable, so should your own documentation regarding the greater purpose of the assessment.

Content

The next task is to decide what is to be assessed. What will we be assessing, and how will it be measured? Are we assessing student knowledge (what does the student know?), skills (what can the student do?) or values (what does the student care about?)

Choose something that is important and meaningful. Although this may seem obvious, this decision requires significant consideration. Deciding to measure whether a student can find the interlibrary loan form on your library's Web site may not contribute to a greater understanding of student learning. A short essay question in which a student describes the process of deciding whether he or she should request an item the library does not have may do so. Use the course's goals and relevant assignments to determine outcomes to assess. Match these to the standards and relevant performance indicators.

To ensure that results are useful, it is essential to keep the assessment simple. Do not get overambitious or end up overwhelmed with data that are too complex and impossible to analyze. Use a simple process that will provide clear, accurate data applicable to your objectives.

Identifying learning outcomes is a first step toward creating concrete objectives. Learning outcomes can be articulated in a number of ways. Battersby defines learning outcomes as "the essential and enduring knowledge, abilities (skills) and attitudes (values, dispositions) that constitute the integrated learning needed by a graduate of a course or program."[16] An outcome includes "the bigger picture." A learning outcome can include an attitudinal, behavioral, or cognitive change and sometimes includes all three of these aspects. For example, although an objective for information literacy instruction may be for a student to identify a peer-reviewed journal article, the learning outcome may be that the student understands the nature of scholarly information exchange (cognitive), seeks out peer-reviewed publications when conducting research (behavioral), and values the peer review process (attitudinal).

Objectives are measurable, specific, definable, and observable behaviors, and indicate the expected level of attainment. Despite having the standards as an initial guide, writing genuinely clear objectives is not so easy. But the process of writing objectives is greatly aided by using the standards as a guide. For example, we may want to test Standard Two, Performance Indicator 2 (Constructs and implements effectively designed search strategies.) Specifically, we are looking at Outcome 2.2 (Identifies keywords, synonyms, and related terms for the information needed) and Outcome 2.4 (Constructs a search strategy using appropriate commands for the information retrieval system selected). Different formulas for writing objectives are available in the literature. In the following example, the ABCD formula is used:[17] Given an information problem, by the end of the semester, students in English 101 will be able to identify appropriate keywords from a list and construct at least 2 search strategies using Boolean operators for the MLA database.

The *A* is for the audience: "English 101 students." Who exactly will participant in the assessment? Will it be the entire course, only some of the students or a sample group, several students in each section of the course? Will students be working in groups or alone? The *B* is for the behavior you hope to measure: "identify appropriate keywords," "construct search strategies," and "using Boolean operators." What do you expect the students to do? This part of the objective begins with a verb describing the expected behavior. The *C* is for the conditions under which the students will demonstrate this behavior. For example, "Given an information problem" and "in the MLA database" both set parameters for this behavior. And finally the *D* is the degree, or how will we know that they have done it well? Or how much they have learned? In this example, we expect students to construct "at least 2 search strategies." Another example is shown in table 2-2.

Within a specific course, the chart in table 2-2 will have a column with the header "lecture" or "activity" specifying where student learning will occur or how the library instruction takes place. Another column is added stating how the learning will be measured or the actual test question. In our example, we might have a short-answer test where this objective is included. An information problem followed by a short list of keywords is provided, and short answers are graded

Table 2-2. Search Strategy Assessment

Standard 1: The information literate student determines the nature and extent of the information needed.	Performance Indicator 2: The information literate student identifies a variety of types and formats of potential sources of information.	Outcome d: Identifies the purpose and audience of potential resources.	Objective: Given a list of database titles, students can match topic with "best" database correctly 80% of the time.

to establish that the students can construct "at least 2 search strategies." However, as we prepare to gather data, we still want to answer the following questions: Can current methods be used or adapted? Are new methods needed? If so, what is the best method for gathering these data? Are qualitative or quantitative measures the best method for our goals? Referring back to your own or the instructor's course materials for sources of data may easily answer these questions. A worksheet you use when conducting instruction or the instructor's annotated bibliography assignment may hold numerous, already existing opportunities for data gathering.

Implementing

Should you determine that the data needed are not already being gathered, proceed with the first assessment. As you finalize your assessment instrument, be sure to conduct a pilot study. Gather a few students who are not in the course and have them take the test or use the first cohort of students to use the instrument as your pilot study group. In this study, you are actually measuring the test itself rather than making judgments about student learning. Expect for some issues with the assessment instrument and administrative problems to be revealed. Instructions may be unclear or the assessment may take too much time. The actual answers from students may reflect problems with the wording of questions. Allow for time to revise and address the problems. This added time will only strengthen the data gathered and what is ultimately taken from the assessment project. The assessment instrument must be valid and reliable for it to effect change. Use the assessment instrument only when you are confident that the instrument measures the objectives you outlined in your plan.

The first assessment also can serve as a benchmark. A benchmark is defined as "A surveyor's mark made on a stationary object of previously determined position and elevation and used as a reference point in tidal observations and surveys." This initial assessment allows us to confirm or change our assumptions and identify gaps in our understanding of what students have learned. These benchmark data allow us to monitor change and demonstrate improvement. Benchmark data are necessary should you choose to assess student learning after a particular class, graduate, or even postgraduation. Longitudinal studies rely on benchmark data.

Also consider that an assessment project may need approval of your campus's human subject review board. Although this is not always the case, it is a good idea to consult with someone familiar with such policies. Doing so will ensure that should you choose to report on your results for publication or through other public means, you are not in violation any policy or procedure.

Results

Data analysis can be very daunting, especially should you choose to conduct some sort of statistical analysis. As it is necessary to clearly articulate learning outcomes and objectives, so it is necessary to carefully plan your approach to analyzing data. Some data may be lost due to administrative problems. Perhaps an outside party may be needed to analyze information. Here again, collaboration with faculty can facilitate and strengthen the assessment project. Classroom faculty can provide guidance as results are gathered and analyzed. Problems with data gathering and analysis sometimes can be as insightful as the perfectly executed assessment plan, and faculty partnerships also can provide assistance in determining how to proceed should this happen. Including campus assessment leaders in your project team can greatly facilitate the data analysis stage.

Assessment is best as a continuous improvement cycle and not as a one-shot experiment. As you gather the data, you will want to review the results to see if your initial objectives are met. Go back to your assessment plan and revisit the goals of the project. Review any questionable items in your assessment instrument and revisit the specific data points. Is it capturing the information you need? Do the students understand the questions?

Conclusion

Assessment can be part of every instructional opportunity and experience. The data you have gathered will serve to improve the instruction and ensure student learning. Best practices for classroom-level assessment are to work collaboratively with faculty to measure student learning outcomes, and the process is iterative, cyclical, and leads to action. Difficulty in determining whether students become information literate as a result of a librarian's instruction or as a byproduct of the course itself should not be a barrier to implementing assessment projects. An effective assessment plan will produce data to show that students are learning and that we are accountable and to illustrate the integral value of librarians to the educational process. A common concern of academic librarians is that our contribution to student learning is not recognized. Formal assessment with classroom faculty collaboration can be a major step toward this recognition. Ultimately, librarians must remember that what is important as a result of the faculty–librarian partnership is that students have had a worthwhile educational experience and are now information literate!

Notes

1. Robert E. Dugan and Peter Hernon, "Outcomes Assessment: Not Synonymous with Inputs and Outputs," *Journal of Academic Librarianship* 28 (6): 376.
2. Patricia Davitt Maughan, "Assessing Information Literacy among Undergraduates: A Discussion of the literature and the University of California-Berkeley Assessment Experience," *College & Research Libraries* 62(1): 71–85.
3. Ibid.
4. Ibid., 83.
5. Patricia Iannuzzi, "We Are Teaching, But Are They Learning? Accountability, Productivity, and Assessment," *Journal of Academic Librarianship* 25 (July): 304–5.

6. Ralph Catts, "Some Issues in Assessing Information Literacy," in *Information literacy around the World: Advances in Programs and Research,* ed. Christine Bruce and Philip Candy (Wagga Wagga: New South Wales, Australia: Center for Information Studies, Charles Stuart University, 2000), 271–83.

7. Much of the content for this chapter can be attributed to the excellent workshops offered as part of the IMLS grant by Dr. Nana Lowell and Dr. Laurie Collins, University of Washington. More information on this grant is found on the ACRL Web site at http://www.ala.org/Content/NavigationMenu/ACRL/Issues_and_Advocacy1/Information_Literacy1/ACRL_Information_Literacy_Web_Site/IL_@_ACRL/IL_@_ACRL.htm.

8. Sharon L. Stewart, "Assessment for Library Instruction: The Cross-Anglo Model," *Research Strategies* 16(3): 165–74.

9. Thomas A. Angelo and K. Patricia Cross, *Classroom Assessment Techniques: A Handbook for College Teachers* (San Francisco: Jossey-Bass, 1993).

10. Dugan and Hernon, "Outcomes Assessment."

11. Iannuzzi, "We Are Teaching, But Are They Learning?"

12. Ibid.

13. Mary Jane Petrowski, "Managing Information Literacy Programs: Building Repertoire," in *Managing Library Instruction Programs in Academic Libraries.* Selected Papers presented at the LOEX of the West 2000 conference, Montana State University-Bozeman, June 7–10, 2000.

14. Institute for Information Literacy, Best Practices Initiative. 2003. *Characteristics of Programs of Information Literacy That Illustrate Best Practices.* [Accessed 27 May 2003.] Available online from http://www.ala.org/Content/NavigationMenu/ACRL/Standards_and_Guidelines/Characteristics_of_Programs_of_Information_Literacy_that_Illustrate_Best_Practices.htm.

15. For an example of an assessment plan, see Indiana University Bloomington Libraries plan at http://www.indiana.edu/~libinstr/Information _Literacy/assessment.html.

16. Mark Battersby, "So What's a Learning Outcome Anyway?" Learning Outcomes Network, Centre for Curriculum, Transfer and Technology, 1999. [Accessed 27 May 2003.] Available online from http://www.c2t2.ca/GoodPractice/Exchange/curriculum-frameworks/sowhatsa.html.

17. The ABCD Format for writing objectives was the method taught to the grant participants by the assessment consultants, Drs. Lowell and Collins, at the training workshops.

Chapter 3: Selecting and Developing Assessment Tools

Bonnie Gratch-Lindauer

This chapter describes several types of assessment instruments and methods for measuring information literacy (IL) learning outcomes. Given the length limitations, only brief descriptions can be included, with referrals to specific readings for in-depth information. Because so many of the projects described in this book use performance-based instruments with accompanying rubrics, more detail is included on the development of rubrics. Table 3-1, "Instructional Settings with Instruments/Methods for Assessing Information Literacy Outcomes," is provided as the chapter organizer. For illustrative purposes, references are made to some assessment projects included in this volume and in the literature.

Before describing the various tools and approaches, it is useful to recall some overall principles that ground assessment work. First, a reminder about the purpose of all assessment—to improve teaching and learning—and, second, this important advice from two of the "Nine Principles of Good Practice for Assessing Student Learning" from the American Association of Higher Education (AAHe):

> Assessment is more effective when it reflects an understanding of learning as multi-dimensional, integrated and revealed in performance over time.
>
> Assessment requires attention to outcomes but also to the experiences that lead to those outcomes.[1]

Table 3-1. Instructional Settings With Instruments/Methods for Assessing Information Literacy Outcomes

Learning Domain	Sample Learning Outcomes	Gen. Educ.	Major/Program	Credit course in Info. Lit.	Course-Related/ Integrated	Stand-alone (workshops; online tutorial)
Cognitive **What do students know?**	Identifies key concepts and terms that represent the information need or research topic question. Knows how information is formally and informally produced, organized, and disseminated. Demonstrates an understanding that date or sponsor/publisher of the information may affect its value.	*1. items on standardized or local tests for general education * 2. online tutorial quiz *3. comprehen-sive IL exam 4. items on alumni or graduate surveys of IL skills	*1. items on standardized or local tests for major *2. online tutorial quiz *3. comprehensive IL exam 4. capstone course exam component; 5. senior exit exam or essay 6. portfolio analysis of research products	*1. tests/quizzes 2. embedded course assignments 3. portfolio analysis of coursework 4. CATs**	*1. tests/quizzes 2. embedded course assignments 3. portfolio analysis of research products/assign. *4. online tutorial quiz 5. CATs**	1. workshop exercise *2. online tutorial quiz 3. CATs**

Table 3-1. Instructional Settings With Instruments/Methods for Assessing Information Literacy Outcomes (cont.)

Learning Domain	Sample Learning Outcomes	Gen. Educ.	Major/Program	Credit course in Info. Lit.	Course-Related/ Integrated	Stand-alone (workshops; online tutorial)
Behavioral (performance-based) **What can students do?**	Constructs and implements the search strategy using appropriate search features/ commands for the inform. retrieval system selected. Uses various technologies to manage the information selected and organized. Selects information that provides evidence for the topic.	1. portfolio analysis of research products/tasks in GE courses *2. performance items on standardized or local tests *3. comprehensive IL exam *4. tutorial quiz	1. portfolio analysis of research products or tasks in major 2. capstone performance/ product 3. senior exit essay *4. performance items on standardized or local tests * 5. tutorial quiz 6. items on alumni/ graduate surveys of IL performance	1. portfolio analysis of coursework 2. embedded course assignments *3. performance-based tests/projects 4. online monitoring 5. direct observation checklist 6. CATs**	1. portfolio analysis of research products/assignments 2. embedded course assignments *3. performance-based tests/projects *4. online tutorial quiz 5. direct observation checklist 6. CATs**	1. workshop exercise *2. online tutorial quiz 3. direct observation checklist 4. CATs**

Table 3-1. Instructional Settings With Instruments/Methods for Assessing Information Literacy Outcomes (cont.)

Learning Domain	Sample Learning Outcomes	Gen. Educ.	Major/Program	Credit course in Info. Lit.	Course-Related/ Integrated	Stand-alone (workshops; online tutorial)
Affective **How do students perceive their abilities?** **What do they value?**	Revises the development process for the product or performance by reflecting on past successes, failures, and alternative strategies. Values the variety of information resources and investigative methods, including the librarian and other experts.	*1. learner self-rating of IL skills via questionnaire, interviews, focus groups 2. employer surveys of IL performance 3. alumni/ graduate follow-up surveys	*1. learner self-rating of IL skills via questionnaire, interviews, focus groups *2. survey of instructor rating of student performance 3. employer surveys of IL performance 4. alumni/ graduate follow-up surveys	*1. learner self-rating of IL skills via questionnaire, interviews, focus groups 2. research diary/ journal or reflective papers *3. survey of instructor rating of student perfor-mance	*1. learner self-rating of IL skills via questionnaire, interviews, focus groups 2. research diary/ journal or reflective papers *3. survey of instructor rating of student perfor-mance	*1. learner self-rating of IL skills via questionnaire, interviews, focus groups *2. survey of instructor rating of student performance

* optional to administer pre and post to compare performance. The use of a control group and effective research design strengthen the findings.

** CATs are classroom assessment techniques, such as the "one-minute paper," "the muddiest point," "the one-sentence summary," "what's the principle," etc. (See Thomas A. Angelo and Patricia Cross, *Classroom Assessment Techniques: A Handbook for College Teachers*, 2nd. San Francisco: Jossey-Bass, 1993).

Assessing student learning is extremely difficult because learning is complex and multidimensional. It is virtually impossible to assess what a learner can do or knows and feels about what he or she knows by a single instrument or method. Therefore, the use of multiple instruments/methods is recommended to try and capture learning from different dimensions—cognitive, behavioral, and affective—and when the purpose merits, to plan research designs that will compare groups of learners across time. Moreover, although not the focus of this book, a true picture of student learning tries to assess the quality of the "experiences that lead to the outcomes." These are the features of the learning opportunities, the extent of penetration of IL assignments across the curriculum, and teaching methods and materials that comprise IL instructional programs.

Maintaining a holistic view of the teaching–learning dynamic in outcomes assessment is especially important for several reasons: first, higher education regional accreditation agencies expect institutions to capture and describe findings that reflect the feedback loop of teaching, instructional support, and cocurricular "inputs" in relation to learning outcomes and resulting improvements made; and second, the choice of an assessment tool is connected to the institutional learning environment and its assessment values and practices. For example, in those institutions, such as Alverno College, that have made assessment part of their organizational culture, librarians would benefit from working within the parameters of local assessment values and practices. Some examples might include scheduling to be part of a collegewide assessment week or day, being part of program portfolio assessment, or using standardized testing. Furthermore, in those institutions where IL has truly become integrated across the curriculum, the library is one among several stakeholders with the institutional responsibility to ensure that IL goals are clearly defined and that the various IL elements scattered across the curriculum are identified and assessed as part of a coherent whole. At this time, the author is aware of only one regional accreditation agency, the Middle States Commission on Higher Education, that has finalized a guidelines document, *Developing Research & Communication Skills: Guidelines for Information Literacy in the Curriculum*, for implementing and assessing information literacy throughout the curriculum.[2]

A few comments relating to table 3-1 are needed. First, the author defines "instruments" broadly to include any learning activity, product, performance, or presentation that can be evaluated to produce a measurable score or grade or provide qualitative information to the learner and/or instructor about learning outcomes. Primarily, the instruments and assessment methods included in the table produce scores or grades that might be used—for example, to compare pre- and postperformance and/or experimental to control group performance or comparisons within a class or group. Many of these instruments—particularly course-embedded assignments, a generic category that includes such products as research papers/projects, annotated bibliographies/Webliographies, research process essays, information task analyses—require a corresponding scoring "tool" to assess performance, such as a rubric, scoring checklist, bibliography rating sheet, observation checklist, and so on. However, classroom assessment techniques (CATS) also are included in the columns for courses and workshops. These formative assessment methods are well known to discipline-based faculty and are taken mostly from the Angelo–Cross book, *Classroom Assessment Techniques: A Handbook for College Teachers*. CATS include activities such as the one-minute paper, the muddiest point, and what is the principle, and are used to clarify for the learner and the instructor what is or is not understood within a course period(s); thus, no score or grade would be generated.

Second, one could organize such a chart in may ways, for example, by learning outcomes. Table 3-1, however, attempts to address a variety of institutional sizes, values, and approaches to teaching information literacy and arranges instruments/methods by institutional programs (i.e., general education and major/program), credit course in information literacy, course-related and course-integrated settings, and stand-alone settings (e.g., drop-in workshops, online tutorial, or other self-paced, independent learning opportunities). The table also includes both summative (e.g., comprehensive IL exam, capstone exam/essay) and formative types of assessments (e.g., workshop exercise, course-embedded assignments) with group/class, individual, or cohorts as the locus of assessment. One can observe from table 3-1 that the instructional setting and learner population, such as assessing all first-year students in several sections of a general education course versus assessing a course-integrated learning experience with one group of students, will partially determine the type of assessment instrument. Tests or questionnaires are much easier to use with large groups of students; whereas, course-embedded performance-based assignments are much more typical of course settings.

Table 3-1 includes instruments that yield both direct and indirect evidence. There are other sources of outcomes, not represented on the chart, for obtaining indirect evidence. The following indirect measures, from Peggy Maki's excellent online article, "Using Multiple Assessment Methods to Explore Student Learning," is offered to supplement the chart:

A) "percentage of students who go on to graduate school, providing evidence of how well an institution prepared students for advanced work;

B) retention and transfer studies, providing evidence of institutional success;

C) job placement statistics, providing evidence of how well an institution has prepared students for entry into the workplace."[3]

Assessment of learning outcomes should always strive to use instruments and methods that yield data to provide both types of evidence reflecting the three learning domains. A limitation of table 3-1, however, is that it may appear to suggest that these instruments produce evidence for only a single type of learning domain. This is not always the case. In fact, the reader will notice that certain instruments (e.g., portfolio analysis, embedded assignments, tests) are listed for two learning domains. Clearly, many performance-based instruments yield quantitative and qualitative data, often both direct and indirect evidence, that address both behavioral and cognitive learning outcomes. Likewise, quizzes and tests can include performance-based items in addition to cognitive items.

Assessing Knowledge/Conceptual Understanding

Tests

Currently, there is no standardized information literacy test, although Project SAILS has one under development.[4] Some state teacher certification examinations, professional association certification, and discipline-specific standardized tests include items that address some IL learning outcomes. Indeed, librarians can and do advocate for the inclusion of IL items in locally developed tests used at the institutional or academic and vocational program level. Although tests are often easier to administer and score, unless performance-based items are included, they measure only what students know. Table 3-2 summarizes some of the advantages and disadvantages of standardized versus locally developed tests.[5]

There are many examples of locally developed multiple-choice and short-answer IL online and paper-copy tests in use. The UCLA Information Competence Survey is a good example of a locally developed cognitive test and survey that was field-tested with several samples and used as part of a research study.[6]

Table 3-2. Standardized vs. Locally-Developed Tests

	Advantages	Disadvantages
Standardized tests	1. normative data from other institutions is available 2. easy to administer 3. validity and reliability established	1. contents may not reflect local intended student learning outcomes 2. normative comparisons may be inappropriate 3. expensive to purchase and score.
Locally-developed tests	1. content can be tailored to match intended student outcomes 2. detailed analysis possible to accomplish 3. more likely faculty will use results 4. amenable to a variety of formats 5. faculty "ownership" assured	1. commitment of great amounts of faculty time to develop, score and maintain. 2. lack of normative data for comparison 3. little external credibility for accountability purposes 4. often an absence of validity and reliability research

Source: Nichols, James O. *Practitioner's Handbook for Institutional Effectiveness and Student Outcomes Assessment Implementation*, 3rd ed. New York: Agathon, 1995.

Nearly half of the projects included in this volume used a locally developed test/questionnaire or a combination self-assessment questionnaire and test. A particularly interesting project is the Austin Peay State University project, which used six assessment instruments that included a pre- and postquestionnaire/test. The project employed a quasi-experimental design within three different instructional settings (i.e., none, active learning, and lecture). Complementing the cognitive assessment is a performance-based Web site evaluation assignment and a self- and peer assessment questionnaire with items that assess the learner's perceptions of his or her IL instruction. Indeed, when testing is used to try and prove that IL instruction causes an improvement in scores, careful attention is required to the research design, sampling, and other features of experimental research. Other examples have used a combination of cognitive and performance-based tests. One project described in this book is the Bay Area Community Colleges Information Competency Assessment Project. This two-year-plus project involved a collaboration of six California community college librarians to develop and administer two field tests of a two-part challenge out exam that can be used at community colleges that have an IL graduation requirement or adapted for other assessment purposes. It is composed of a forty-six item cognitive test and a fourteen-item performance-based activity. In addition to the information provided in this volume, the reader can obtain more information about its development at the project Web site and in an upcoming Jossey-Bass publication.[7]

Three other well-known examples connected to IL requirements are the Information Literacy Competency Exam used at Weber State University, which combines twenty-five multiple-choice questions with approximately twelve performance-based items;[8] the Web-based tutorial "Go for the Gold" with its Information-seeking Skills Test used at James Madison University for its general education IL requirement;[9] and the Web-based tutorial with quizzes, OASIS: Online Advancement of Student Information Skills, used at CSU-San Francisco State University.[10] The ACRL Information Literacy Assessment Issues Web page has links to many other examples of tests and tutorials employing quizzes that test the cognitive dimension of IL skills.[11]

Test developers must pay close attention to the design and wording of multiple-choice and other item formats commonly used on locally developed objective tests. A very concise and useful source can be found in the chapter, "Using Multiple Choice and Other Objective Measures," in *Natural Classroom Assessment* by Smith, Smith and De Lisi listed in the Selected Sources at the end of this chapter.

Performance-based Instruments and Methods

A growing number of colleges and universities are using performance-based instruments to assess specific IL skills in a variety of instructional settings, but particularly in course-related and integrated settings. There is almost no limit to the variety of performance-based instruments, largely because of the many course-embedded assignments developed by faculty and collaborating librarians, such as speeches, presentations, research papers/projects, annotated bibliographies/ Webliographies, and research essays/journals that describe the process of doing research, and direct observation with behavior checklists or online monitoring of performance on specific tasks. Slightly more than half of the assessment projects showcased in this book are performance based and use scoring rubrics to evaluate and quantify the performance. Authentic assessments are nearly always some type of performance-based task or project that simulates a real-world information retrieval, evaluation, and/or communication activity. As previously noted, quizzes and tests can be designed to include both cognitive and performance-based items, especially those administered online. A couple of larger institutional or systemwide IL assessment projects using an analysis of student work/products, information scenarios, or information-seeking and evaluating tasks include:

• Washington Assessment of Information and Technology Literacy Project, a consortium of six higher education institutions in the state of Washington that has been working in this area for several years and has based its work on the following assumptions: "that student ability to access and use information is a complex task best observed in samples of student work; work products should be supplemented by some type of student reflection to provide a more complete picture of the process used; and because information is stored and used somewhat differently within various subject areas, assessment of information and technology literacy should take place within the academic discipline."[12]

• California State University (CSU) Information Competence Initiative, along-standing and impressive systemwide initiative dating back to 1995 that has spawned a variety of instructional products and assessment instruments, such as Web-based tutorials with quizzes, curriculum integration projects with course-embedded assignments, summer faculty development workshops to reshape curricular offerings, outreach effort to high schools and community colleges through teacher–librarian collaboration, support for a campus online information competence graduation requirement, and the creation of various information competence courses and programs at the undergraduate and graduate levels.[13]

A major initiative of the Educational Testing Service (ETS), announced in May 2002 on the information literacy page of the ETS Web site (http://www.ets.org/research/ictliteracy/index.html), is the proposed development of an information and communication technologies literacy assessment. The report, *Digital Transformation: A Framework for ICT Literacy*, from ETS's International ICT Literacy Panel, provides a foundation for the design of instruments.[14] The report's appendixes include examples of sample ICT tasks, which are authentic assessment tasks of practical information seeking assessing multiple learning outcomes.

Portfolios

Some academic programs use portfolios, which are a collection of student work across a semester, a year, or several years. They can be used to assess student learning through several assignments in a course or through assignments in several courses required in a program. They also can help a student become more aware of his or her learning process if the student is required to reflect upon and evaluate his or her own learning. In this book, the Millersville University project, "Assessing Abilities of Freshmen to Reconcile New Knowledge with Prior Knowledge," is an example of a portfolio of several drafts of a research essay accompanied by a reflective essay and corresponding rubric. Several of the sources listed about portfolios at the end of this chapter elaborate on the purposes and related portfolio entries depicted in table 3-3.

Rubrics

Performance-based instruments that include written, presented, or performed work typically require the development of some type of scoring tool, such as a checklist, a rating scale/sheet, or a scoring rubric to differentiate and quantify performance. In this book, Appalachian State University's project, "Information Literacy Assessment for Introductory Music," illustrates the use of a project checklist, and an example of a rating sheet is the bibliography rating sheet used by the Hunter College project, "Past Lives: An Exercise in Historical Research with an Annotated Bibliography Requirement."

Rubrics are defined by Craig A. Mertler "as scoring guides, consisting of specific pre-established performance criteria, used in evaluating student performances or products resulting from a performance task."[15] The two types of rubrics are holistic and analytic. A holistic rubric is designed to score the overall process or product as a whole, without judging the separate parts. Mertler explains that "holistic rubrics are probably more appropriate when performance tasks require

Table 3-3. Portfolio Goals and Related Entries

Goal/Purpose	Entries in Portfolio
To evaluate the achievement of intended learning outcomes.	Best work exemplifying outcomes
To demonstrate the breadth with which learning outcomes have been achieved.	Work representing a range of accomplishments
To illustrate the process associated with achieving a learning outcome.	Multiple drafts or versions that represent a chronology of progress.
To understand one's own learning.	Written reflections about learning.

Source: Huba, Mary E., and Jann E. Freed. *Learner-Centered Assessment on College Campuses.* Boston: Allyn & Bacon, 2000.

Table 3-4. Template for Holistic Rubrics

Score	Description
5	Demonstrates complete understanding of the problem. All requirements of task are included in response.
4	Demonstrates considerable understanding of the problem. All requirements of task are included.
3	Demonstrates partial understanding of the problem. Most requirements of task are included.
2	Demonstrates little understanding of the problem. Many requirements of task are missing.
1	Demonstrates no understanding of the problem.
0	No response/task not attempted.

Source: Mertler, Craig A. "Designing Scoring Rubrics for your Classroom." *Practical Assessment, Research & Evaluation*. 7 (25). 2001. http://ericae.net/pare/getvn.asp?v=7&n=25.

students to create some sort of response and where there is no definitive correct answer.... and when errors in some part of the process can be tolerated provided the overall quality is high."[16] (See table 3-4.)

Nearly all of the rubrics included in this book's projects are analytic rubrics, as they were designed for scoring individual parts of the product/performance first, then summing the scores to obtain a total score. The only example of a holistic rubric is the one created for the Illinois Wesleyan University assessment project, which was for an ethnographic journal assessment. Mertler explains that "analytic rubrics are usually preferred when a fairly focused type of response is required¼. for performance tasks in which there may be one or two acceptable responses and creativity is not an essential feature of the students' responses."[17] As the reader has probably noticed, analytic rubrics are more time-consuming to develop and score, but they provide more feedback to the student and the instructor than do holistic rubrics. There are twelve examples of analytic rubrics in this book. One project, the Highline Community College's project, "Using Rubrics to Assess Information Literacy Attainment in a Community College Education Class," provides examples of three rubrics for orally presented and written work.

Developing rubrics requires several steps and decisions about criteria, levels of achievement, and dimensions of quality. The development process includes:

1. stating the specific information literacy learning outcomes;
2. identifying specific observable attributes in the product, process, or presentation;
3. brainstorming characteristics that describe each attribute;
4. writing narrative description for the levels of performance ranging from excellent to poor work for each attribute;

5. collecting samples of student that illustrate each level;
6. using these samples to evaluate the rubric and make revisions.

Before getting too far into the development of the rubric, these three questions could be useful, as they might suggest the need for an additional assessment instrument, such as some type of instrument to capture student self-reflection, for example, if the process is as important as the outcome.

1. What content must students master in order to complete the task well?
2. Are there any important aspects of the task that are specific to the context in which the assessment is set?
3. Is the process of achieving the outcome as important as the outcome itself?

Table 3-5 lists six essential questions to help structure the development process.

Rubrics typically include several elements (i.e., statement of criterion to be assessed; description of performance levels; scores) illustrated in table 3-6, a template that was adapted from three different rubrics.

In addition to these elements, rubrics might include examples derived from student work to illustrate each of the performance levels and possibly notes on scoring. One of the more challenging tasks is to devise language that clearly distinguishes the meaning of the various performance levels. For example, most scorers would correctly recognize a research topic that has been sufficiently narrowed to be appropriate for a three- to five-page research paper. However, coming up with a description of what characterizes a sufficiently narrow research topic that could be applied across research questions is another matter. The example above tries to delineate aspects of an exemplary research topic. To improve interrater reliability it is especially important to have clear descriptions with examples so that any librarian-scorer would be likely to rate the criterion with the same score.

Table 3-5. Questions to Ask When Constructing/Revising Rubrics

1. What criteria or essential elements must be present in the student's work to ensure that it is high in quality?
2. How many levels of achievement (mastery) do you want to illustrate for students?
3. For each criteria or essential element of quality, what is a clear description of performance at each achievement level?
4. What are the consequences of performing at each level of quality?
5. What rating scheme will you use in the rubric?
6. When you use the rubric, what aspects work well and what aspects need improvement?

Source: Huba, Mary E., and Jann E. Freed. *Learner-Centered Assessment on College Campuses.* Boston: Allyn & Bacon, 2000.

Table 3-6. Template for Analytic Rubrics—Example of Part of a Rubric for a Research Paper

	Beginning 1	Developing 2	Accomplished 3	Exemplary 4	Score
Criteria #1 Research topic	Topic is not narrowed; topic is poorly narrowed.	Topic has been somewhat narrowed but not sufficiently for a 3-5 page paper.	Topic is passably narrowed for a 3-5 page paper	Topic is well narrowed by specifying time frame, or persons, or organization or group, or location, or event or incident, or some combination of these **AND** is suitable for a 3-5 page paper.	Range= 0-4 pts.
Criteria #2 Develop-ment of ideas	Minimal idea development, limited, limited and/or unrelated details	Unelaborated idea development; unelaborated and/or repetitious details	Deep idea development supported by elabo-rated, relevant details	Deep and complex ideas supported by rich, engaging, and pertinent details; evidence of analysis, reflection and insight	Range= 0-4 pts
Criteria #3 Grammar and format	Numerous errors in grammar and format (e.g. spelling, punctua-tion, capitalization)	Several errors in grammar and/or format that do not interfere with communication	Few errors in grammar or format relative to length and complexity	Virtually no errors in grammar or format.	Range= 0-4 pts
Criteria #4 Organiza-tion	Random or weak organization	Lapses in focus and/ or coherence	Logical organization	Careful and/or suitable organization	Range= 0-4 pts
Criteria #5 Voice and tone	Limited awareness of audience	An attempt to communicate with the audience	Evidence of voice and/ or suitable tone	Evidence of distinguished voice and/or appropriate tones.	Range= 0-4 pts

The reader is directed to the documents in the Selected Sources by Emmons and Martin, Moskal, Mertler, Huba, and the ERIC Clearinghouse on Assessment and Evaluation for more information about developing rubrics. Moreover, a free rubric generator is available on the Web that provides many templates used by teachers and the option of generating one's own rubric, "Rubrics and Rubric Makers—Automated Web-based Rubric Maker for Teachers" (http://www.teachnology.com/web_tools/rubrics/).

Instruments to Measure Affect and Survey Use of Research Tools

Instruments that measure what students feel they know, how confident they are, and how they use research tools and feel about doing research include self-rating checklists, questionnaires, focus groups, interviews, and research diary/journals that include reflective comments. As indicated in table 1, these can be used in a pre- and posttest setting and can be combined with surveys of classroom faculty members' perceptions about student IL skills. Surveys, whether by mail, phone or on the Web, have the advantage of potentially reaching a large number of people, both inside and outside a typical classroom setting.

Focus groups, though more useful to probe for more detail and interpretations behind questions, are extremely time-consuming and typically reach a smaller number of people. If a research diary/journal or reflective essay is used, some type of content analysis employing a checklist or simple rubric will be required to assess them. It is not uncommon to find libraries using questionnaires that are actually cognitive tests with some questions about previous library use and IL instruction. Perhaps the thought is that students will not be as alarmed by the word *questionnaire.* These types of instruments are particularly useful in combination with performance-based and/or cognitive instruments because items can be included that ask about previous IL instruction, use of research tools, and self-rating of IL skills. The results of such items can then be cross-tabulated with scores on a cognitive test and/or performance-based activity so that a comparison can be made between the direct evidence of the actual performance and the indirect evidence of the student's self-rating. Just one example of this type of comparison in the literature is the University of California-Berkeley's Teaching Library's Information Literacy Survey (http://www.lib.berkeley.edu/TeachingLib/Survey.html), where it was found that those scoring higher on the cognitive items had previously received some library instruction. Several of the projects in this book combine a survey/questionnaire of student perceptions about what they learned with performance-based or multiple-choice style tests, such as the Oberlin College project, "Assessing Student Learning in Sociology," and the Regent University project. The reader is referred to the following writers for more information about developing and using qualitative instruments for surveys, interviews, and focus groups: Dillon, Fowler, Krueger, Rubin and Rubin, and Shannon.

Conclusions

The choice of an assessment instrument is made after consideration is given to the purpose, audience for and use of the assessment findings, and resources available. The institutional purpose, such as accreditation self-studies or institutional program review, is likely to influence the type of instrument selected. What is most important to remember is that (1) the specific learning outcome(s) to be assessed usually determines the instrument/method; (2) the use of multiple instruments/methods yields richer data for more than one learning domain; (3) collaborating with various academic stakeholders in the selection, development, and use of instruments results in better instruments and findings; and (4) there is support and help on every campus in such places as a research services office or a faculty assessment center or from faculty colleagues who have experience in developing learning outcomes assessments.

Notes

1. Alexander W. Astin, et al., "Nine Principles of Good Practice for Assessing Student Learning," *Assessment Forum*, American Association of Higher Education. [Accessed 23 May 2003.] Available online from http://www.aahe.org/assessment/principl.htm.

2. Middle States Commission on Higher Education, *Developing Research & Communication Skills: Guidelines for Information Literacy in the Curriculum* Draft #6 (March 2001). For information contact Oswald Ratteray at Middle States Commission at http://www.msache.org.

3. Peggy Maki, "Using Multiple Assessment Methods to Explore Student Learning and Development inside and outside the Classroom," *NetResults* (Jan. 2002). [Accessed 23 May 2003.] Available online form http://www.naspa.org/NetResults/PrinterFriendly.cfm?ID=558.

4. Lisa G. O'Connor, Carolyn J. Radcliff, and Julie A. Gedeon, "Applying Systems Design and Item Response Theory to the Problem of Measuring Information Literacy Skills," *College and Research Libraries* 63 (2002): 528–43. Also see the Project SAILS site at http://sails.lms.kent.edu/index.php.

5. Derived from the handout "Pros and Cons of Testing for Cognitive Learning," Research and Planning Group Student Learning Outcomes and Assessment Workshops, California Community Colleges, Mar. 2003.

6. UCLA Library, "Information Competence at UCLA: Report of a Survey Project" (spring 2001). [Accessed 15 May 2003.] Available online from http://www.library.ucla.edu/infocompetence/index_noframes.htm.

7. Background information, revised performance outcomes, and other documents related to the Bay Area Community Colleges Information Competency Assessment Project are found at http://www.topsy.org. A chapter describing the development and field-testing of the instruments is forthcoming (fall 2003) in the Jossey-Bass book, *Integrating Information Literacy Competency into the Disciplines.*

8. Weber State University Stewart Library, Information Literacy Example Sample Questions (Jan. 2003). [Accessed 23 May 2003.] Available online from http://library.weber.edu/il/infolit/infolitcomp/sample.asp.

9. James Madison University Libraries, Information-seeking Skills Test. [Accessed 23 May 2003.] Available online from http://www.lib.jmu.edu/library/gold/isst.htm.

10. California State University at San Francisco, J. Paul Leonard Library, OASIS (updated May 2003). [Accessed 23 May 2003.] Available online form http://oasis.sfsu.edu/.

11. ACRL, "Information Literacy Assessment Issues." [Accessed online 23 May 2003.] Available online from http://www.ala.org/Content/NavigationMenu/ACRL/Issues_and_Advocacy1/Information_Literacy1/ACRL_Information_Literacy_Web_Site/IL_in_Classrooms/Assessment_Issues.htm.

12. See the project Web site at http://depts.washington.edu/infolitr/project.htm.

13. See the results of the early phases of the CSU Information Competence Assessment Initiative at http://www.csupomona.edu/~kkdunn/Icassess/ictaskforce.html. More current information about the CSU Information Competence Initiative is available at http://www.calstate.edu/LS/infocomp.shtml, and some links to assessment and evaluation instruments are available at http://www.calstate.edu/LS/Assessment.shtml.

14. Educational Testing Service (ETS), *Digital Transformation: A Framework for ICT Literacy—A Report of the International ICT Literacy Panel* (Princeton, N.J.: ETS, 2002). Also available online from http://www.ets.org/research/ictliteracy/ictreport.pdf.

15. Craig A. Mertler, "Designing Scoring Rubrics for Your Classroom," *Practical Assessment, Research & Evaluation* 7 (2001). [Accessed 23 May 2003.] Available online from http://ericae.net/pare/getvn.asp?v=7&n=25.

16. Ibid.

17. Ibid.

Selected Sources

General/Multi-instrument

Angelo, Thomas A., and K. Patricia Cross. 1993. *Classroom Assessment Techniques: A Handbook for College Teachers*, 2nd ed. San Francisco: Jossey-Bass.

Borden, Victor M., and Jody L. Owens. 2000. *Measuring Quality: Choosing among Surveys and Other Assessments of College Quality.* Washington, D.C.: Association for Institutional Research and the American Council on Education.

Educational Resources Information Center (ERIC) Clearinghouse on Assessment and Evaluation. At this URL, click on the "Scoring Rubrics" link for an automatic search of this clearinghouse at http://ericae.net/sinprog.htm.

Huba, Mary E., and Jann E. Freed. 2000. *Learner-centered Assessment on College Campuses.* Boston: Allyn & Bacon. (See chapter 6 on developing rubrics and chapter 8 for use of portfolios.)

Maki, Peggi. 2002. "Using Multiple Assessment Methods to Explore Student Learning and Development inside and outside the Classroom." *NetResults* (15 Jan. 2002). Available online from http://www.naspa.org/NetResults/PrinterFriendly.cfm?ID=558. [Accessed 1 May 2003.]

Merz, Lawrie H., and Beth L. Mark. 2002. *Assessment in College Library Instruction Programs: CLIP Notes #32.* Chicago: ALA.

Nichols, James O. 1995. *Practitioner's Handbook for Institutional Effectiveness and Student Outcomes Assessment Implementation,* 3rd ed. New York: Agathon.

Pellegrino, James A., Naomi Chudowsky, and Robert Glaser, eds. 2001. *Knowing What Students Know: The Science and Design of Educational Assessment.* Landover, Md.: National Academies Press. Available online from http://www.nap.edu/books/0309072727/html/.

Rubin, Herbert J., and Irene S. Rubin. 1995. *Qualitative Interviewing: The Art of Hearing Data.* Thousand Oaks, Calif.: Sage.

Smith, Jeffrey, Lisa Smith, and Richard De Lisi. 2001. *Natural Classroom Assessment: Designing Seamless Instruments and Assessment.* Thousand Oaks, Calif.: Corwin. (See chapter 6, "Using Multiple Choice and Other Objectives Measures," for a checklist of dos and don'ts.)

Wiggins, Grant. 1998. *Educative Assessment: Designing Assessments to Inform and Improve Student Performance.* San Francisco: Jossey-Bass.

Portfolios

American Association for Higher Education, The Portfolio Clearinghouse. 23 May 2003. Available online from http://www.aahe.org/teaching/portfolio_db.htm.

Cambridge, Barbara, ed. 2001. *Electronic Portfolios: Emerging Practices in Student, Faculty and Institutional Learning.* Washington, D.C.: AAHE.

Surveys, Interviews, and Focus Groups

Dillon, Don A. 1999. *Mail and Internet Surveys: The Tailored Design Method,* 2nd ed. New York: John Wiley.

Fowler, Jr., Floyd J. 1995. *Improving Survey Questions: Design and Evaluation.* Thousand Oaks, Calif.: Sage.

Krueger, Richard A., and Mary Anne Casey. 2000. *Focus Groups: A Practical Guide for Applied Research,* 3rd ed. Thousand Oaks, Calif.: Sage.

Shannon, David M., Todd E. Johnson, Shelby Searcy, and Alan Lott. 2002. "Using Electronic Surveys: Advice from Survey Professionals." *Practical Assessment, Research & Evaluation* 8(2). Available online from http://ericae.net/pare/getvn.asp?v=8&n=1. [Accessed 23 May 2003.]

Rubrics

Emmons, Mark, and Wanda Martin. 2002. "Engaging Conversation: Evaluating the Contribution of Library Instruction to the Quality of Student Research." *College & Research Libraries* 63(6): 545–60.

Mertler, Craig A. 2001. "Designing Scoring Rubrics for your Classroom." *Practical Assess-*

ment, Research & Evaluation 7(25). Available online from http://ericae.net/pare/getvn.asp?v=7&n=25. [Accessed 23 May 2003.]

Moskal, Barbara M. 2000. "Scoring Rubrics: What, When, and How?" *Practical Assessment, Research, & Evaluation* 7(3). Available online from http://ericae.net/pare/getvn.asp?v=7&n=3. [Accessed 23 May 2003.]

Moskal, Barbara M., and Jon A. Leydens. 2000. "Scoring Rubric Development: Validity and Reliability." *Practical Assessment, Research & Evaluation* 7(10). Available online from http://ericae.net/pare/getvn.asp?v=7&n=10. [Accessed 23 May 2003.]

Chapter 4: Analyzing Data

Cynthia H. Comer

After the assessment instruments have been administered, the researcher will have collected a body of data—the information obtained during the project—that must then be analyzed and interpreted. The types of data collected and the steps necessary to process and understand them are a product of the research design. This chapter provides an overview of various approaches to an assessment project and of the types of data that may be collected during the project. It discusses the characteristics, advantages, and disadvantages of both quantitative and qualitative data and outlines the basic steps necessary to analyze and interpret data.

Frequently in an assessment project, a sample group is studied. Based on the findings, the researcher makes generalizations from the sample to the larger population from which the sample was drawn. This is known as an inductive approach—that is, developing general principles, hypotheses, or theories based on specific observations. An assessment project also may follow a deductive approach—first developing a theory or hypothesis, and then developing measurements and tests to determine whether a predicted or expected pattern or set of behaviors actually occurs.

An assessment project may attempt to answer a variety of questions. Some are descriptive in nature, focusing on understanding the existing situation. This can be thought of as examining "what is." How do students evaluate Web sites? What do they understand about the use of Boolean operators in searching databases? Do they understand the differences between popular and scholarly materials? How adept are they at distinguishing among different types of bibliographic citations? Other questions take an experimental approach, focusing on changes that may be affected by introducing something new into the existing situation. This can be thought of examining "what if." Will student scores on an information literacy (IL) test improve after they complete a tutorial? Do students locate more relevant and timely resources for research assignments after attending an instruction session? Are seniors better able than first-year students to cite references appropriately? Does the quality of students' research papers improve after a faculty member introduces IL instruction into a course? These questions can be studied using various types of assessment tools and instruments, each of which produces a particular type of data. Chapter 6 contains many useful examples that have been used by different types of academic libraries.

Because no single instrument is likely to measure everything the researcher may want to know, it may be desirable to incorporate various methodologies into the assessment plan in order to produce multiple measures. This is sometimes referred to as triangulation—that is, using multiple means to study a subject from different angles to increase the evidence in support of the project findings. Different types of data can be used together to complement one another, provide more complete analysis, and build a stronger case. As a result, research frequently employs both quantitative and qualitative methods, as each method gathers quite different types of data.

The methods of data collection and analysis described in this chapter are based largely on social science research methods, particularly those used in education and sociology. Although an overview of quantitative and qualitative data is provided, detailed explanations of statistical analysis techniques, as well as in-depth discussions on software for analyzing quantitative and qualitative data, are beyond the scope of this chapter. Some methods of data analysis are relatively simple and straightforward—computing percentages or averages, for example. Others are much more complex and may require a fair amount of expertise and experience to carry out and fully understand. During the design phase of an assessment project, the researcher should develop a clear understanding of the types of data to be collected, as well as the analytical methods to be used in interpreting the data. If the researcher lacks the skills and expertise to carry out the data analysis part of the project independently, a source of support for this phase of the project should be identified and recruited to the project before it is implemented.

Quantitative Data

The major characteristic of quantitative data is that they deal with information that can be meaningfully represented by *numbers*. They collect information in a form that can be analyzed using objective measures and standard methods of analysis. A certain error of measurement or level of probability is assumed in using quantitative data; estimating that error or probability level is one of the primary purposes of statistical analysis.

Typical instruments used in quantitative research include surveys, tests, and questionnaires. There are numerous ways to collect information on such instruments, all of which generally involve the use of closed- or fixed-response questions that offer a finite and predetermined range of answers. Examples include:

- checklists or options to select;
- rating scales (e.g., Likert);
- multiple-choice questions;
- true/false or yes/no questions;
- ranking or ordering choices.

Quantitative measures offer certain advantages, includng:

- Data are relatively easy to collect. In many cases, the researcher simply distributes an instrument and ask participants to complete it.
- Instruments are usually fairly simple and straightforward, and therefore easy for participants to complete.
- Due to the ease of data collection, data are relatively inexpensive to collect.
- It is possible to have large sample sizes, gathering large amounts of data from many subjects.
- Analysis of data is objective; there is no need to interpret or categorize responses.
- With a well-designed instrument, responses are consistent among participants.
- Data can be analyzed using established statistical methods.
- Web-based tools are available to simplify both data collection and analysis.

Quantitative measures also have substantial disadvantages, including:

- The use of closed questions limits the range of potential responses because participants can only select from among options already provided.
- It is difficult to gather a lot of detail—quantitative instruments do not allow for considered, thoughtful, and in-depth responses that provide insight into participants' feelings, attitudes, or values.
- Questions must be phrased in such a way that answers can be given a number or value.
- There is little or no opportunity for participants to clarify the meaning of questions.
- Instruments that accurately assess what they are intended to (i.e., are both valid and reliable) are difficult and time-consuming to develop— ambiguities are surprisingly difficult to eliminate.
- It can be difficult to design good questionnaire or test items. For example, it is challenging to create plausible distracters (incorrect responses) for multiple-choice questions. Wrong answers must be believable enough to be selected by someone who does not know the correct answer, but not so plausible that someone who really does know the correct answer will be unreasonably drawn away from it.

• Depending on how the instrument is administered, there may be a low response rate (particularly for surveys sent by mail).

• Because questions tend to be fairly specific, more questions may be required to assess accurately a particular skill or bit of knowledge.

• The researcher may need training or assistance with data analysis, which can prove difficult and complex without a thorough understanding of statistical methods.

Because they are based on numbers, quantitative data are summarized numerically, using conventions such as frequencies, averages (mean, median, mode), and percentages. The data may consist of *categorical variables*, those that fit responses into separate, distinct categories. Examples include gender or the subject in which the student in majoring. Categorical variables are commonly represented by a number and summarized by computing the percentages that comprise each category (e.g., 217 or 54% of the participants were women; or 86, or 23%, of the students were natural science majors). Data also may consist of *continuous variables*, those whose values form a steady progression or can be ranked along a scale or dimension. Examples include age or placement in a rating system. Continuous variables are commonly summarized by computing averages (e.g., median age = 20.7 years; mean answer based on a scale of 1 to 5 = 4.2).

These numbers may be compared to one another to detect or confirm patterns, causal relationships, correlations between variables, and changes over time. The later could result from a cohort study (studying the same group or participants over time, for example, a group of students from their freshman year until their senior year of college), a longitudinal study (studying different groups of participants over time 0, for example, students enrolled each semester in a particular course), or a cross-sectional study (simultaneously studying difference groups, for example, freshman and juniors). A number of different tests for determining relationships among variables and the degree of statistical significance are available for analyzing data. The type and quantity of data collected will determine the appropriate tests for use.

To analyze quantitative data, the first step is to create a data file. For small amounts of data, this can be as simple as a tally sheet on which responses are marked up by hand. For large amounts of data, or to conduct more complex methods of analysis, it is helpful to use some sort of computer software for data entry. A spreadsheet program such as Excel, a database program such as Access or FileMaker Pro, or a statistical analysis package such as SPSS can be used to input and analyze data effectively.

The next step is to develop descriptive statistics, which are statistics that simply describe the sample. For example, the researcher might note the frequency of responses to particular questions, indicate the average score participants achieved on a test, or provide a breakdown of participants by gender, class year, or other characteristic. The researcher may then compute inferential statistics by subjecting the data to various statistical procedures and tests. Inferential statistics help identify relationships among variables, as well as determine whether the results are truly meaningful rather than simply due to chance. Based on the results of this analysis, the researcher may be able to make inferences about the larger population based on the sample that has been studied. The bibliography at the end of this book lists several useful works for working with statistical data for those who desire more detail.

Finally, interpret the data. What are plausible explanations for the data? What do the results really mean? Even if results are shown to be statistically significant, do they matter? Which findings are of greatest importance? What are the broader meanings and implications of the findings?

Qualitative Data

The major characteristic of qualitative data is that they are expressed in *words* or *language*. They are nonnumerical. The information gathered is often narrative, with the participant providing opinions, explanations, and descriptions. The focus of qualitative assessment is frequently *process oriented* rather than *product oriented*, meaning that the steps, thoughts, feelings, and other subjective information supplied by or gathered from participants may be as or even more important than whether they get an answer right or wrong. Qualitative research often requires the researcher to interact with participants through conversation, observation, or providing feedback on assignments.

As with quantitative research, the way the assessment is conducted will determine the kinds of data collected. Typical qualitative approaches include:

- open-ended questions on tests, surveys, and questionnaires;
- interviews;
- case studies;
- focus groups;
- observation (revealing what people actually do rather than what they say they would do);
- essays;
- portfolios;
- research journals/logs;
- bibliometrics (e.g., analysis of bibliographies from student research papers);
- transaction log or session monitoring (e.g., search statements typed by users in the library's online catalog or links users select on the library's home page).

Some of the advantages of qualitative measures include:

- They allow freedom of response, including answers the researcher did not anticipate.
- They allow more reflective, thoughtful, and complex responses.
- Questions, such as those for surveys or focus groups, are relatively easy to construct.

• They often permit clarification, both by the participant, who may not understand a question or assignment, and by the researcher, who may not understand a response.

• The format often permits follow-up, allowing the researcher to probe further and get more detail.

• They allow the collection of information about emotions, thoughts, feelings, and experiences.

• There is generally a high response rate, as participants may be self-selected volunteers, hand-selected willing participants, or students enrolled in a class and completing required assignments.

• They allow the assessment of actual, rather than hypothetical, performance.

There also are a number of disadvantages to qualitative measures, including:

• Data collection is labor-intensive, often requiring considerable time on the part of both participant and researcher.

• Due to the time-consuming nature of data collection, data are therefore relatively expensive to collect (especially when interviews, focus groups, observation, or the review of lengthy documents are involved).

• Cost and time constraints, as well the large amounts of data collected from participants, may make it necessary to limit the sample size.

• Developing codes and then coding data, or developing and then applying rubrics, can be a lengthy, arduous process.

• Responses may be inconsistent or misinterpreted by the researcher.

• It can be difficult to maintain consistency when using different interviewers, questioners, or observers.

• There is potential for the researcher to introduce bias and distortion because the process and data are both subjective.

• The researcher may end up with a lot of irrelevant data that cannot be used.

It is useful to distinguish between three broad types of data frequently gathered from qualitative research, as the procedure for analyzing each type of data varies. First, extemporaneous *comments* may be provided in writing by participants on questionnaires or surveys, or spoken aloud by participants and recorded by the researcher on tape or in notes during interviews or focus groups. A second type of qualitative data consists of *observations* made by the researcher while participants perform an exercise or activity. Often the researcher will record on tape or write down comments describing the behaviors and actions of the participants. A third type of qualitative data are *documents* created by participants as they write essays and term papers, maintain journals and research logs, build portfolios, compile bibliographies, or complete other assignments.

To analyze qualitative data in the form of comments, the researcher must first transcribe comments or otherwise prepare them for analysis. An accurate and complete account in the participants' own language is preferable, but if constraints of time and money only permit the researcher to take notes, these notes should be written up in a detailed, comprehensive summary.

The next step is to read through a sample of the data to get an idea of their overall range and quality and then, based on recurrent patterns, ideas, themes, and topics that appear in the data, develop a code to represent important, frequent, or significant categories. Noteworthy deviations or contradictions that appear in the data should be included, as well. To remove ambiguities about how comments are to be coded, categories should be distinct and mutually exclusive. The initial questions, assumptions, and predictions of the assessment project should be reviewed to ensure that the code addresses the original research topic. This is an ongoing, reflective process that may continue while data are being coded and analyzed; as the researcher becomes more familiar with the data, existing categories may be clustered or combined and new categories created.

Next design a coding system. This could be as simple as using colored pens to mark up the text (using copies, not originals) or a more complex system of letters or words that represent each category. Read all comments closely and thoroughly and systematically assign codes to ideas expressed in them. Count the frequency of responses that contain each theme, keeping in mind that some responses may contain multiple ideas.

Finally, develop theories or explanations from the data. What are the prevalent themes and ideas that emerge? What is really going on, and why is it important? Are there inconsistencies that need to be noted? What is the "story" the data reveal, and what can we learn from the study?

The process for analyzing data collected in the form of observations is similar to that for comments. The main difference is that the researcher is working with his or her own words, rather than those supplied directly by the participants. With that difference in mind, the steps above for coding comments can be applied to coding and analyzing data produced from observations. Note that there are software programs that can assist in analyzing language; one commonly used is NUD*IST (also known as NVivo).

Before reviewing the steps for analyzing documents, it is well worth having a brief discussion of rubrics. A rubric is a set of scaled criteria used to judge performance. It can help to quantify information that is essentially qualitative in nature, make rating more objective and consistent, and keep the focus on essential criteria. Ideally, rubrics are constructed in advance and shared with participants so that participants have a clear understanding of the expectations for the assignment and what they must do to demonstrate different levels of proficiency. Because the rubric is developed before the researcher has seen any resulting performance, it can be difficult to predetermine scoring criteria. Obviously, as the researcher repeats the process over time, both the assessment instruments and the rubrics used to score them can be modified and improved.

To create a rubric, the researcher first determines the criteria on which performance will be judged and distinguishes varying ranges and levels of performance quality. Criteria and performance levels must be described clearly and unambiguously. It is important to have a well-articulated rubric that can be applied consistently—by different raters, by the same rater at different times, and across different groups or individuals. (See chapter 3 for a broader discussion of rubrics.) To analyze qualitative data in the form of documents using a rubric, first read through a sampling to get an idea of overall range and quality of the data; this will help in applying rubric. Then read all documents closely and thoroughly, and systematically apply the scoring rubric to each criterion on which performance is to be judged.

Getting Help

For inexperienced researchers or those unfamiliar with the tools and methods necessary to conduct a thorough and accurate analysis of their data, there are ways to get help. On many campuses, there is an office devoted to research or assessment for the institution as a whole. Staff in this office may be prepared—and perhaps even expect—to assist with research projects conducted on campus; if not, they at least may be able to consult and provide advice. Another source for on-campus help is faculty who teach statistics or research methodology courses; they are well versed in the intricacies of quantitative analysis. Faculty in sociology, psychology, and education are also likely to be familiar with qualitative research methods. Similarly, graduate students may be available to assist. If grant money or other financial resources are available, it may even be possible to hire a graduate student to do the initial data analysis.

For researchers who wish to hone their own analytical skills, there are dozens of recent books on conducting quantitative and qualitative research. Many are used as textbooks in college courses and are frequently revised. A brief bibliography of useful titles is included in this book. It may also be possible to take or audit a course on statistics or social science research methodology. Professional associations often have committees, sponsor mentorship programs, and offer workshops to aid inexperienced researchers. Within the ALA, ACRL's Research Committee and RUSA/MOUSS's Research and Statistics Committee may be able to provide advice and assistance.

Selected Bibliography

Babbie, Earl. 2004. *The Practice of Social Research,* 10th ed. Belmont, Calif. Thomson/Wadsworth.

Bell, Judith. 1999. *Doing Your Research Project: A Guide for First-Time Researchers in Education and Social Science,* 3rd ed. Buckingham, England: Open University Press.

Bryman, Alan. 2001. *Social Research Methods.* Oxford: Oxford University Press.

Burns, Robert B. 2000. *Introduction to Research Methods.* 4th ed. London: SAGE, 2000.

Creswell, John W. 2003. *Research Design: Qualitative, Quantitative, and Mixed Methods Approaches*, 2nd ed. Thousand Oaks, Calif.: SAGE.

de Vaus, David A. 2002. *Analyzing Social Science Data*. London: SAGE.

de Vaus, David A. 2001. *Research Design in Social Research*. London: SAGE.

Glazier, Jack D., and Ronald R. Powell, eds. 1992. *Qualitative Research in Information Management*. Englewood, Colo.: Libraries Unlimited, Inc.

Hernon, Peter, and Robert E. Dugan. 2002. *An Action Plan for Outcomes Assessment in Your Library*. Chicago: American Library Association.

Hernon, Peter, et al. 1989. *Statistics for Library Decision Making: A Handbook*. Norwood, N.J.: Ablex Publishing Corporation.

Loertscher, David V., and Blanche Woolls. 2002. *Information Literacy: A Review of the Research: A Guide for Practitioners and Researchers*, 2nd ed. San Jose, Calif.: Hi Willow Research and Publishing. [Although this book is written for school library media specialists with a focus on children and teenagers, it includes some interesting material that may be of use to academic librarians.]

Neuman, William Lawrence. 2003. *Social Research Methods: Qualitative and Quantitative Approaches*, 5th ed. Boston: Allyn and Bacon.

Powell, Ronald R. 1997. *Basic Research Methods for Librarians*, 3rd ed. Greenwich, Conn.: Ablex Publishing Corporation.

Slater, Margaret, ed. 1990. *Research Methods in Library and Information Studies*. London: The Library Association, 1990.

Chapter 5: Reporting Results

Cynthia H. Comer

It is important to share the results of an assessment project with an appropriate audience, whether it be the library administration, one's colleagues in the broader profession, or even the project participants themselves. The main objective of the report is to clearly describe the topic that was investigated, present the main findings, and discuss the importance or implications of the project. This chapter reviews the various elements that make up the report about the assessment project, including a discussion of the purpose and types of information to include in each section.

For data to be meaningful and useful to others, it must be organized, summarized, and presented in a clear, thoughtful manner. There are standard components of a research report within the educational and social sciences disciplines. All reports need not include every element listed below; rather, each should be tailored to the particular purpose for which the assessment project was originally conducted and for the particular audience in mind. A report submitted for publication in a peer-reviewed scholarly journal might well include most or even all of these categories, whereas one submitted for internal review by an individual or small group may require only some. The researcher may find it useful to combine, alter, reorder, or even rename the sections listed below to suit the nature of the report.

Although the focus of this chapter is on written reports, the elements described here also are useful for organizing research presented in other venues and settings, such as conference presentations, seminars, poster sessions, and workshops.

Elements of the Report

Title

Select a report title indicative of the subject studied. Including words that accurately describe the subject matter may be useful for later retrieval from a database.

Abstract

The abstract should provide a clear summary of the main focus, aims, methods, and results of the research. It is usually no more than about two hundred words. A well-written abstract provides a crucial service by helping readers determine their interest in reading further. As with the title, careful and descriptive phrasing in the abstract may enhance later retrieval of the report from a database. Abstracts usually are written in the third person, in past tense, and often in passive voice. Following are sample sentence constructions that might appear in an abstract:

- "The purpose of the study was to determine what undergraduate students know about…";
- "Participants were asked to discuss how they look for information…";
- "A majority of participants indicated that they had used…";
- "An analysis found that there were no statistically significant differences in…";
- "Implications for instruction librarians are discussed…."

Introduction

The introduction to the report frames a meaningful context for the research—what was done, why it was done, and what was hoped or expected would be discovered. It may itself include several subsections, including: an overview of the issues and problems germane to the research; the cause, need, or reason for the study; the scope, purpose, and goals of the study; questions and hypotheses to be tested; background information relevant to the study; a description of the institutions and participants involved in the study; and a description of the assessment instrument(s) used. Because the introduction encapsulates the entire project, it may, in fact, be the last section to be written.

Literature Review

The literature review sets the research in a larger context by providing additional background, reviewing work previously done in this area, and further detailing the need for the current research. It also provides relevant references the reader may wish to explore. As appropriate, the literature review may draw on fields tangential to or outside the field of librarianship.

Methodology

The methodology provides a detailed description of how the research was done.

It describes how the investigation was carried out, details the methods and techniques used, and explains why the particular methodology was selected. It should include an overall description of the research design, variables and controls incorporated into the research design, the procedures followed in carrying out the research, a description of the assessment instrument, and definitions of any terms that need clarification or may otherwise be useful to the reader.

Information about the participants should be provided, including a general description of who they were, the method used to select them, and the sample size (number of participants). The methods used to analyze data are described in this section as well; for example, the tests of measurement and statistical analysis used. Ideally, the methodology section is complete enough to enable later researchers to replicate the study or at least design a comparable project.

Results, Analysis, and Findings

In this section, the researcher selects ways to summarize and present the data clearly and succinctly. This section also may include additional detail on how the data were analyzed. If the data were subjected to statistical analysis, there should be an explanation of the descriptive and inferential statistics derived from the data. Quantitative data are generally represented through illustrations such as figures, pie charts, tables, bar graphs, line graphs, or radar charts. (A radar chart vaguely resembles an archery target or dart board; it is useful for grouping questions into broad topical categories and then indicating patterns of choices, behaviors, or attitudes that appear in the answers chosen by participants.) A brief statement or label must accompany each illustration. Qualitative data are generally represented by illustrative quotes or extracts from the comments, observations, or documents studied. For both quantitative and qualitative methods, this section also will include a narrative description of what the data show.

Discussion

The discussion provides an opportunity for the researcher to undertake a critical analysis of the research project as a whole. In terms of the findings, topics that might be addressed include a discussion of whether the initial hypotheses were supported by the research, the significance of the outcomes, and the relationship between the initial goals of the project and the final results. In terms of the methodology, areas to cover could include problems with the research design, unexpected challenges or difficulties encountered during the research, how the project could have been improved, and acknowledgment of any limitations, weaknesses, or shortcomings. This section also might address the extent to which the findings are generalizable to other libraries and how others might relate the findings to their own particular situations.

Summary, Conclusions, and Recommendations

This is the final "wrap-up" section in which the researcher reiterates the major themes and topics addressed by the research and briefly summarizes the most important findings. The concluding remarks also should contain speculation on the implications of the research and suggestions for how the findings fit into the bigger picture. Moreover, the researcher may offer suggestions for directions for future research in related areas.

References, Bibliography

The references and/or bibliography include all items referred to in the literature review. Depending on the nature of the report, the author also may decide to include recommended resources of potential use to the reader or future researcher.

Appendices

The appendices provide a place to include material that is not integrated elsewhere into the report and not essential to understanding the text but may still be of interest to the reader. Examples include copies of assessment instruments and scoring rubrics used, and charts, graphs, and so on that further illuminate the text.

Acknowledgments

The researcher may wish to recognize individuals or institutions that provided assistance, funding, advice, or other support with some aspect of the research project.

Chapter 6: First-year Experience Research Skills Survey

Alison Armstrong

Institutional Description

The University of Cincinnati (UC) is a Carnegie Research I institution serving a diverse student body of more than 34,000 students through eighteen colleges and divisions offering more than five hundred degree programs from the associate to the doctoral level. UC is a public, comprehensive system of learning and research. In 1998–1999, 26,839 undergraduate and 7,185 graduate and professional students were enrolled in the university's majors and preprofessional programs. African American students numbered 3,900, Asian American 1,000, Hispanic 350, and international students 1,500. About 89 percent of the university's total enrollment are residents of Ohio. The average age of full-time students is nearly twenty-three years. The average age of part-time students is nearly thirty-two years. Approximately 3,000 students live on campus and another 750 live in fraternity and sorority housing. Approximately 2,000 full-time faculty members and 1,200 part-time faculty members are employed universitywide. Ninety percent of the full-time faculty hold a doctorate or terminal degree in their field.

The university's strong commitment to information literacy (IL) was clearly demonstrated in its incorporation into the redesign of the General Education (http://www.uc.edu/gened/) program begun two years ago: *Information literacy is integral to the undergraduate baccalaureate experience and permeates every component of the general education program.* UC's Gen Ed program's definition of and standards for information literacy are based on the ACRL's *Information Literacy Competency Standards for Higher Education.* The university has charted a rigorous course for assessment. This is an institutional priority and as such, two senior administrative positions, vice-provost for institutional effectiveness and director, academic for enrollment management, are focused on assessment.

Project Participants

Primary participants include the head of training and educational services (TES), the first-year experience (FYE) librarian, coordinator of the information commons, other professional librarians, peer student assistants, and faculty who teach first-year students (FYS).

Project Description

The overall project goal is to help increase student retention by working directly with first-year students (FYS), and faculty who teach them, by increasing their understanding of research resources and services. This will enable those students to perform better in their classes and reduce the tendency to drop out due to the frustration of not knowing how and where to find high-quality resources for research. Our efforts went beyond the scope of the IMLS grant and included teaching IL classes focused on course content in collaboration with college faculty, an information commons in Langsam Library (the main library) where students get hands-on, personalized attention to their research needs, a virtual presence in the form of two Web sites (http://www.libraries.uc.edu/libinfo/FYE/index.htm and http://www.uc.edu/first_year/Index.htm), and outreach to Cincinnati Public Schools students with the goal of better preparing them for success when they reach the university.

The FYE librarian was hired to work directly with FYS and faculty who teach FYS to increase information literacy. Increased IL translates into better-informed students who perform better academically. By making the large university library system smaller and more manageable to the FYS, the likelihood is increased that the FYS will succeed in his or her first year and have a solid foundation of research skills on which to build in succeeding years. A student without these skills is more likely to become frustrated and do poorly in his or her courses and, perhaps, choose not to continue at the university. The efforts of the FYE librarian, coordinator of the information commons, other librarians, and peer student assistants are designed to counter this possibility and to produce students who not only have the ability to survive academically, but also to also thrive with superior research skills.

There are three key areas of FYS engagement. The first is through teaching IL classes custom tailored to the course content needs of faculty in the various colleges. These classes are most often "one-shot" sessions where the fundamentals of research are explored through hands-on exercises related to the individual class research needs. The second area of engagement is through an information commons where professional librarians and peer student assistants provide hands-on, personalized assistance with research to FYS and others at the point where the students are engaged in those efforts. A PR campaign is under way to inform FYS and university faculty of this new resource. The third area of FYS engagement is a virtual presence designed to help FYS and others to find and use information resources.

Planning for Assessment

In planning for the assessment of the IMLS project, we considered the number of and type of classes we were teaching. We wanted to gather both quantitative and qualitative data. The use of a survey tool (pretest/posttest) allowed us to gather both types of information. This tool is employed only with classes that meet for more than one session with the FYE librarian as the typical one-shot library instructional sessions are not conducive to its use. This tool has been implemented from the very beginning of the FYE librarian's tenure at the university. Other, less structured and more qualitative assessment includes feedback from faculty with whom the FYE librarian has collaborated in multiple and one-shot library sessions.

Developing the Assessment Instrument

The tool was developed primarily through a review of the literature for other similar tools. It was then adapted through consultation with colleagues to fit local needs. In addition, our classroom experience helped us further refine the questions. Finally, we had a few student workers review the assessment instrument and we incorporated their suggestions.

Analyzing the Results

Assessment thus far has consisted of a survey tool designed to evaluate the level of information literacy. The research skills surveys, given to IL classes that met more than once, indicate a significant improvement in understanding of research tools and services by the students who participated in those classes. This demonstrates the necessity of the research skills training available through the library in teaching those skills to students who otherwise may not receive it. The surveys, although only given to classes that met more than once, indicate that most students who take the survey fail to complete it successfully or just barely pass. After the multiple-class interaction most students pass the survey. This seems to indicate that at least some research skills instruction, even for those who meet only once with the FYE librarian, produces a better understanding of the research tools and services available than no instruction at all. The library's efforts have produced better-informed students who understand how to find, evaluate, and use information more skillfully than they did before they had a class in the library.

Results

Our data from the survey is as follows:

FYE Research Skills Survey—Autumn 2001 Preevaluation
(Totals from five sections of A&S FYE Courses 001, 002, 004, 005, 006)
Pass = eight correct answers; fail = less than eight correct answers
64 total respondents: 29 pass, 35 fail

FYE Research Skills Survey—Autumn 2001 Postevaluation
(Totals from five sections of A&S FYE Courses 001, 002, 004, 005, 006)
Pass = eight correct answers; fail = less than eight correct answers
61 total respondents: 51 pass, 10 fail

Challenges

One of the biggest challenges was getting started and then maintaining our focus. We tried to work with too many classes too soon and at the same time. As well, the IMLS grant was rolled into a larger initiative and that caused some overload. Although we were able to work with many interested colleagues, we were unable to formally bring them into the IMLS grant as we had hoped. In addition, it was crucial for us to have more than one backup plan. Two of our three initial courses we had intended to work with became unavailable. Flexibility and perseverance were key, as were the willingness and dedication of staff. Building on and creating good relationships with teaching faculty were important factors. Finally, one of our biggest supports was our institution and its commitment to assessment. We were able to draw on the strengths and expertise of the director, academic for enrollment management.

Conclusion

The efforts thus far have been highly successful. In the first year, the FYE librarian has reached more than 1,200 students, including more than 900 FYS, through 83 information literacy classes. These classes, combined with the virtual availability of research services and the information commons, will be valuable resources in the coming years to new students who need the skills the library offers and who will be more likely to succeed with those skills.

Additional Key Findings

Areas of strength include the large number of students reached and satisfaction with the FYE librarian's efforts: 1,257 students in 83 classes (904 of which were FYS). In addition, feedback from faculty relating to the importance and value of the research skills classes was positive.

Opportunities for improvement include better assessment strategies for the one-shot library sessions.

Library instruction for FYS increased from 400 during the FYE librarian's first six months to 504 in his second six months. The program is anticipated to continue to grow.

The FYE Librarian will collaborate with an increasing number of faculty as word gets out about the availability of instruction at the library.

The information commons and Web sites are important components of the effort to reach FYS and enable them to better succeed academically at the university. Outreach to CPS students is a growing component of preparing those students for college and attracting them to UC.

Next steps include forming a more complete assessment strategy and promoting the information commons as a first-stop place in the library where FYS and others can get personalized attention to their research needs.

Assessment Instrument

FYE Research Skills Survey—Autumn 2001

Please note that this form will not be graded.

1. Books in a college library are normally located through the use of:
   A. The card catalog
   B. Periodical indexes
   C. Printed lists that are updated each month
   D. An online library catalog

2. A place in a library staffed by someone who answers questions and provides help in using the library, conducting research, and locating information is:
   A. A reference desk/reference consultation area
   B. A computer lab
   C. A periodicals room
   D. A security office

3. Choose the most accurate statement:
   A. All information is available on the Internet.
   B. The Internet contains a mix of information of varying quality.
   C. The Internet contains mainly popular information sources.
   D. The Internet contains nothing of value.

4. Where is the best place to begin research on a term paper if you don't know where to start?
   A. In the book stacks
   B. In the periodical department
   C. In the reserve collection
   D. At the reference desk

5. Which would you normally <u>not</u> find listed in a library catalog?
   A. A book
   B. An article
   C. A government document
   D. A video

6. Anything you find on the Internet is yours for the taking.
   ____ TRUE
   ____ FALSE

7. The most accurate statement about Boolean operators is:
   A. They retrieve information by responding to infrared commands.
   B. They manage the switchboard in college libraries.
   C. They are words like AND, OR, and NOT which limit or broaden a search.
   D. They are replacements for the old card catalogs.

8. When performing a search in an Internet Search Engine or online database, which of the following uses a term that broadens the search results?

   A. election OR presidential
   B. election AND presidential
   C. election NOT presidential
   D. national AND security

9. To find articles in periodicals you will use:

   A. A library catalog
   B. Online indexes or databases
   C. An encyclopedia
   D. An Internet search engine

10. Which of these would be a citation to a journal article?

   A. Smith, R. *Bones.* New York: Big Press, 1999.
   B. Smith, R. "Bones." *Paleoanthropology* 10.1 (1999): 34–66
   C. Smith, R. *Bones.org.* 6 Nov. 1999 <http://www.bones.org/>
   D. Smith, R. *Bones.* 1999: Unpublished manuscript.

11. Performing a subject search in a library catalog is likely to produce the same results as a keyword search.

   ____ True
   ____ False

12. Which of the following is not a feature of OhioLink:

   A. It is an online central catalog of the holdings of member libraries.
   B. It links libraries from all around the country.
   C. It provides online access to research and reference databases.
   D. Its services are available only to faculty, students, and staff of OhioLINK participating institutions.

Comments or suggestions concerning library instruction? Thank You.

Chapter 7: Information Competency as Historian's Craft

Michael Barrett

Institutional Description

California State University, Northridge, a Carnegie Master's Colleges and Universities I, is one of the largest campuses of the California State University System. Located in the San Fernando Valley, twenty-five miles northwest of downtown Los Angeles, it is the only public university serving this metropolitan suburb of 1.4 million people. The student body of approximately 32,000 reflects the ethnic and cultural diversity of the region. There are approximately 950 full-time tenure-track faculty and 650 part-time faculty. CSU, Northridge, is a comprehensive university offering undergraduate and graduate degrees in more than fifty fields as well as credentials in the field of education. The university is committed to creating a community in which individuals form different backgrounds can live, learn, and work together.

In 2000, a series of information competency goals and standards were added to the curriculum standards for general education courses. All general education courses are evaluated in light of these standards during recertification processes. The university has a strong tradition of faculty–librarian collaboration concerning bibliographic instruction. In 2001–2002, more than 19,200 students participated in some form of formal bibliographic instruction.

Project Participants

During the fall semester of 2002, I collaborated with a faculty member in the Department of History on the initial development of an assessment instrument that was administered for trial purposes in one section of his History 301 class. After refinement of the instrument and analysis of expressed needs and identified areas of student weakness, during the spring semester 2002, I collaborated with another faculty member of the Department of History, this time with both sections of her History 301 classes. History 301 is entitled "The Historian's Craft: Reading, Research, and Writing History." It is a three-unit class normally open only to history majors. It is an entry to the major class and an introduction to the search for and criticism of historical sources, the issues and controversies concerning interpretation of the sources, "schools" of historical interpretation, organizing the materials and data of research, and the rearwards and pitfalls of historical writing. The syllabi for sections of this course are individually developed by instructors and are highly customized to reflect the topics, themes, issues, and so on the instructor wishes to cover. A copy of the syllabus for the course, Spring 2002, is at the end of this chapter.

Project Description

In collaboration with instructors during the fall semester 2001, I developed a detailed information competency plan specifying outcomes, objectives, and assessment means for each of the five information competency standards. In collaboration, the instructors identified several major areas of student difficulty. These included nonunderstanding of individual media advantages and disadvantages, choice of appropriate database indexes and abstracts, confusion concerning primary and secondary source material, unawareness of specific factual reference sources in history, inability to decipher periodical citations, problems in developing an appropriate search strategy, and problems in determining which sources to investigate for individually assigned research projects.

The Assessment Instrument

We decided to use pre- and posttests to assess the impact of the instruction. There were four separate, but similar, instruments (a sample is included at end of chapter). These tests covered the areas that were to be the assignments.

Class assignments included the following: an academic journal report (analysis of two journals), submission of an annotated bibliography, a book précis, and either a family history research paper or a research paper on some aspect of Los Angeles history. Research papers were presented both in writing and orally. During the first week of class, a twenty-question Information Competency Survey was administered. Each class then participated in three hours of bibliographic instruction presented by myself (Checklist of Selected Library Sources). At the conclusion of the final bibliographic instruction session, each student was provided both a Research Strategy Development Template and a Proposed Source Checklist (included at end of chapter). Each student was required to fill in the templates and return to me for review. After my review, I returned the templates along with a Review of Research Proposal with strategy and source suggestions.

In addition, students were required to consult with me on an individual basis at least once, although in actuality, several consulted many more times. During the last week of April, the Information Competency Survey was again administered.

The Results

Initial analysis indicates that areas of student strength at the pretest included: a knowledge of primary sources (both by definition and type), the ability to correctly identify a correct abstracting source for modern history periodical articles, comprehension of the term *bibliography*, and the ability to match media type with information need. These areas improved in strength and remained the areas of greatest strength on the posttest. Analysis indicates that the greatest areas of student weakness both at the pretest and posttest included: the ability to correctly identify a current source for ancient or medieval history periodicals, the ability to decipher citations and determine holdings information for periodicals, a knowledge of the contest of the online catalog, and the ability to construct a complete search statement. Areas showing the greatest improvement between pre- and posttest included knowledge of the contents of the online catalog, identifying types of primary sources, ability to match media with informational need, ability to decipher periodical citations, and the ability to identify the correct abstracting source for articles on modern history. Areas of the least improvement included comprehension of the term *bibliography*, types of primary sources, determination of periodical holdings, and the ability to construct a complete search statement. Out of a possible score of 70, aggregate pretest average was 34.15 correct. The posttest average was 48.68, or an average increase of 14.51 correct points.

Challenges

Challenges were mainly related to time available on my part. Shortly after award of the grant, I was elected chair of the Reference and Instructional Services Department and also reelected faculty senate secretary. During this academic year, I was involved on three separate search and screen committees for tenure-track positions. Basically, I found that I had to establish definite office hours to work on the project and often needed to take other work home in evenings and over weekends. Feedback from individual students has been exceedingly positive, and I plan to continue to administer the survey as well as to provide templates for students to submit strategy and source choices for review.

Conclusion

Although there was improvement across all question areas, effective understanding of periodical access and the ability to construct complete search statements remain highly problematic. I plan to do some comparison based on class level, gender, library use, participation in library instruction, computer use, and availability of Internet access.

History 301: The Historian's Craft (SAMPLE)
Information Competency Survey

1. What is your class level? junior ___ senior ___ other ___
2. What is your gender? male ___ female ___
3. Do you use the University Library?
   not at all ___ rarely ___ sometimes ___ frequently ___
4. Have you had library instruction? yes ___ no ___
5. Do you use computers at home? ___ in the library? ___ both? ___
6. Do you have Internet access at home? yes ___ no ___
7. Match the format with the advantage

Internet site ___	a) fast imprint information
Periodical article ___	b) photo-reduced imagery
Micro card ___	c) background and detail
Book ___	d) currency
Dissertation ___	e) high originality
Newspaper article ___	f) multimedia availability
JStore ___	g) provides out-of-print materials
	h) online journal articles

8. A Primary Source is (choose one)
   a. the first book written on the event
   b. the most important journal article written on the event
   c. a biography of someone involved in the event
   d. an eyewitness account of the event
   e. a newspaper article written after the time of the event
   f. I don't know

9. Primary sources may include (circle all appropriate):
   a. letters
   b. diaries
   c. a ship's log
   d. minutes of an organization meeting
   e. court decisions
   f. all of the above
   g. I don't know

10. Where is the Oviatt Library?

11. To find references to scholarly articles about ancient Egypt, which is the best source to consult?
   a. Poole's Index
   b. American: History and Life
   c. Historical Abstracts
   d. Humanities Abstracts

e. Social Sciences Abstracts
f. I don't know

12. To find references to scholarly articles about the Panama Canal, which of the following sources would be best to consult?
a. American: History and Life
b. Readers Guide
c. Historical Abstracts
d. Los Angeles Times Index
e. Public Affairs Information Service
f. I don't know

13. Match: Media Format	Advantage
a) Internet site ___	1. Local emphasis
b) Periodical article ___	2. Photo-reduced imagery
c) Micro card ___	3. Extensive background
d) Book ___	4. Currency
e) Dissertation ___	5. High originality
f) Newspaper aticle ___	6. Multimedia
	7. Out-of-print material

14. A Bibliography is:
a. A person's life story
b. A style guide for witting papers
c. A list of documents
d. A directory of names and address
e. I don't know

15. You may use the library's online catalog to find information on:
a. all books published about history
b. CSUN history faculty and the courses they teach
c. books for sale
d. book and journal titles owned by the University Library
e. all of the above
f. I don't know

16. Match the Reference Source with

Encyclopedia of the Holocaust ___	a. timelines
Dictionary of American Biography ___	b. a research guide
The Asian American Almanac ___	c. overview articles
Oxford Companion to World War Two ___	d. explanation of terminology
Atlas of Westward Expansion ___	e. miscellaneous data
The People's Chronology ___	f. information about people's lives
Dictionary of Historical Terms ___	g. graphic depictions

17. In evaluating an Internet Web site, which of the following are very important?
a. stated coverage

b. qualifications of authors
c. organizational affiliation
d. length of time in existence
e. special features
f. a, b, e,
g. b, c, d
h. all of the above

18. Please identify the following in the reference below
a. _______________
b. _______________
c. _______________
d. _______________
e. _______________

a>Siobhan Moroney b> Widows and Orphans: Women's Education beyond the Domestic Ideal c> Journal of Family History 25 d> (1) (Jan 2000): e> 26-38

19. To find if the Library carries this article you would:
a. search by author's name in the library's online catalog
b. search by article's title in the library's online catalog
c. search by title of the journal in the library's online catalog
d. ask library staff
e. I don't know

20. Question:
Based on the fairness of the trial and evidence presented, was Bruno Richard Hamptman guilty of kidnapping and killing Charles A. Lindberg's son?

What are the key concepts in the above statement?

History 301: The Historian's Craft
Research Strategy Development Template

Statement of Topic [e.g., Who started the Spanish-American war?]:

Key Concepts [e.g., Spanish-American War, War of 1898, War of the First Revolution]:

Key Modifiers [e.g., Caus*, imperialism, foreign investment, yellow journalism, social Darwinism, foreign relations]:

Key Participants [e.g., Mckinley, Roosevelt, Hearst, Pulitzer, de Lome, Weyler, Marti, Maceo, Gomez]:

Key Corporate Entities [e.g., U.S.S. Maine, New York World, New York Journal]:

Key Geographic Areas Involved [e.g., United States, Cuba, Spain]:

Key Dates [e.g., 1898, 1895–1898]:

Other Limiters [e.g., languages, publication dates, type of material]:

Based on the Above, I Would Express My Search Strategy(ies) as:
History 301: The Historian's Craft

Proposed Source Checklist

Factual Reference Sources to Consult:

Literature Survey Sources to Consult:

Monograph/Book Catalogs to Consult:

Journal Indexes/Abstracts to Consult:

Newspaper Sources to Consult:

Internet Sources to Consult:

Primary Documents Sources to Consult:

Other Sources to Consult:

Chapter 8: Assessing Liberal Arts Classes

Lori E. Buchanan

Institution Description

Austin Peay State University (APSU), Tennessee's designated public comprehensive liberal arts university is located in urban Clarksville (pop. 103,000), forty-five miles northwest of the state capital, Nashville. Of the 7,200 students enrolled at APSU, 63 percent are full-time, 80 percent commute, and 35 percent are nontraditional (22 years or older). Nearly 1,750 students attend the nearby Fort Campbell (Army) Center. More than 1,500 students are enrolled in distance learning courses. APSU's educational emphasis is the liberal arts and professional programs; the Nursing and Education Programs are considered among the best in the state.

The APSU administration's commitment to information literacy (IL) instruction and assessment began in 1986 when the first user education librarian was hired. An instructional facility equipped with twenty-four computers and instructional equipment, including a video networking system and LCD projector, was built in 1994; a third equipment replacement cycle just occurred. In 2000, the user education librarian's participation in the ACRL Information Literacy '00 Immersion Institute received full financial support from the university. Most recently, APSU matched the ACRL national assessment training project's funding and approved leave for the user education librarian to attend training sessions during ALA midwinter and annual conferences. APSU faculty and librarians have a long history of collaboration, including work in the Heritage Program (see below). Most recently, library faculty partnered with a communications professor to develop and teach a new online graduate multimedia literacy course in fall 2001. For more information about IL instruction and assessment at APSU, see http://library.apsu.edu/library/3_5.htm.

Project Participants

A pilot project involving five library faculty members working with five English and communication faculty members occurred during fall 2001. This project built on a thirteen-year relationship among English, communication, and library faculty members who collaborated to create two courses (HUM 1010-1020) that are part of an alternative liberal arts core. The assessment instruments used with HUM 1010 students were then modified and used during spring 2002.

The user education librarian worked with four English instructors in six English 1010 class sections during spring 2002. Instructors selected for the project had involved their students in library instruction during previous semesters and the user education librarian had worked with each of them before. Assessment conducted with these six English 1010 composition classes is the subject of this project. Demographics of the students involved are as follows:

Gender: 87 women, 50 men

Ethnicity: 90 caucasian, 31 African-Americans, 9 Hispanic, and seven other

Age range: 17 to 50; mean age = 22

Student status: 83 first-time, 31 continuing, 12 reentry, and 11 transfer

Class level: 115 freshmen, 16 sophomores, 4 juniors, and one senior

Residence: 100 commute and 37 live on campus

Instruction: 106 had no prior college library instruction, 31 had prior instruction

Project description

Assessment at APSU prior to involvement in this national project was limited primarily to student perception survey questionnaires and essays, as well as instructor feedback and a review/revision process conducted by librarians each semester. In this project, APSU librarians focused on learning outcomes related to evaluative criteria. By the end of the project, librarians had gained assessment experience with nine classes involving more than 150 students. The following information relates directly to the six English 1010 class sections with which the user education librarian worked during spring 2002.

Planning the Assessment

The selected instructional planning process utilized a framework (model) taught by Deb Gilchrist (Pierce College Library director) during the Information Literacy Immersion Institute and in various other workshops. Learning outcomes, curriculum, pedagogy, assessment, and criteria, including questions that address each of these instructional design elements, are the focus of this model. A chart was used to record these elements as they were planned. First, specific **learning outcomes** were identified. This was accomplished by examining both the ACRL/IS *Objectives for Information Literacy Instruction* (http://www.ala.org/acrl/guides/objinfolit.html) and the ACRL *Information Literacy Competency Standards for Higher Education* (http://www.ala.org/acrl/ilcomstan.html). The instruction and assessment targeted one manageable skill area (e.g., evaluative criteria) that was not overly ambitious and which was achievable by the level of students being taught. Next, the **assessment** instruments were developed. The learning outcomes that students were expected to achieve were carefully considered in the design of the instruments. When assessment instruments were developed, the **criteria** describing the expected level of student performance were written. Having the learning outcomes, assessment, and criteria in mind was crucial when it came time to consider **curriculum**, which would prepare students to perform well in the assessment stage. Finally, employing good **pedagogy** (learning activities) ensured that students met the learning outcomes.

Developing the Assessment Instrument

Six assessment instruments for gathering information on student learning outcomes related to ACRL IL Competency Standard Three were developed by the APSU user education librarian in consultation with other librarians teaching in the Heritage Program. The instruments include:

- A preliminary questionnaire (pretest) and a follow-up questionnaire (posttest) designed to measure student knowledge of the five established evaluative criteria (authority, accuracy, coverage, currency, and objectivity). These instruments also gathered information concerning the degree to which students use evaluative criteria and verification methods. The pretest and posttest asked identical questions.
- A Web site evaluation assignment was designed to measure student application of the five criteria listed above, as well as application of information verification methods. A grading criteria (rubric) sheet with which to score the Web site evaluations was incorporated into the Web site evaluation assignment so that students were aware of how the assignment was to be graded.
- A questionnaire designed to assess student perceptions of their own abilities to successfully apply the established evaluative criteria.
- A questionnaire designed to assess student perceptions of their peers' abilities.
- Finally, a questionnaire was created to assess the library instructor's perceptions of students' abilities to successfully apply the established evaluative criteria.

Copies of these instruments are at the end of the chapter.

Analyzing the Results

The study employed a quasi-experimental design using primarily a pretest/posttest analysis, which utilized both parametric and nonparametric techniques. All data were matched (i.e., pretest, posttest) within three different instructional conditions (i.e., none, active learning, lecture). Data were entered into a spreadsheet-type statistical program, SYSTAT (Version 10, ©SPSS Inc., 2000). Following the study's research questions, response frequencies were calculated and comparisons made using statistical tests such as Chi square analyses and analyses of variance (ANOVA).

Six classes (141 students) were divided into three groups as follows:

• A control group of forty-eight students participated in the same activities (see below) as the other groups with one exception, which is that they did not receive instruction from the librarian until after all assessment was completed.

• An active learning experimental group of forty-seven students completed the same activities and participated in an active learning instructional session on evaluative criteria.

• A lecture experimental group of forty-six students completed the same activities and participated in a lecture-formatted instruction session on evaluative criteria.

Activities completed by all students included:

• a preliminary questionnaire (pretest) prior to receiving instruction;
• an instructional session (except for the control group);
• a Web site evaluation assignment;
• a self-assessment questionnaire;
• a peer assessment questionnaire;
• a follow-up questionnaire (posttest).

Of 141 students, 112 completed both the pre- and posttests. The Web site evaluation assignment was completed by 109 students.

Results

Student knowledge, application, and perceptions relating to evaluative criteria are the focus of this project. For detailed results, see http://library.apsu.edu/library/3_5.htm.

Knowledge

As a whole, students listed an average of one criterion on the pretest, while averaging three criteria on the posttest. No significant differences appeared among groups on the pretest; however, posttest results among the groups were significantly different. Although only four control students listed three to five criteria, 32 active learning and 10 lecture students successfully listed three to five criteria, $F(2, 109) = 60.47, p = .001$. Notably, 19 of the 41 active learning students listed all five criteria on the posttest, compared to two lecture and no control students.

Student knowledge as a whole increased between the pre- and the posttest with respect to individual criteria. As evidenced in the table 8-1, the number of students who identified specific criteria is listed for both the pre- and posttests.

Significant differences among groups emerged as a function of instruction.

Table 8-2 illustrates the differences in students' knowledge of the evaluative criteria.

Table 8-1. Pre and Post test knowledge

Criteria	Pretest (# of students)	Post test (# of students)
authority	11	63
accuracy	9	56
coverage	2	34
currency	8	53
objectivity	3	41

Application

When students completed the Web site evaluation assignment, 49 percent were able to successfully apply all five criteria. Students appeared to have the easiest time applying the coverage and currency criteria and more trouble applying authority, accuracy, and objectivity. All forty-one active learning students successfully applied both coverage and currency; all thirty-one of the control students successfully applied coverage. Four (lecture) students were unsuccessful with coverage; ten (five control and five lecture students) were unsuccessful with currency. The accuracy criterion was successfully applied by all but five active learning students; nine control students and sixteen lecture students had trouble applying accuracy

Perceptions

Student perceptions of the number of criteria they could list increased over the course of the study. Initially, they were able to list only one criterion. Immediately following the Web site assignment, they believed they were able to list four. However, in reality, they were only able to accurately recall three criteria, $F(2, 196) = 193.38$, $p = .001$. Of the students completing self-assessments, 88 of the 105 believed they could list three to five of the criteria at that point in time; on the posttest, 46 of the 112 students actually did list three to five criteria. Finally, when students were asked to self-assess the number of criteria they applied in the Web site evaluation assignment, their assessments were significantly correlated to that of the instructor, $r(98) = .32$, $p = .003$. However, peer assessments were not correlated to either the instructor or the self.

Challenges

Challenges encountered in this project were overcome through persistence and hard work. First, the three HUM 1010 sections assessed during fall 2001 contained too few students to produce significant results. Therefore, a new assess-

Table 8-2. Knowledge gained as a function of instruction method.

Group	Authority	Accuracy	Coverage	Currency	Objectivity
Control n = 41	10	6	3	3	4
Active n = 41	36	34	26	34	30
Lecture n = 33	17	16	5	16	7

ment study was developed to use with the six English 1010 classes in spring 2002. A second challenge was that of coordinating the timetable for gathering data; with six instruments to administer in six classes, careful planning and time management were vital. The third and final challenge involved obtaining a good assessment return rate. A thorough analysis of the assessments received and persistent follow-up with students who had not turned in all their work paid off in a reasonably high return rate (approximately 79%).

Conclusion

Assessment is a logical extension of the groundwork laid in establishing information literacy partnerships at APSU. The training and experience gained through participation in this project will allow APSU to continue assessing IL instruction. Specific knowledge gained in this project addresses the need to employ active learning in instruction to achieve the best outcomes. Ongoing assessment activities will enable APSU librarians to shape instruction to best meet the needs of a changing student population.

Preliminary Questions about Evaluating Information

Your Name ______________________________

1) I use criteria to evaluate information. Circle one.

Never   Almost never   Sometimes   Almost always   Always

2) List five criteria for evaluating information.

1.
2.
3.
4.
5.

3) Mark the steps listed below that apply to the following statement.
I verify information by

___ communicating with the author
___ consulting another source
___ asking a friend
___ I don't; instead, I assume the information is correct
___ write any other steps you take below

Follow-up Questions about Evaluating Information

Your Name ______________________________

4) I use criteria to evaluate information. Circle one.

Never   Almost never   Sometimes   Almost always   Always

5) List five criteria for evaluating information.

1.
2.
3.
4.
5.

6) Mark the steps listed below that apply to the following statement.
I verify information by

___ communicating with the author
___ consulting another source
___ asking a friend
___ I don't; instead, I assume the information is correct
___ write any other steps you take below

Web Site Evaluation Assignment

Due in Class on ____________________

Your Name ____

Search and select a high-quality Web site about a paper topic you plan to write this semester. Examine the Web site closely. Use the five established evaluative criteria (accuracy, authority, currency, coverage, and objectivity) and associated questions below, as a resource for completing this assignment.

Write a thorough typed double-spaced paper (at least 500 words) covering the Web site you identified. Give specific examples from your Web site. Your grade on this assignment will be based on how well you incorporate your responses to all of the questions below, as well as how well you address the criteria (accuracy, authority, currency, coverage, and objectivity).

1) What is your topic?
2) What is the complete/full URL of your Web site? Print out and attach the **first page only** of your Web site to your paper.
3) How well does this Web site cover your specific topic or information need? How useful will it be in your paper? (Be specific.)
4) How accurate is this Web site? Are there spelling or grammatical errors? Does the Web site contain outrageous or misleading information?
5) Who wrote or sponsored this Web site? Is it an educational, commercial, governmental, or organizational Web site? What audience was the Web site written for? Be sure to look in the Web site's header, footer, and any links for clues.
6) How objective is the Web site? Is a particular viewpoint presented in the Web site? If so, what is the viewpoint? If not, give evidence of how the Web site covers more than one viewpoint. Be sure to state what viewpoints are covered.

   Does the Web site present
   - Facts
   - Opinions
   - Both facts and opinions

   Give at least one specific example of a fact and/or an opinion covered by the Web site.
7) How current is this Web site? When was the information first posted? Has it been updated within the past year? If present, how current are the sources cited or links contained in the Web site?
8) What is the breadth and depth of the Web site's coverage? What is its purpose? Does it cover a highly specialized topic area in great detail, or does it merely provide a general overview of a broad topic?
9) What are some steps you can take to verify the accuracy of the information contained in this Web site? (Be specific.)

These are the **grading** criteria:

Score Levels	**Number of Criteria Covered**	**Information Verification**	**Content of Essay**
A	Applied all 5 evaluative criteria (accuracy, authority, coverage, currency, and objectivity)	Stated 2-3 possible steps to take in verifying information on Web site	Detailed, in-depth, clear descriptions of appropriately applied criteria
B	Applied 4 of 5 evaluative criteria listed above	Stated 1-2 possible steps to take in verifying information on Web site	Understandable and clear, but insufficient detail and depth
C	Applied 3 of 5 evaluative criteria listed above	Stated 1 possible step to take in verifying information on Web site	Understandable, but abbreviated and not entirely clear or simply copying some class materials
F	Applied less than 3 of the 5 evaluative criteria listed above	Stated no verification steps	Vague or nonsensical sentences, or copies class materials with no original work

Self-Assessment of Information Evaluative Skills

Your Name ______________________________

Circle the **ONE** answer out of the available choices that comes closest to what you perceive your abilities to be. Please be honest. Completing this questionnaire is **required**, but your specific answers to the statements will **NOT** impact your grade.

1) Overall, based on the established evaluative criteria, I think the Web site I selected was of high quality.

Yes No

2) As it relates directly to the topic about which I plan to write a paper, the Web site I selected is

of no use of very limited use of some use useful very useful

3) I successfully applied the following number of the established evaluative criteria in my Web site Evaluation Assignment.

one two three four five

4) Before taking this class, I applied evaluative criteria to information and its sources.

never almost never sometimes almost always always

5) At the present moment, I can list from memory the following number of established evaluative criteria covered in the assignment.

one two three four five

6) Before taking this class, I was in the habit of checking other sources to either confirm or question the point of view or bias of an information source.

never almost never sometimes almost always always

Peer Assessment of Information Evaluative Skills

Your Name ______________________________

Circle the **ONE** answer out of the available choices that comes closest to what you perceive your classmate's abilities to be, based on your examination of her or his completed Web Site Evaluation Assignment. It will be helpful to review the assignment (attached) and the Web site your classmate evaluated **before** you read your classmate's work and answer the questions.

Please be honest. Taking the time to complete this questionnaire in a serious fashion is **required**, but your specific answers to the statements below in no way impact your grade or your classmate's grade. Your classmate will **NOT** see the results of your assessment.

1) Overall, based on the established evaluative criteria, my peer selected (see attached completed Web Site Evaluation Assignment) is of high quality.

Yes No

2) In relation to the paper topic my peer has selected (see attached completed assignment), the selected Web site is

of no use of very limited use of some use useful very useful

3) In my opinion, my peer successfully applied the following number of established evaluative criteria that were either discussed in class and/or found within the assignment.

one two three four five

Instructor Preliminary Assessment of Information Evaluative Skills

Student Name ______________________________

Circle the **ONE** answer out of the available choices that comes closest to what you perceive the student's abilities to be, based on your examination of her or his completed Web Site Evaluation Assignment. It will be helpful to review the assignment (attached) and the Web site the student evaluated **before** you read the student's work and answer the questions.

The student will **NOT** see the results of this particular assessment. Please forward this sheet to the librarian as soon as you complete the preliminary assessment.

1) Overall, based on the established evaluative criteria, the student selected (see attached completed Web Site Evaluation Assignment) is of high quality.

Yes No

2) In relation to the paper topic the student has selected (see attached completed assignment), the selected Web site is

of no use of very limited use of some use useful very useful

3) In my opinion, the student successfully applied the following number of established evaluative criteria.

one two three four five

Chapter 9: Assessing Student Learning Outcomes: Training Academic Librarians

Barbara Burd

Institution Description

Regent University, a small private university offering graduate degrees in twenty-six programs from eight schools, enrolls approximately 2,000 students, about half of whom participate in distance learning. Many of the students are nontraditional, seeking to further their education while pursuing careers. All students are required to take an online course in library research and resources during their first year.

Project Participants

When redesigning the curriculum for the MBA program, it was decided that introduction to information literacy would be integrated throughout one of the introductory classes to familiarize students with the strategy, resources, and processes that they would need to successfully complete the program. Dr. Greg Stone invited me to participate in designing this course so that it would include a librarian's perspective and expertise in developing activities focused on meeting information literacy (IL) competencies. Because this is a large class and requires considerable individual student–teacher interaction, the class is taught by a team of faculty, including myself.

BUSN620: Ideas, Customers, and Competition (6 credits) is one of the introductory courses in the MBA program. As such, it is designed to introduce students to the research skills they will need throughout the program. The goals of the course are to:

- generate creative, innovative business ideas;
- evaluate business ideas in light of
  - -corporate purpose;
  - -customer demand;
  - -technological feasibility;
  - -competition;
  - -internal capabilities;
- craft a succinct and compelling strategy to pursue a business idea;
- develop and present a feasibility study for a business idea, incorporating all of the above elements.

This course typically has about fifty students divided into groups of approximately eight to ten, with each group being the responsibility of an instructor. The course is taught both on campus and distance, all modules and activities are administered through Blackboard, and both on-campus and distance students are integrated through online discussions and activity postings. For the spring 2002 class enrollment numbered forty-eight: fourteen students were registered as distance students; twenty-nine were on-campus; and five were registered in the EMBA (Executive MBA) program.

Project Description

Planning for Assessment

Each of the modules in the course is designed with specific learning outcomes judged by faculty to be integral to the MBA program. Relating these outcomes to the *ACRL Information Literacy Competency Standards for Higher Education* helped us to clearly formulate the competencies we wanted to address as we sought to align these competencies with a business environment.

According to our course syllabus:

> In BUSN 620, the objective is to create a feasibility study for an idea, product, or service that you develop. The feasibility study is an examination, analysis, and investigation of key factors surrounding the marketing, production, and financial aspects of a business venture. The final output is a go/no go recommendation with qualifications.
>
> BUSN 620 will cultivate your ability to create, generate, and innovate new ideas, products, and services (Modules 1 through 3). Once you actually cultivate an idea you want to pursue, you will conduct extensive research related to the industry that is the environment for that idea, prod-

uct, or service (Module 4). Modules 5 through 11 walk you step-by-step through the process of gathering data and information that will let you determine the feasibility of your idea. In other words, is your idea, product, or service possible? Modules 12 and 13 are where you present your feasibility study to a public audience and then construct your written feasibility report.

The course consists of thirteen modules, each of which is designed with specific objectives. The objectives of modules 4, 5, 6, and 7 are directly built around the IL standards.

Module 4—Researching an Idea
Objectives: After completion of this module, and given a business idea, you should be able to:

1. frame the key questions upon which its success depends;
2. describe the evidence and information needed to answer the questions;
3. locate, organize, and summarize the information needed to answer the questions;
4. draw conclusions about your questions based on the evidence you gathered.

Module 5—Researching an Industry: Building an Industry Analysis
Objectives: Upon completion of this module, you should be able to:

1. demonstrate your ability to research an industry and identify key competitors;
2. define the dynamics of a given industry using Porter's Five Forces Model of Competition and Porter's Value Chain System.

Module 6—Key Competitor Analysis
Objectives: Upon completion of this module, you should be able to:

1. identify how you intend to position your company in your industry;
2. clearly define the benefits and value added of your product/service idea;
3. identify and evaluate the firms that "do business" in your specific "competitive arena" *and* provide products and services that are similar to the benefits and value added you intend to provide;
4. analyze and explain the competitive environment *for the firms in your "competitive arena,"* including the overall structure (e.g., fragmented, mature, declining, emerging, global) as well as the overall competitive climate;
5. identify and evaluate the technology advances within your competitive arena that you will need to consider in order to "gain entry" and maintain competitive parity in your "competitive arena";

6. identify and analyze your most critical key competitor using Porter's Company Value Chain to contrast *specifically* how your organization will function compared to theirs;

7. evaluate the strategy of your most critical key competitor and identify sources of competitive advantage.

Module 7—Market Analysis

Objectives: Upon completion of this module, you should be able to:

1. evaluate the market for certain products/services, divide customers into segments based on key characteristics, demonstrate the homogeneity of each segment, and compare/contrast key characteristics of the customers in the various segments;

2. compare and contrast customer and consumer;

3. compare and contrast customers in the consumer market (B2C) and in the business-to-business market (B2B).

With each module, students must respond to activities by posting in Blackboard. Students are required to write summary papers for Modules 8, Market Feasibility, and 10, Operations Feasibility. The culminating project is a comprehensive feasibility study.

Developing the Assessment Instrument

Because the IL competencies were integrated within the structure of the course, activities in each module were graded on how well the student was able to complete the research, evaluate, and synthesize the information and communicate his or her findings to others for discussion. We developed a grading rubric for the summary papers that included recognition of performance indicators of information literacy.

In addition, I asked students to complete a self-evaluation at the end of the course. For this self-evaluation, I asked students to address the following: (1) to briefly describe what they learned about doing research in this course; (2) to comment on their success in using the tutorials on Locating Industry Information and Locating Company Information; (3) to comment on which databases they used and their success in obtaining information; (4) to describe other resources they used to complete their projects; and (5) to assess their level of confidence in being able to find appropriate business information.

Assessment Instrument

Because a different professor grades each group and assessment is based on summary papers and studies, it was important to have some kind of common understanding of concepts. Developing a rubric that all could use helped to ensure that grading was uniform among professors. Included at the end of the chapter are two examples of the grading templates that we use throughout the course.

Results

Overall assessment was reflected in the course grade. Students could not pass the course without completing the necessary research components. All teaching faculty assessed the projects based on the quality of the research. Reference lists were checked to make sure that students were including information obtained from a variety of sources. In discussions of the quality of the final feasibility study, all teaching faculty felt that the emphasis on information literacy was resulting in better-quality papers and presentations.

Responses to the self-evaluation varied greatly in some areas. Some of the students felt they were already proficient in doing research and that emphasizing this was a waste of their time. More responded that they had completed their undergraduate many years before or that their undergraduate education had not included this information, so this focus on research was very important to them. Most used the business databases mentioned throughout the course, and almost half used the tutorials or other study guides that were available. Although we strongly encouraged students to "get away from" reliance on the Web as their sole information provider, many students said that searching on the Web was much easier than searching databases. One person wrote a comment that I think may be a reflection of why students prefer Web searching to searching databases, "Simplify the process!! Not so many rules and procedures for all the different databases! How can you remember them all?? The system appears to be designed for a librarian who enjoys the "search," not an average "Joe" who just needs some information." Almost all expressed a greater level of confidence in being able to do the research that would be needed for them to complete the program.

Challenges

One of the biggest challenges for me as a librarian was managing the time to devote to this course along with my other responsibilities. Besides teaching certain modules, individual consultations by phone, e-mail, or in person increased substantially. Some other challenges involved the actual process of integration of the competencies into the subject-specific format and speaking a "common language" with faculty who had very definite ideas about the outcomes from a business perspective. Although I was the librarian in this project, more important, it was a team project and focusing on the development of the course with student learning in mind overcame many of the obstacles.

Conclusion

Overall, this course was well received by students. Faculty expressed satisfaction with the content and the achievement of course objectives. We continue to learn and refine both the content and learning objectives as we see areas where we feel we can improve. For summer we will be adding a videoconferencing component that will allow us to experiment with bringing together classes on the main campus and in a satellite location. In keeping with the theme of developing creativity and innovation in students, we try to use various pedagogies, especially in the area of technology, to enhance the student learning experience.

This project afforded me the opportunity to be involved in course development and collaborate with faculty on a project that we believed would set the foundation for students to successfully complete the MBA program. While the project is time-consuming and work intensive, it gives me the opportunity to expand my teaching and to add a new dimension to my role as librarian. The integration of information literacy throughout the course provides a "point of need" approach, that hopefully reinforces the skills being taught.

BUSN 620-EVALUATION SHEET (Market Feasibility Section – Modules 5 through 8)		
Student Name		**Section** **Date**
% of Total	**Score**	
20%	____	**I. Industry Analysis (from Mod 5 assignments)** a. Industry structure, characteristics & trends b. Description of industry forces and their impact (use Porter 5 Forces) c. Key success factors d. Description of industry players & competitive structure of industry (Industry Value Chain Analysis is useful here) e. Identification & analysis of key competitors
20%	____	**II. Key Competitor Analysis (from Mod 6 assignments)** a. Defining/positioning your product—concept (see activity 1 of Mod 6). b. Identify & analyze your key competitors. c. Analysis of the marketing strategy/programs of your key competitors. d. Identify the competitive advantages of your key competitors (company value chain analysis is useful here).
20%	____	**III. Market/Customer Analysis (from Mod 7 assignments)** a. Describe key market characteristics, trends & how the market is segmented. b. Identify and describe the customers (segment) you intend to target. c. Describe why these customers will buy your product/service over the products/services of your key competitors. What will be your competitive advantage?
20%	____	**IV. Channel Analysis (from Mod 8 assignments)** a. Describe how each member of your potential channel (value chain) adds value to the members it serves. b. Identify the critical partnerships/relationships with channel members that you will need to "do business" and reach your target customers. c. Discuss whether any of these relationships provides a source of competitive advantage for your business. d. Summary of your entry strategy given the conclusions you developed from your industry and market analysis.
20%	____	**V. Process Issues** a. Logical consistency from start to finish b. Thoroughness of analysis c. Clarity of presentation (including use of supporting materials such as Porter Five Forces, Value Chain Analysis, charts and graphs which summarize information more clearly) d. Spelling, punctuation, and grammar
100%	____	

BUSN620 Feasibility Study Comment Form for: **Date:** **Reviewer:** **Points Possible:** **Points Earned:**	
Element	***Comments***
Executive Summary	
Concept (mod 4)	
Industry/competitor analysis (overall) **Industry composition and trends (mod 5)** (Industry overview, Porter's Five-Forces Model, industry situation [emerging, high-velocity, maturing, stagnant/declining, fragmented, international], Porter's Value Chain [upstream-downstream])	
Key competitor analysis (mod 6) (Your fit in industry, competitors' worksheet, differentiation, KSFs, biblical perspective, your worldview, technology)	
Market/customer analysis (mod 7) (Characteristics, trends, target markets, benefits of your role, demographics, psychographics, lifestyle, rank segments, stage of adoption and hierarchy of effort, information to decision makers)	
Channels of sales and distribution analysis (mod 8) (Types in your industry, advantages, disadvantages, needs, your partnership)	
Operations/Production Feasibility (overall)	
Internal Capabilities and assessment (mod 9)	
SWOT (mod 10)	
Financial Feasibility (mod 11)	
Conclusions and Recommendations (Is it feasible, and why or why not?)	
Overall evaluation criteria (Command of topic, thoroughness, analytical models, writing style, spelling, grammar, format, appearance)	
General Comments	

Grading Criteria

The following table shows the graded assignments for each module within BUSN 620. The details for grading criteria are explained within each module.

Mod. #	Module Title	Assignment	Activities 1	2	3	4	5	Participation Points	Graded Activities
1	Conceiving an Idea	BB Participation	Y	N	Y	Y	.	3	0
2	Strategic Fit	BB Participation	Y	Y	Y	Y	.	4	0
3	Strategic Choice	BB Participation	Y	Y	Y	.	.	3	0
4	Researching an Idea	BB Participation	Y	N	Y	Y	Y	4	0
5	Building Industry Anal	BB Participation	N	Y	Y	Y	Y	4	0
6	Competition	BB Participation	Y	Y	Y	Y	Y	5	0
7	Customer Segments	BB Participation	Y	Y	Y	.	.	4	0
8	Marketing Channels	BB Participation	Y	Y	Y	.	.	3	0
		Mkt Feasibility	.	.	.	Y	.	0	10
9	Internal Capabilities	BB Participation	N	N	Y	.	.	2	0
10	SWOT	BB Participation	N	N	.	.	.	0	0
		Ops Feasibility	.	.	Y	.	.	0	10
11	Financial Feasibility	BB Participation	N	N	N	N	Y	2	0
12	Presentation Skills	BB Participation	N	.	.	.	.	0	0
		FS Presentation	.	Y	.	.	.	0	20
13	Report Development	BB Participation	N	Y	.	.	.	3	0
		Final Report	.	.	Y	.	.	0	30
Potential Bonus Points								0	8
Total Points								37	78

MAXIMUM POSSIBLE POINTS FOR BB PARTICIPATION	30
MAXIMUM POSSIBLE POINTS FOR GRADED ACTIVITIES	70
MAXIMUM POSSIBLE POINTS FOR THE CLASS	100

Chapter 10: Assessing Student Learning Outcomes in Sociology

Cynthia H. Comer

Institutional Description

Founded in 1833, Oberlin College combines a distinguished undergraduate college of arts and sciences with one of the nation's leading music conservatories. A Carnegie Baccalaureate Colleges—Liberal Arts institution, it enrolls approximately 2,850 students and employs approximately 290 full-time faculty. The library has worked actively in cooperation with faculty to address information literacy concerns. A 1996 report by the faculty library committee articulated the need for better integration of information literacy (IL) skills into the curriculum. Subsequent to the report, a faculty task force, working in close collaboration with library staff, designed a nine-session workshop on information literacy that was offered to faculty during the 1997 winter (January) term. The workshop served the dual purpose of better acquainting faculty with the library's rapidly expanding electronic resources and initiating discussion of information literacy as a curricular concern. Each winter term since, the library has offered workshops for faculty that focus in some way on information literacy.

In 1998, the libraries of the Five Colleges of Ohio consortium received an AT&T Learning Network Teaching and Technology Grant, which it used to develop a Web-based IL tutorial aimed at lower-level undergraduates. An extensive assessment was made of the tutorial, using a pre-/posttest and qualitative questionnaire. Results showed that students' scores improved after taking the tutorial. In 1999, the consortium was awarded a major grant from the Andrew W. Mellon Foundation to support a three-year program called Integrating Information Literacy into the Liberal Arts Curriculum. The grant project focuses on building collaborative partnerships between librarians and faculty members at each of the campuses, with the ultimate goal of increasing undergraduate students' IL skills and capabilities. Each faculty member who participates in the project is asked to address in a final report student success in mastering IL content in their courses; librarians have worked closely with faculty to design a variety of assessment methods to address this issue. Although the library has not had, in general, a strong culture of assessment, in recent years it has begun to give more attention to assessment through an extensive self-study, participation in the LibQUAL+ survey, and grant-related activities.

Project Participants

We worked with a professor of sociology, who teaches Sociology 211, Social Research Methods. According to the fall 2000 course syllabus, "This course is an introduction to the types of methodology used in the social sciences—both quantitative and qualitative. Emphasis will be placed on which type of methodology is appropriate for given situations as well as understanding the underlying logic and assumptions of each method. Time will also be spent discussing how method must be used concurrently with theory. Two goals of this course are to develop information literacy (how to locate, manage, and use information) and to introduce students to the various methods used within the discipline so that they will be able to interpret scholarly articles in order to utilize fully this academic resource. Some basic data analysis will be covered in conjunction with the employment of various methodological techniques."

The course is offered each fall semester and usually enrolls forty-plus students. There is a prerequisite of one introductory-level sociology course. The methods course is required for the sociology major and is generally taken by students in their sophomore or junior year.

Project Description

Introduction

Prior to receiving the ACRL/IMLS assessment grant, the instructor and I had collaborated in redesigning the course in the summer of 2000 to focus on social research methods as a means to *manage information*. As a result, it already included many aspects of information literacy. Most of this content is presented in a series of hands-on IL labs cotaught by the librarian and the instructor. As part of the redesign, we had developed an evaluative questionnaire that students completed near the end of the course that measured student opinions, self-assessment of skills, application in other classes of skills learned in this class, and resources students both used and determined to be useful in research projects. Through this project, I expanded the questionnaire to include new questions designed to assess student learning and to seek more in-depth student evaluation of resources used. This instrument was then administered at the beginning of the semester as a pretest and again at the end of the semester as a posttest. Students also completed assignments for each of four IL labs, all of which were reviewed by the instructor. Also, students worked in small groups on a major research project over the entire semester; for this project, students were required to prepare an annotated bibliography and literature review and to give a formal presentation of their research results to class peers. These also were reviewed and evaluated by the instructor.

Planning for Assessment

Our assessment plan had to meet the following needs: We (the instructor and the librarian) wanted to give students feedback on their progress and on the information they were finding in support of their final projects. We wanted to know whether students learned the concepts we had identified to be covered in the information literacy labs. Because this project was a continuation of a course initially revised under a grant program, we wanted to continue to build on our earlier work, as well as report to the grant administrators how the project was progressing in the year following that when the course redesign was supported by the grant.

When the course was initially redesigned to incorporate information literacy, the instructor and I had outlined the major IL concepts we wanted students to learn; this list of concepts determined what we covered in the various IL labs. We also designed several assignments to accompany the labs. For the assessment project, we refined the broad goals we had articulated earlier. Although not stated in the exact language of the *ACRL Information Literacy Competency Standards*, the concepts we chose to cover are all represented in the standards in one form or another; the instructor generally phrased these goals in her own words.

Developing the Assessment Instrument

Unfortunately, there was not a great deal of time between the summer workshop offered through the ACRL/IMLS grant project and the beginning of the fall semester, so the instrument was redesigned primarily without the collaborative input of the instructor. Because we already had articulated our goals for student learning outcomes, I wrote items for the pretest that would help us determine where students were in their knowledge at the beginning of the course and which could be used at the end of the course to measure whether students had mastered each concept. This part of the instrument took the form of several multiple-choice questions. We included several checklists of resources and repeated a number of open-ended self-assessment questions we had asked students on the evaluative questionnaire the year before in order to compare responses to those from last year. There was no time to pretest the questionnaire, nor to check the questions for validity and reliability. I simply did as well as I could and hoped for the best! The pre- and posttest are at the end of this chapter

Analyzing the Results

At the time of this writing, all of the qualitative data and some, but not all, of the quantitative data have been analyzed. Because some of the questions on the new assessment instrument were carried over from the previous year's evaluative survey, for some questions we now have two years of data available, although these data focus primarily on students' self-assessments of their abilities and their self-reports on the resources they used and found helpful. All of the narrative comments students made on the forms were transcribed and coded by different categories.

Results of the Assessment

Initial results are available for some of the data, and there are some interesting findings, discussed below.

Course Assignments

When compared to work completed by students in prior years, before IL labs were developed for the course, the instructor found that students performed much better on the annotated bibliography and literature review assignment. The sources students cited came from more diverse sources, were more on target and relevant to the students' project topics, were more current and up-to-date, and were more likely to come from scholarly journal literature. The final research project peer presentation was a new element in the course, replacing the final exam students were given in previous years. The instructor found that this assignment equipped students with new skills related to presenting research to an audience, that the quality of student research was strengthened by the cumulative approach that took place in the IL labs and related assignments, that a synergy developed among group members that had not been present in previous years, and that students' group presentations were of high quality.

Assessment Instrument

There were four parts to the assessment instrument: closed-ended questions that measured student attitudes, behaviors, and self-assessed abilities related to IL skills; open-ended questions that obtained detailed information on students' experiences and opinions; checklists on which students indicated resources used for this class, which were most useful and which would be useful in other courses; and questions—mostly multiple choice—designed to measure student learning of various IL concepts and skills. As of this writing, data are available only for the first three parts; contact the author for results from the fourth part of the assessment instrument (e-mail: cynthia.comer@oberlin.edu).

The following four charts compare student responses from fall 2000 and fall 2001. The exact wording of questions is included in the assessment instrument section.

As shown in table 10-1, approximately 90 percent of respondents indicated that they believed themselves to be more efficient at retrieving relevant search results from electronic databases as a result of the IL material covered in the course. High percentages of students also indicated that the IL instruction they received in this course would be useful in other sociology courses, as well as other non-sociology courses. The last measure on table 1 indicates that 70 percent or more of students had already applied IL skills taught in this course in other courses and situations where they needed to find information, suggesting that students are able to transfer these skills to new situations and environments.

In table 10-2, students reported that they felt better equipped to critically evaluate information, refine their research topics, and obtain information. However, many students also reported that they still lacked confidence in critically evaluating information. Their ratings of their abilities in this area dropped significantly in the second year, despite our decision to spend more lab time on the topic of evaluating information. The lower score could indicate that we did a poorer job of imparting this information to students the second year, or it may indicate that the more students learn, the more they realize how much they do not know. Approximately 80 percent of students indicated they believed that the development of sound information literacy skills should be an integral part of a liberal arts education.

Table 10-1. Attitudes and Behaviors

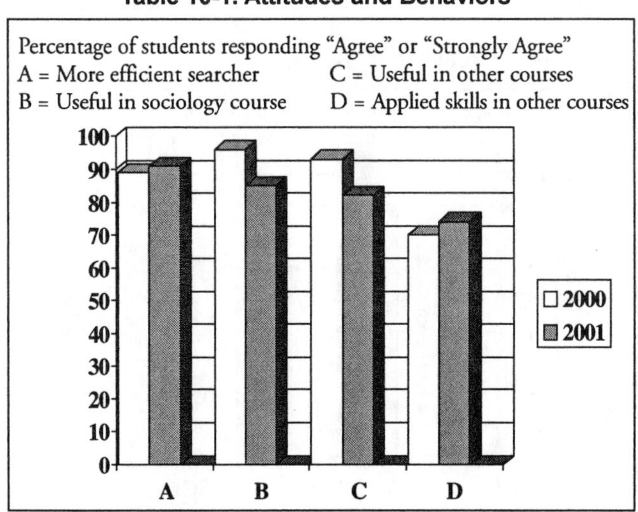

Table 10-2. Attitudes and Behaviors

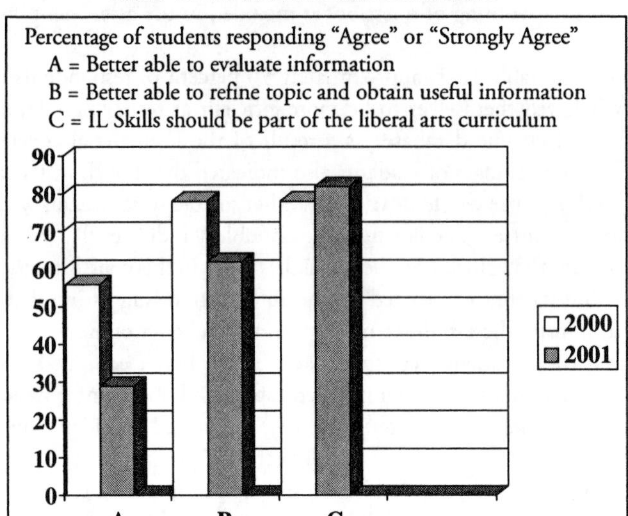

Table 10-3 lists the top five resources (selected from a list of more than a dozen) that students indicated they had used for their research in the class. The top five sources were the same in each of the two years and offer no particular surprises. Students also were asked to indicate from among the same list those sources they actually found useful for their research. Table 10-4 shows how the top five sources fared in terms of usefulness. It is interesting to note that although most students used the Web in their research, few found it actually useful. Socio-

Table 10-3. Resources Used

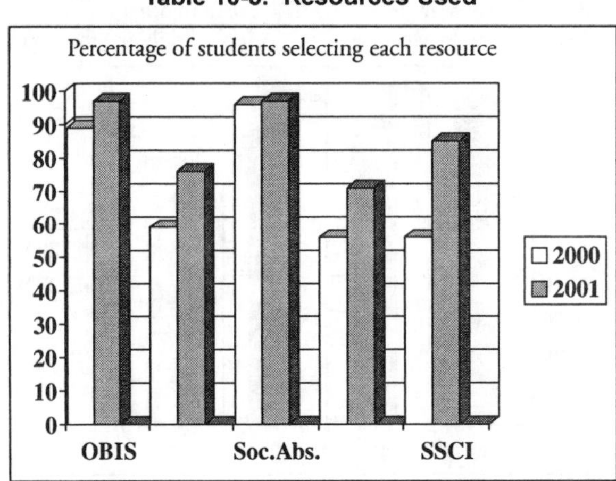

Table 10-4. Resources found most useful

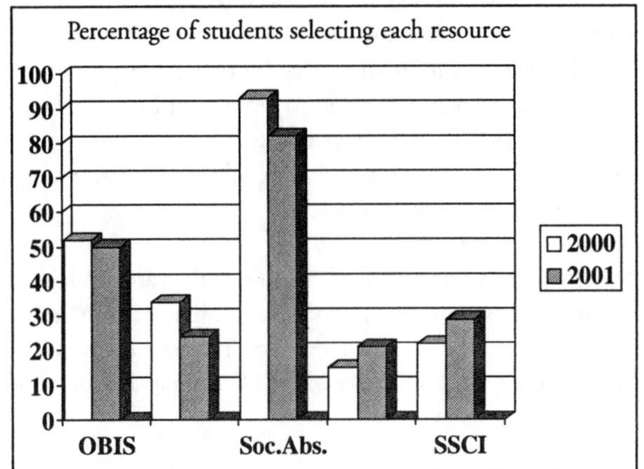

logical Abstracts, and to a lesser extent, the library's catalog (OBIS) received the highest ratings both years.

The assessment instrument also generated a good deal of qualitative data in the form of comments from students to various questions. In general, these comments were positive and students indicated they were more successful at conducting research, knew more about the resources available to them, would (or already had) applied their new skills to other courses and situations, and felt that information literacy was an important aspect of a liberal arts education. A number of students also reported that they were already familiar with much of the information and that some of the lab content was a repeat for them. This often came from students who had previously attended library instruction sessions in other courses. Following is a selection of typical student comments in several of the areas in which we asked questions.

On whether the course was successful in meeting information literacy goals:

- "The labs at the beginning of the semester were an excellent guide to how to locate materials relevant to your research."
- "The part on evaluating web sites was helpful, because I haven't done that before."
- "I feel like I learned a few tricks, a few places to search, that open doors and make researching a little easier."

On what information literacy skills the course helped develop:

- "Using the skills I learned in this class can increase research effectiveness, thus minimizing time wasted on fruitless searches."
- "I feel confident that I've gained much more knowledge regarding the research process."

- "The course exposed me to many sources of information that I had not used before. I also learned new skills for search retrieval."

On whether the information literacy instruction will be useful in other courses:

- "This has helped a lot in preparing for research papers in other courses."
- "I have another research paper to write, and I was able to find relevant sources more quickly that I would have before."
- "Only problem is that I wish I took this course early in my college life. It would have been useful in other classes."

On the issue of redundancy:

- "It helped me to be refreshed on things that are available to me, but I had already learned most of it before and was familiar with the material."
- "Some of this type of instruction was interesting and informative, but most of it was redundant for students who had taken a class in which a research paper was required."

Challenges

The two major challenges I have faced with this project are communication and time. Although the instructor is very interested in, and receptive to, incorporating information literacy into the course, the amount of time she can devote to this task is limited. The assessment work adds another level of complexity to teaching the course, and although the data are there, she will not be able to give them her full attention until this summer. Although I have access to much of the data, those for the newly written multiple-choice questions have only recently been input into SPSS for in-depth analysis. Because I am not trained in using that software, I will not know the results of that aspect of our assessment until the instructor has time to review the data and meet with me to discuss the results.

Conclusion

The data suggest certain changes we should consider the next time the course is taught. Students would continue to benefit from increased opportunities for hands-on learning. We also need to devote more attention to critical evaluation skills, in particular getting students to the point where they feel confident in their ability to evaluate information resources. Perhaps through more careful screening of pretest results, we might seek ways to address the issue of redundancy for students who enter the course with a higher level of IL skills. Some students could opt out of the first lab session, for example. Another approach would be to encourage the incorporation of IL instruction in all introductory sociology courses. As one introductory course is a prerequisite for enrollment in the Social Research Methods course, this would better ensure that students enter the methods course in a more equal footing in terms of their knowledge of IL concepts.

I also realize that there is much more I could be doing to assess students' work. One place this could happen is the series of assignments connected to each IL lab.

These assignments cover basic reference sources in the discipline, such as encyclopedias and printed bibliographies; the library's online catalog; research databases; online full-text resources; effective searching techniques; modifying search statements in order to yield more pertinent references; comparing and evaluating databases; locating relevant information from diverse sources; and evaluating the value and relevance of citations retrieved. Another place this could happen is with the annotated bibliography and literature review, as well as the students' research presentations. Currently, I am not involved in reviewing any of these assignments, but I realize that the feedback from these would be very useful in evaluating my own teaching and could help me find ways to present the material more effectively. My input also would provide a perspective that differs from the instructor's on how well students performed on each assignment. Even if I were not involved in grading student work, it would be helpful to review how well students are completing these various assignments.

Assessment Instrument

Sociology 211
Information Literacy Questionnaire and Pretest

Name: ____

Currently, I am a: ___ Soph. ___ Jr. ___ Sr.

___ Other (explain): __________________________

I have previously attended a session given by a librarian in a college-level *sociology* course about using libraries and doing library research.

____ Yes ____ No If yes, how many times? ____

I have previously attended a session given by a librarian about using libraries and doing research in a college-level course *other than in sociology.*

____ Yes ____ No If yes, how many times? ____

1. Rate your experience/ability in using each of the following kinds of software (check one level for each kind of software):

	None	A little	Moderate	Lots
Word processor (e.g., Microsoft Word)				
Presentation (e.g., PowerPoint)				
Library catalog (e.g., OBIS)				
Research databases (e.g., Periodical Abstracts)				
Web browser (e.g., Netscape)				
Spreadsheet (e.g., Excel)				

2. Describe how a popular magazine differs from a scholarly journal in each of the three categories listed below:
Example: Availability: Popular magazines available widely in bookstores and at newsstands; scholarly journals are generally available only in libraries or by subscription

a. readership/audience:

b. how articles are selected for publication:

c. who writes the articles:

3. You are writing a research paper about employment discrimination against people who are HIV positive. If your research strategy is to start by looking at works that provide a general, broad overview of the topic before looking at those that are more specific, in which order would you consult the sources below? (Circle one.)
   a. books, research articles, encyclopedias
   b. encyclopedias, books, research articles
   c. research articles, books, encyclopedias
   d. research articles, encyclopedias, books

4. Which of the following searches in an online database would likely result in the greatest number of records retrieved? (Circle one.)
   a. children and divorce
   b. children or divorce
   c. children not divorce

5. Which group of words would be most useful to use in a database for researching the following: "Does the racial composition of a jury affect the likelihood that it will choose the death penalty for a convicted murderer?" (Circle one.)
   a. race, jury, affect
   b. murder, race, death penalty
   c. likelihood, jury, death penalty
   d. murder, capital punishment, race
   e. jury, race, death penalty

6. If your keyword search "schools and violence" in the research database Sociological Abstracts retrieves 932 records, what would be the next best step to help focus the search? (Circle all that apply.)
   a. Switch to a different research database
   b. Add a third term that is related to your topic and search again
   c. Search instead for "schools or violence"
   d. Look only at the first 30 records
   e. Search the two terms again, but as subject words rather than as keywords

7. When evaluating the quality of a Web site for possible use in a research paper, which domain (URL ending) would be most likely to cause you to be cautious?
   a. .org
   b. .com
   c. .gov
   d. .edu

8. Suppose you read an article that is relevant to your research paper. In which instances should you include a footnote for the article in your own paper? (Circle all that apply.)
   a. When you copy an entire paragraph from the article word for word
   b. When you rewrite the paragraph using your own words
   c. When you directly quote a sentence from the article
   d. When you summarize the key findings of the article using your own words
   e. None of the above

9. Rate your ability level for each of the following kinds of research skills:

	Poor: Need to improve skill level	Fair: Could use some good tips	Excellent: Confident and skilled
Choosing and focusing an appropriate topic for my research			
Finding a broad range of material and information suitable to my research			
Efficiently retrieving a relevant set of search results from an electronic database			
Critically evaluating information for quality and authority			
Critically evaluating information for relevance and usefulness			
Knowing when and how to appropriately cite other sources in my own writing			

10. List any aspects of doing research for which you feel you could benefit from more instruction, hands-on practice, or assistance:

11. Which of the following resources/types of materials have you used before? (Check all that apply.)

___ OBIS ___ OhioLINK ___ Internet/Web ___ printed bibliographies
___ EJC (OhioLINK Electronic Journal Center) ___ JSTOR
___ Sociological Abstracts ___ PsycINFO ___ ERIC
___ LEXIS/NEXIS Academic Universe ___ SSCI (Social Sciences Citation Index)
___ Periodical Abstracts ___ Ingenta ___ Annual Review of Sociology
___ printed journals ___ government publications

12. Which of the following library services have you used before? (Check all that apply.)

___ Checked out a book from the Oberlin College Library
___ Requested a book through OhioLINK
___ Asked for research help at the reference desk
___ Requested an individual research appointment with a reference librarian
___ Requested an article through interlibrary loan
___ Used the library's home page as a starting point for finding useful information

Sociology 211
Additional Questions asked on the Posttest

Please check the response that best fits your level of agreement/disagreement with the following statements:

Rating scale:
___ Strongly Agree___ Agree___ Neutral___ Disagree___ Strongly Disagree

1. I am more efficient at retrieving a relevant set of search results from an electronic database as a result of the instructional material covered in the labs.
Comments:

2. The instruction I received on identifying, locating, and using information will be useful to me in other **sociology** courses.
Comments:

3. The instruction I received on identifying, locating, and using information will be useful to me in other **non-sociology** courses.
Comments:

4. I have applied these skills in other courses and situations where I needed to find information.
Comments:

5. As a result of the instruction in the labs, I feel better equipped to critically evaluate information that I find.
Comments:

6. As a result of the instruction in the labs, I am better able to refine my research topics and obtain information useful to my project.
Comments:

7. The development of sound information literacy skills should be an integral part of a liberal arts education.
Comments:

8. Working in research groups throughout the semester was productive.
Comments:

9. Collaborative learning helped make the research process more clear to me.
Comments:

Please check all that apply:

10. Which resources did you use for your research in this class?

___ OBIS ___ OhioLINK ___Internet/WWW ___ Printed Bibliographies
___ JSTOR ___ EJC (OhioLINK Electronic Journal Center)
___ Sociological Abstracts ___ SSCI (Social Sciences Citation Index)
___ Printed Journals ___ Annual Review of Sociology On Line
___ Psych INFO ___ERIC ___LEXIS/NEXIS ___ Periodical Abstracts
___OTHER (Please specify) ______________________________

11. Which resources did you find most useful for your research in this class?

___ OBIS ___ OhioLINK ___Internet/WWW ___ Printed Bibliographies
___ JSTOR ___ EJC (OhioLINK Electronic Journal Center)
___ Sociological Abstracts ___ SSCI (Social Sciences Citation Index)
___ Printed Journals ___ Annual Review of Sociology On Line
___ Psych INFO ___ERIC ___LEXIS/NEXIS ___ Periodical Abstracts
___OTHER (Please specify) ______________________________

12. Which resources do you think you will be most likely to use for research in other classes at Oberlin?

___ OBIS ___ OhioLINK ___Internet/WWW ___ Printed Bibliographies
___ JSTOR ___ EJC (OhioLINK Electronic Journal Center)
___ Sociological Abstracts ___ SSCI (Social Sciences Citation Index)
___ Printed Journals ___ Annual Review of Sociology On Line
___ Psych INFO ___ERIC ___LEXIS/NEXIS ___ Periodical Abstracts
___OTHER (Please specify) ______________________________

Please give detailed written comments for the following questions.

13. One goal of this course was to develop students' information literacy skills how to locate, manage, and use information). In what ways was this course successful, or not successful, in reaching that goal?

14. Did this course help you develop any specific skills related to information literacy? If yes, what were they?

15. In what ways has this course helped you understand better the research process and the function of information management within that process?

16. Do you feel that your ability to use electronic information management tools (e.g., database search tools, Internet search engines, etc.) was enhanced as a result of this class? How?

Chapter 11: Information Literacy Assessment Tool

Jennifer Dorner

Institutional Description

Lewis & Clark College, located in a residential area in the southwest hills of Portland, Oregon, is a private liberal arts college primarily devoted to teaching. The college falls into the Carnegie Institution Category of Baccalaureate Colleges—Liberal arts. Although primarily an undergraduate school, Lewis & Clark College has some advanced programs. It merged with the Northwestern School of Law in 1965 and added graduate programs in education and counseling psychology in 1984. Educational offering at the college are varied, with strong offerings in the sciences as well as the humanities. Enrollment as of fall 2000 was 1,709 students in the undergraduate College of Arts and Sciences, 616 students in the Graduate School of Education, 689 students in the Northwestern School of Law, and 39 students in the Study of American Language and Culture.

The college has included information literacy (IL) as a general education requirement in the college catalog for over seven years. Information literacy is defined in the catalog as "having the ability to locate, acquire, analyze, synthesize and structure information. This includes the ability to understand the variety of contents and formats of information; to understand systems for organizing information; to retrieve information; and to evaluate, organize, and manipulate information." But even though the college has recognized the importance of information literacy, no one took steps to see that it is taught. Certainly, no academic department has taken responsibility for it; instead, the faculty has relied on librarians and information technology staff to provide the necessary instruction. But without proper facilities and an extensive amount of contact with the students, neither librarians nor information technologists can teach the students all they need to know.

In the past few years, the faculty has recognized that new standards for information literacy must be set to ensure that students acquire the appropriate competencies for the information age. In the spring of 1999, the faculty unanimously passed a resolution calling for the design of a comprehensive IL program at Lewis & Clark College. The library director worked with the president of the college and the dean of the College of Arts and Sciences to write a grant proposal that was funded by the M.J. Murdock Charitable Trust. This grant funded a program of faculty development that would facilitate the integration of information literacy within the general curriculum of the college. It also provided funding for my position of information literacy coordinator.

Project Participants

The assessment team consisted of myself and two faculty members: a senior lecturer in the humanities and an associate professor of history. Funding from the IMLS grant allowed me to provide stipends to these faculty members for their participation. Lewis & Clark College librarians also assisted in the development of the instrument. The freshman core class, Inventing America, was selected as the most appropriate vehicle for delivering the assessment. This class is a first-year requirement for all incoming freshmen and transfer students.

Project Description

The project was a Web-based assessment tool that would measure the IL competencies of incoming freshman and transfer students. The instrument was developed over the summer of 2001 and implemented in the first few weeks of the fall semester.

Planning for Assessment

Measuring the IL competencies of incoming freshmen and transfer students was meant to serve a twofold purpose. First, the information collected would allow us to determine a baseline of skills possessed by these students. Second, with the information gathered, we could intelligently inform the administration and faculty about the need for IL instruction for these students.

Then the two faculty members and I met for the first time to discuss this project, we discussed the purpose of the assessment, the scope of the assessment, and how it would be delivered. We proposed a time line that would allow us to complete the project by the beginning of fall semester 2001.

Developing the Assessment Instrument

Our decision to mount the assessment instrument on the Web rather than distribute it on paper was based on multiple considerations. We wanted a tool that could be easily accessed by students from around campus, one that could be completed outside the classroom and outside class time, and one that could be easily and quickly modified. A primary consideration was reducing the work that would be required to compile the results. There were approximately 400 freshmen and transfer students in that year's class, and compiling results from a paper instrument would have been too burdensome. Because the questions in the assessment instrument were multiple-choice and true/false, the results submitted to the electronic instrument could be automatically recorded to a delimited text file, which could be viewed by any spreadsheet or database program. This saved hours of processing time.

With the participation of the librarians, our assessment team reviewed the *Information Literacy Competency Standards for Higher Education.* From that document we selected those competencies that we expected the students would have achieved by the end of their first year. The students would achieve these competencies through instruction that would be integrated into the Inventing America course. These competencies were:

1.1.3 Explores general information sources to increase familiarity with the topic

1.1.5 Identifies key concepts and terms that describe the information need

1.2.3 Identifies the value and differences of potential resources in a variety of formats (e.g., multimedia, database, Web site, data set, audiovisual, book)

1.2.4 Identifies the purpose and audience of potential resources (e.g., popular vs. scholarly, current vs. historical)

1.2.5 Differentiates between primary and secondary sources, recognizing how their use and importance vary with each discipline

2.1.3 Investigates the scope, content, and organization of information retrieval systems

2.1.4 Selects efficient and effective approaches for accessing the information needed from the investigative methods or information retrieval system

2.2.2 Identifies keywords, synonyms, and related terms for the information needed

2.2.3 Selects controlled vocabulary specific to the discipline or information retrieval source

2.2.4 Constructs a search strategy using appropriate commands for the information retrieval system selected (e.g., Boolean operators, truncation, and proximity for search engines; internal organizers such as indexes for books)

2.3.2 Uses various classification schemes and other systems (e.g., call number systems, or indexes) to locate information resources within the library or to identify specific sites for physical exploration

2.4.2 Identifies gaps in the information retrieved and determines if the search strategy should be revised

2.5.3 Differentiates between the types of sources cited and understands the elements and correct syntax of a citation for a wide range of resources

3.2.1 Examines and compares information from various sources in order to evaluate reliability, validity, accuracy, authority, timeliness, and point of view or bias

5.2.6 Demonstrates an understanding of what constitutes plagiarism and does not represent work attributable to other as his or her own

Reviewing IL assessment instruments created by other institutions allowed us to generate ideas for how questions could be constructed. Each of the questions developed related to a selected competency. There were a few competencies selected that could not be tested using the multiple-choice method and were therefore left out of the instrument.

The Assessment Instrument

When the instrument was developed, it was tested first by the assessment team and librarians. After some small changes were made, we tested it early in the semester on two Inventing America classes. This is where we began running into difficulties. Part of the problem was the timing of the process. Just a few short weeks before the fall 2001 semester began, our library hired a library technology coordinator. Immediately upon his arrival, he began working on a PHP script that would process the results of the assessment instrument. This script created a text-delimited file of the results, which we viewed in Microsoft Excel. Relieved to see that the script was working and the results were being recorded, I did not at that time look very carefully at the results. We planned to make the instrument available to the remaining Inventing America students just one week later, and my time was occupied with making the changes suggested by testing period.

After we made the instrument available to the remaining Inventing America students, they only had one week to complete it. Because we were measuring the students' *incoming* IL skills, we wanted them to complete it before they received any instruction. Because of some problems with student identification numbers, discussed later, the final number of results we recorded was 100, out of approximately 400 students.

The Information Literacy Assessment tool is located at the following URL: http://watzekpx.lclark.edu/infolit/assess/.

Analyzing the Results

This number was sufficient for us to extrapolate some conclusions, but it was at this point that I realized that the information being recorded was insufficient for our purposes. I had designed the tool to record whether a student answered a question correctly or incorrectly, but not to record which answer was selected. This meant that I was unable to do any question analysis to check the validity of the questions being asked.

These errors were caused by not allowing sufficient time for testing and analysis of the test results. Since then, we have redesigned the instrument and have tested it more carefully. We also have shared the assessment instrument and the script with similar institution, George Fox University, and plan to compare our results from our administration of the instrument this fall.

Results of the Assessment

Because we were not able to record the information we had intended to record when developing the instrument, we did not process the results.

Challenges

Unfortunately, we had some technical problems. For their scores to be recorded, the students had to enter their last name and student ID, which matched by the script to an existing library database of student information. Student IDs at Lewis & Clark College are eight digits long, but only the last seven digits are used by the library system. Being new, our library technology coordinator was unaware of this and I never thought to mention it. By the time we realized what was causing the problem, we had reaching our own deadline.

Conclusion

Recent developments indicate that we may not be using the assessment tool at Lewis & Clark this fall, though it will probably be used by another school I am working with.

Chapter 12: Midlands Technical College: Information Literacy Assessment Project

Catherine Eckman

Institutional Description

Midlands Technical College (MTC) is a comprehensive, urban, public, two-year college serving the primary region of Richland, Lexington, and Fairfield counties of South Carolina, which serve approximately 10,000 students and have approximately 600 full-time faculty (200 full-time and 400 adjunct faculty). College programs and services provide accessible, affordable, high-quality postsecondary education that prepares traditional and nontraditional students to enter the job market, allows them to transfer to senior colleges and universities, and assists them in achieving their professional and personal goals. The college provides educational opportunities to some 40,000 students on three campuses. Education in ethics, problem solving and critical thinking, research, and technology literacy are integrated into all curricula. MTC recognizes that information literacy (IL) competencies are crucial to student success and has incorporated IL into its strategic planning process as a priority initiative.

Project Participants

During spring semester 2001, the director of the library and I began a dialog with the chair of the English department and the English 101 program coordinator to discuss using two sections of English 101 as a pilot project to assess student learning outcomes for information literacy. English 101 became the target course because its objectives reflected the five IL standards as defined by ACRL. Our goal was to use the ACRL *Information Literacy Competency Standards for Higher Education*, performance indicators, and outcomes to enhance the course's objectives. Project participants included students in four sections of English 101 and their instructor.

Project Description

Library instruction at MTC is an important service designed to support its teaching mission and to promote information literacy across the curriculum by supporting the academic, professional, and personal information needs of our students. Library instruction supports the curriculum of specific classes, the programs of academic departments, and the research efforts of individual library users. Librarians developed and teach the IL components of College 105 and Engineering Technology 106, MTC's first-year experience courses.

In 1999, the MTC library piloted a faculty–library internship project to help faculty develop IL skills that they could transfer to their classrooms. In 2000, MTC was one of sixteen community colleges in the nation invited by the League for Innovation in the Community College to participate in the 21st Century Learning Outcomes Project whose goal, by 2003, is to increase the capacity of community colleges to define, implement, and assess new and modified sets of learning outcomes that students need to succeed in the knowledge economy. In response, MTC established a committee of faculty members to identify a set of core competencies and skills crucial to student success. The committee identified information literacy as one of these skills, and the academic division added IL to the general education core. Thus, the infrastructure needed for this project (i.e., experience of the library faculty and support from the college administration and classroom faculty) was firmly in place.

Planning for Assessment

English 101 is a three-credit-hour college-transfer course emphasizing the study of composition in conjunction with appropriate literary selections. Frequent theme assignments serve to reinforce effective writing skills. Information finding and basic research techniques are an integral component of the course curriculum.

One of the original course objectives was that students develop research skills. The instructor and I agreed to revise and enhance the research skills objective to include the components of information literacy as defined in our college's general education core. The new objective stated that students will develop IL skills, including (1) defining and articulating the need for information, (2) accessing information efficiently, (3) evaluating information critically, and (4) using information effectively to accomplish a purpose.

The next step in the planning process involved working with the instructor to identify learning outcomes to target for assessment. The following five basic goals with accompanying objectives were agreed upon:

Basic Goal 1. The student recognizes, defines, and articulates the need for information to solve a specific problem.

Objective 1.1. The student identifies the need for information by developing a thesis statement and formulating questions based on the information need.

Basic Goal 2. The student constructs and implements an effectively designed search strategy tailored to his or her specific information need.

Objective 2.1. The student identifies keywords, synonyms, and related terms for the information needed.

Objective 2.2. The student distinguishes between various types of finding tools such as periodical indexes and online catalogs.

Objective 2.3. The student formulates and executes an appropriate search strategy using multiple finding tools.

Objective 2.4. The student records all pertinent citation information for future reference

Basic Goal 3. The student locates basic information in appropriate resources.

Objective 3.1. Given a citation for an information source, the student is able to identify the elements needed to locate the information source.

Basic Goal 4. The student knows how to use information effectively to solve a problem or answer a research question.

Objective 4.1. The student is able to synthesize the information he or she has found to document his or her thesis statement.

Basic Goal 5. The student appreciates standards for the attribution of ideas, for handling quoted materials, and for the presentation of various perspectives.

Objective 5.1. The student demonstrates an understanding of what constitutes plagiarism and does not represent work attributable to others as his or her own.

Objective 5.2. The student selects an appropriate documentation style and uses it consistently to cite sources.

Developing Assessment Instruments

A trial pretest was administered at the beginning of the fall semester to assess student competencies for each objective. The pretest was then revised and administered at the beginning of the spring semester, followed by a more comprehensive posttest at semester's end. An additional instrument, a resource check sheet, was issued to each student so that the students could record pertinent citation information for resources retrieved as documentation for their class essays. The assessment instruments are included at the end of this chapter.

Analyzing the Results

An Excel spreadsheet was created to tabulate each student's response to each question on the pre- and posttests. A preliminary analysis was completed by computing average pre- and posttest scores for each class and comparing results. In addition, average scores were compared for similar questions on the pre- and posttests. A more detailed analysis using statistical comparisons of the data is under way.

Results

Thirty-two (32) students completed the pretest, and twenty-six (26) students completed the posttest. Our preliminary results show an overall improvement in the posttest scores as compared to pretest scores, indicating that students developed some level of competency in most of the learning outcomes outlined in our goals and objectives. The overall average test score for the pretest was 67. The overall average test score for the posttest was 86. Improvement also was seen between similar questions on the pre- and posttests. For example, when asked the best place to begin research on a topic such as the American Revolution, the average score on the posttest was 81 as opposed to an average score of 63 on the pretest. There were two questions in which the scores were lower on the posttest than on the pretest. The reason for this discrepancy is unclear at the present stage of analysis. (See table 12-1.)

Table 12-1. Results of Assessment

	Pretest	Post Test
Average Test Score	67	86
Best Place to Begin Research on a History Topic	63	81
Best Place to Begin Research on a Topic of Current Importance	94	92
The Library Catalog is...	75	81
If you want to find magazine articles on a particular topic	63	58
Citation: Identifying Author	100	100
Citation: Identifying Journal/Magazine Title	81	96
Citation: Identifying Title of Article	81	96
Citation: Identifying Date of Publication	100	100
Citation: Identifying Page Numbers	100	100
Citation: Identifying Issue Number	22	100
Citation: Identifying Volume Number	22	100

Challenges

Designing an effective instrument that could generate meaningful and useful results was by far the most difficult challenge of the project. Questions that included implicit assumptions and/or expectations on my part, questions with potential for different interpretations, or questions that gave away answers to other questions on the tests were difficult to avoid. I rewrote many of the questions, some of them several times. I received a great deal of help from assessment experts provided by the IMLS/ACRL project director as well as experts at my college. I also pilot-tested the instruments on a student worker in the library to gain her insight into the questions before administering the instruments to my test groups. Determining how to analyze data and report results also was challenging. Again, I relied on help from assessment experts at my college and will continue to do so throughout the remainder of the project.

Conclusion

Midlands Technical College prides itself in creating innovative learning environments that enhance student success. The college supports students in becoming self-sufficient and in clarifying their lifelong goals. Information literacy competencies are essential to lifelong learning. This project will serve as a model for librarian–faculty collaboration in weaving information literacy into the MTC curriculum and for assessing related student learning outcomes.

Assessment Instruments

Pretest

I. Circle the best response(s) to the questions below.

1. If you are looking for information about the decline of the Roman Empire, which would be the best place to begin your research?
   a. the Internet
   b. a newspaper article
   c. a periodical article
   d. an encyclopedia
   e. I don't know

2. If you are looking for information about the current war in Afghanistan, which would be the best place to begin your research?
   a. encyclopedias
   b. books
   c. newspaper articles
   d. your friends
   e. I don't know

3. The library catalog is a list of
   a. books held in the library
   b. periodicals held in the library
   c. videos held in the library
   d. CDs held in the library
   e. all of the above
   f. I don't know

4. If you want to find magazine articles on a particular topic, you should
   a. search the library catalog for your topic
   b. search a periodical index (for example, Infotrac) for your topic
   c. leaf through the library's magazines until you find your topic
   d. all of the above
   e. I don't know

5. If you were searching a database for information about the effects of crime on the elderly, which words should you type into the database's search box? (Circle all that apply.)
   a. effects, crime, elderly
   b. effects, of, crime, on, elderly
   c. crime, elderly
   d. (crime or criminals), (elderly or aged)
   e. I don't know

II. Use this citation to a journal article to answer the following questions:

Baker, Laura K. "The use of lap dogs for prenatal cardiopulmonary monitoring: an epistemology of terrier intuition. " *Archives of Canine Channeling* 26.1 (2001): 479–93.

This article was written by____________________________________
The title of the journal is____________________________________
The title of the article is____________________________________
The publication date of the article is____________________________
The page number(s) of the article is/are__________________________
The issue number of the article is______________________________
The volume number of the article is_____________________________

Posttest

I. Circle the best response(s) to the questions below.

1. Gathering information is important before engaging in which of the following activities:

    a. writing a term paper for a college course
    b. buying an appliance
    c. buying a car
    d. buying a home
    e. investing in the stock market
    f. all of the above

2. If you are looking for information about the American Revolutionary War, which would be the best place to begin your research?

    a. the Internet
    b. a newspaper article
    c. a periodical article
    d. an encyclopedia
    e. I don't know

3. If you are looking for information about the winners of last month's Grammy Awards, which would be the best place to begin your research?

    a. encyclopedias
    b. books
    c. newspaper articles
    d. your friends
    e. I don't know

4. The library catalog is a list of

    a. books held in the library
    b. periodicals held in the library
    c. videos held in the library
    d. CDs held in the library
    e. all of the above
    f. I don't know

5. If you want to find magazine articles on a particular subject, you should

    a. search the library catalog for your topic
    b. search a periodical index (such as Infotrac) for your topic
    c. leaf through the library's magazines until you find your topic
    d. all of the above
    e. I don't know

6. When searching for information on a topic, the Internet is the only place you need to go

    a. true
    b. false

7. All information on the World Wide Web is true and accurate.
   a. true
   b. false

8. MTC students can use any of the library's databases from home if they have an Internet connection.
   a. true
   b. false

9. If you were searching a database for information about differences in academic achievement between middle-school aged boys and girls, which keywords should you type into the database's search box?
   a. differences in academic achievement between boys and girls in middle school
   b. sex differences, academic achievement, middle school
   c. gender differences, school achievement, adolescents
   d. any of the above
   e. b and c only
   f. I don't know

10. Documenting a source is important when you are
   a. using a direct quotation from it
   b. using facts or statistics from it
   c. paraphrasing it
   d. all of the above

II. Place the letter of the term next to the definition that it matches.

11. _____ periodical that publishes scholarly articles	a. magazine
12. _____database that contains updated daily news, international news, transcripts, and radio/TV news broadcasts	b. Infotrac
	c. journal
13._____ periodical that publishes current, general interest articles	d. serial
	e. Lexis Nexis
14._____ database that contains some full-text articles	

III. Use this citation to a magazine article to answer the following questions:

A love story: our bond with dogs. Angus Phillips. *National Geographic* Jan 2002 v201 i3 p12.

15. The author of this article is ______________________________

16. The title of the magazine is ______________________________

17. The title of the article is ______________________________

18. The publication date of the article is ____________________________

19. The page number (s) of the article is/are _________________________

20. The issues number of the article is_______________________________

21. The volume number of the article is_______________________________

IV. In our library orientation session, we discussed several types of information sources. List three types of information sources that we discussed.

22. ____

23. ____

24. ____

Check Sheet

Source #1

Database used ______________________________

Keywords used ______________________________

Title of source ______________________________

Author of source ______________________________

Date of publication ______________________________

Record the following information for books only:

Place of publication ______________________________

Publisher ______________________________

Record the following information for periodicals or newspapers only:

Title of periodical/newspaper______________________________

Pages of article______________________________

Volume number______________________________

Issue number______________________________

Source #2

Database used ______________________________

Keywords used ______________________________

Title of source______________________________

Author of source______________________________

Date of publication______________________________

Record the following information for books only:

Place of publication ______________________________

Publisher ______________________________

Record the following information for periodicals or newspapers only:

Title of periodical/newspaper______________________________

Pages of article______________________________

Volume number______________________________

Issue number______________________________

Chapter 13: Information Literacy Assessment at a Small Commuter Campus

Janet Feldmann

Institutional Description

Indiana University Purdue University Columbus (IUPUC) is a commuter campus that serves approximately 2,000 undergraduate students. Most students are first-generation college students from a rural background. More than half the students are nontraditional and do not attend classes full-time. Thus, the student population is very fluid. The campus itself and the library are part of a much larger campus, Indiana University Purdue University Indianapolis (IUPUI), which is about fifty miles away. The IUPUC campus views its library as a teaching library. The term "information literacy" embraces concepts, goals, and a philosophy that have always been basic elements of library service on this campus.

Project Participants

Several courses were included in our assessment activities this past year. These included the campus's basic speech communication course required of most students; the introduction to college course (often called a freshman seminar or first-year experience course), which is required for all traditional full-time freshmen, and several subject-specific courses. In each of them, a different assessment approach was used. For the purposes of this report, we chose the speech classes because the initial assessment raised as many issues as answers.

Project Description

Several instructors involved in teaching speech communication classes, all of them adjunct lecturers. They use a common textbook developed by the speech communications faculty at IUPUI and take pains to teach the same skills. The speech communications class is required for numerous degrees and is taken by most students on the campus. Thus, several years ago, IUPUI designated this class as the one in which the introductory level of information literacy (IL) instruction would be presented.

Planning the Assessment

Before classes began, the librarian met with several speech instructors to discuss the assignments and desired learning outcomes for the library instruction. As a result, there is an agreed-upon list of goals on which the librarians based the topics to be covered and to be used in the assessment. Although the assessment instruments were designed primarily by the librarian, the speech instructors were encouraged to make comments and suggestions. Because all of the speech instructors are on campus only during class time (they are all adjunct lecturers), we had various levels of involvement in this process. All of them, however, liked what the librarians designed. Their major concern had been that we address the specific learner outcomes that they wanted their students to gain. They agreed that these outcomes were satisfactorily addressed. Instructors attended the instruction sections and were very pleased with the information that was discussed by the librarians.

Developing the Assessment Instrument

The knowledge and skills identified to be addressed included the following:

- ability to do basic searching of IUCAT, Indiana University's online catalog;
- awareness that most reliable information was better found on the invisible Web rather than via a search of Google, etc.;
- awareness of journal indexes as the primary means to find journal articles with emphasis on the campus's primary general academic index, Gale's Expanded *Academic Index;*
- awareness of criteria that can be used in making reasoned judgments regarding the reliability of Web resources;
- awareness of the library's interlibrary loan service;
- awareness of the existence of electronic journals;
- ability to locate the electronic journals to which the library subscribes;
- awareness that the library is a friendly place where questions will be welcomed by librarians;

- understanding of the services and kinds of resources available in the library;
- awareness of certain specific resources that would be of particular interest to students researching their "speech to persuade."

One of the pedagogical techniques the librarians use in the speech class and others is to give the students a questionnaire to fill out during the first five minutes of class. The original purpose was to provide questions that would let students know what would be covered and enable them to realize what they do not know. The speech instructors are very much in favor of this technique and request that it be a standard part of library instruction. However, by design, the questions are open ended. This made the comparison of preinstruction knowledge and end-of-the semester questionnaire results more difficult interpret. We realized later that some students filled out the sheet and turned it in with the answers they learned during the class. This is an acceptable learning technique, but it makes the instrument much less useful as an assessment instrument.

This year was the first one in which the librarians used an end-of-the-semester questionnaire for several courses, including speech. The instrument proved to be a work in progress. Each time a class filled it out (and each was course specific), we learned what worked and what needed to be improved. Because of some unfilled positions, the librarians' workload was much heavier than had been anticipated at the beginning of the project. Thus, the assessment process was not well tested before being used in class.

Results

Initially, we were disappointed in some of the results. However, as we analyzed the process and the results, we found that the instrument we used raised as many questions as it did results. Our expectations regarding student learning may not have been realistic. The amount of research required for the speech classes is limited. Students must use outside resources for only one five-minute speech. Students are not required to use the campus library to do their research. Because many students live an hour or more away from campus, they may well have relied on local resources. If they did so, they may not have used the resources the librarians introduced them to. In the fall, there will be questions regarding the library they used, their access to the Internet, the specific resources they used in writing their speech, the number of credits already completed by each student, and whether they have used the library previously for research.

Some of the questions will be rewritten in multiple-choice format rather than fill in the blanks. For example, you may know where to find a specific resource on the shelf, but not remember its title. The way in which the questions are phrased also needs to be examined. Until we include these questions, we do not have sufficient information to use to fully analyze the results.

In talking over the results with the speech instructors, we found that they were pleased. They pointed out that the majority of their students are in their first year of college. Many of them do not even know if they want a degree. Thus, they lack the motivation to put much effort into their research. Only after they have given their speech and gotten the results from their peers and instructor may they begin to realize that research can be valuable.

We know from previous research that entering students are not aware of the existence of an online catalog or have any idea how to use it. They were totally unaware of the existence of journal indexes, electronic journals, the accessibility of the librarians, and the various services and resources that the library offers. Thus, even a 50 percent correct response rate may indicate that the instruction was successful. Using this as our benchmark, we may have met the goals that had been established prior to the semester. Next semester, after we have instituted the changes we have discussed, we should have some very useful data to guide us in future instruction.

Challenges

The librarians had planned to do the first iteration of assessment in the fall of 2001, learn from that attempt, and make changes for the second semester. For a variety of reasons, however, the trial run had to wait until spring 2002. We learned a great deal; our assessment instrument for this class next fall and the methods we use for analysis will be quite different. As can be seen above, our analysis this past semester was simple and straightforward. We simply calculated the percentage of correct responses for each question. Although we gained useful information, the results raised as many questions as answers.

Conclusion

From the standpoint of information literacy assessment at this campus, this grant project has been extremely useful. Previously, assessment had seemed a monumental challenge requiring much more knowledge about assessment techniques than we possessed. As we learned in this grant project, assessment need not be as difficult as we had thought. Our results this past semester may not have been as useful as we would have liked, but the information we gained about our techniques will enable us to make the changes we need for the next semester. Assessing IL instruction is critically important and not nearly as difficult as we had assumed.

Assessment Instrument and Raw Data

This is *not* a test. It is your librarians' way of learning what worked in the library instruction session for Communication R 110 so that they can do a better job of teaching in the future: Thank you!

1. Where do you look for books belonging to any of the IU libraries? 59%
2. How do you truncate words in IUCAT? 71%
3. What are subject headings, and why are they important? 60%
4. What kind of a "finding aid" will lead to articles on a specific topic? 60%
5. In general which journal index should you look at first to find articles? (Choose one.)
   - a. Cambridge Scientific Index 2%
   - b. IUCAT 26%
   - c. Expanded Academic Index 52%
   - d. Alta Vista 9%
   - e. Applied Science and Technology Index 2%
6. What specific weekly resource is a good starting point for information on many subjects of current interest? 19%
7. Can you find most of the information in the world by searching the World Wide Web?
   Yes: 40% No: 50% Blank: 10%
8. You found an article that you'd like to read, but the library does not own a print copy of the journal that the article appears in. Where should you look *next* to find a full-text copy of the article? (Choose one of the following.)
   - a. Electronic journals list 45%
   - b. Yahoo 7%
   - c. IUCAT 10%
   - d. Encyclopedia Britannica Online 5%
   - e. Interlibrary loan 21%
9. What is a periodical?
   - a. a mathematical symbol 7%
   - b. a Web site 7%
   - c. a journal or magazine 83%
10. What service does the library offer that allows you to borrow a copy of a specific book if the library does not own it? (Fill in the blank.)
    - a. Interlibrary loan 50%
    - b. Incorrect answer or no answer 50%
11. Are all Web sites reliable?
    No: 81%
12. Did the Web site "Feline Responses to Bearded Men" help you learn to look at Web sites more critically?
    Yes: 60%
13. As a result of the librarian's presentation, are you now more comfortable asking the librarians for help?
    Yes: 60% No: 17% Blank: 23%
14. Did the library instruction session help you with your class research?
    Yes: 48% No: 38% Blank: 4%
15. Do you now use the library more often than you did before?
    Yes: 48% No: 43% Blank: 9%

Chapter 14: Assessing Student Learning for Information Literacy in a Core Business Class

Ann Fiegen and Bennett Cherry

Institution Description

California State University San Marcos, a Master's Colleges and Universities I Carnegie Institution, was founded in 1989 and draws its student body from the local counties. It is a growing campus currently enrolling 7,600 students in three colleges: Arts & Sciences, Business Administration, and Education. In the College of Business Administration, students choose between four concentration options in accountancy/finance, global business management, high technology management, and service sector management.

Information literacy (IL) and its assessment are incorporated into the strategic plan of the university. The twenty-three-campus California State University System has considered information competence and its assessment a priority for more than five years and has funded a number of system and campus initiatives. The curriculum at CSUSM requires a writing requirement in all courses. Students are introduced to the campus research environment and library resources in the university's lower-division general education program. Instruction librarians participate actively across a broad spectrum of research and information activities, including guest lectures to classes, a three-week module on library research in a freshmen success course, team teaching in learning communities, and faculty of record in general education and discipline courses.

Project Participants

Participants were the students enrolled in the College of Business Administration's Services Management (SSM 304) course in fall 2001. The course is the entry course for the option in the major, with most of the students taking it in their first semester upper-division course work. Students enter the upper-division program with a wide range of previous library research experience, with approximately 70 percent transferring in at the junior level from community colleges. Twenty of the thirty-three students in the course indicated they had participated in a library instruction session at either Cal State San Marcos or one of the local community colleges prior to the course.

The goal of the services management course is to provide students an understanding of organizational behavior so that they may appreciate and are able to manage the complexities and challenges associated with modern service organizations. The largest research-based requirement in this course was a team project designed to expand the students' knowledge and analysis of management-related questions in the delivery of services. When working in their teams, students were expected to formulate a specific research question and find solutions and answers to that question based on the extant literature. Each project's success hinges on the team's depth of understanding of the topic, including multiple and possibly conflicting perspectives. The rationale for the inclusion of this project maps nicely onto the IL standards. The final deliverable was a presentation to the class at the end of the semester. In addition to the presentation, students composed annotated bibliographic references, wrote an executive summary, and provided citations of the sources they used in their research.

Project Description

The overarching goal of the project was to begin development of an assessment instrument that could accurately reflect each student's IL competence. The course objectives that related to this project included: articulate a formal research statement, identify main research concepts, and use the research statements to develop a search strategy for their research. In that context, Standard 1, *Students determine the nature and extent of the information needed,* and Performance Indicator 1, *Student defines and articulates the need for information,* were central to guiding our search for assessment instruments that would provide learning opportunities for students to master that and other measures by the end of the semester.

Planning the Assessment

We initially envisioned multiple measures for the assessment. Pre- and posttest questions were designed to capture the critical elements of the student research process. The course objectives and the IL competencies served to guide our initial brainstorming to develop questions for the assessment instrument. An exercise in critical thinking directed students to read and then write a critical annotation of two articles. (Standard 3, *The information-literate student evaluates information and its sources critically and incorporates selected information into his or her knowledge base and value system.*) Bibliographical item counts would provide a measure of the variety of resources used. (Standard 1 Performance Indicator 2: *Student identifies a variety of types and formats of potential sources of information.*) Analysis in this report is limited to the pre-/posttest instrument.

Developing the Assessment Instrument

The pre- and posttest questionnaire was chosen in order to measure improvement in student learning we deemed central to the course objectives. We developed the pretest by beginning with the course objectives and asking the question, What did we want the students to learn? Starting with sketchy ideas for questions, we used the learning outcomes mapped to the course objectives to refine the questions. Pre- and posttest questions were similar, and each question was tied to one or more of the learning outcomes. To remove potential bias by the researchers from the student responses, we developed a coding instrument and asked business librarians at other institutions to code for evidence of a more precise statement among the pre- and posttest response pairs.

The Assessment Instrument

A pretest of the survey instrument was given to students in one of the first class periods at the beginning of the semester. Students were asked to answer the questions as best they could in light of their team's selected project topic. The answers formed a baseline measure of each student's competence in information literacy. Following completion of the pretest instrument, the librarian led the class in an hour-long discussion describing how to write a critical annotated bibliography and how to search business databases. Within the two weeks following this instruction, students were assigned to find, critically evaluate, and annotate an article related to their topic. The purpose of the annotation exercise was to help students think more critically about their research and retain a better record for their analysis of their topic. Feedback was given on these projects, but no grade was given. This task was designed to be a developmental tool that students could use to reflect on their research experience and to assist in the synthesis of disparate pieces of information that would eventually form the basis for their team project. The assignment provided an application of Standard 3, *The information-literate student evaluates information and its sources critically and incorporates selected information into his or her knowledge base and value system.*

Students then spent the remainder of the semester working with their teammates on their projects. Executive summaries of their projects were turned in one week prior to the presentation date. Immediately following the presentations, all students were asked to complete a posttest assessment. The posttest included essential components from the pretest instrument to allow for comparison. The assessment instrument is included at the end of this chapter.

Analyzing the Results

Three business librarians who were unaware of the intent of the research project independently coded student responses. The coders were instructed to identify which of the paired responses (pre- or post-) was more specific or precise. The order of pre- and posttest responses was changed on some of the pairs. We expected that a more precise statement exhibited greater understanding and knowledge of the question or research method being tested. If a high percentage of posttest responses are found to be more specific, we can extrapolate that the question is an accurate measure for that outcome and that student learning occurred. We recorded whether all three coders chose the posttest response, whether two coders chose it, and whether only one coder chose the posttest response as the most specific of the pair. Initial analysis was limited to the consensus response.

Results

Table 14-1 reports the percentage of cases where all three coders agreed that the posttest response was more specific or precise. If a high percentage of posttest responses are found to be more specific, we can extrapolate that the question is an accurate measure for that outcome, and that student learning did occur from the pretest to the posttest.

The learning goals for the students were that they would be able to articulate a statement, identify the main concepts, and develop a strategy for their research. Results show a clear increase in extracting main concepts in order to develop a search strategy. Forty percent of responses cited the posttest response as more precise. Twenty-five percent of students responded with more precise statements in the questions designed to assess critical thinking, perhaps a result of the additional critical annotation assignments. Articulating the problem statement and recalling where to locate information to solve the problem were a distant 15 to a low 5 percent of responses. These low percentages may have been affected by timing of the posttest administration. Again, the researchers emphasize the preliminary nature of this instrument and expect that further refinement of the instrument and its administration would test data validity.

Challenges

Throughout the process, we felt overwhelmed by the sheer number of the IL learning outcomes. When we now reflect on our experience, we tend to think that we were trying to use the outcomes too early as a way to identify what we needed to measure. We overcame that obstacle by keeping the outcomes in the

TABLE 14-1. Three Coders Agreement

Question	Post Test % of Total Responses	Learning Outcomes
Question 3: Constructing a search	40	S2.P2.O2
Question 4B: Where to find press releases	26	S1.P2.O3
Question 5B: Citation evaluation, valid reputable study	25	S3.P2.O1
Question 5C: Citation evaluation, accuracy	25	S3.P2.O1
Question 5A:Citation evaluation, reliable, trustworthy	25	S3.P2.O1
Question 5E: Citation evaluation, timeliness	20	S1.P2.O3
Question 5F: Citation evaluation, bias	20	S1.P2.O3
Question 4D: Where to find background reading	15	S1.P2.O3
Question 4A: Where to find current examples of industry practices	14	S1.P1.O5
Question 1: State problem	13	S1.P1.O5
Question 5D: Citation evaluation, authority of author	13	S1.P1.O5
Question 4C: Where to find employment law and regulations	11	S1.P2.O3
Question 2: Describe information needed for research	5	S1.P1.O5

back of our mind and then delving deeper into the pedagogical goals of the project. In particular, it was helpful for us to remember that *all* of the outcomes were not important to measure, but only the ones that were the most important elements the professor wanted to see from the students. After we clearly identified five specific outcomes (S1.P1.O5; S1.P2.O2,O4; S2.P1.O3; S2.P2.O2; S3.P2.O1), it was much easier to proceed and begin building the instrument.

Originally, we envisioned the multiple measures described earlier would be used to test the learning outcomes. We discarded a bibliographical analysis of student references because we did not want to study the references in isolation from the papers. In the case of this course, much of the content of the research was presented orally rather than in writing. Also, with each of these ideas we had to subject them to the realism question—Is this too much or are we asking too many questions of the students? Again, we realized that for this project, we were not building the mother of all IL instruments. Instead, we were attempting to create a part of a tool that can be used to assess whether information literacy increased as a result of our training and that could be easily administered semester after semester.

The timing of the administration of the posttest was not optimal. The instrument was distributed to the students immediately after the conclusion of their final presentations (around 8:00 p.m.). In future administrations of such instruments, it is wise to recognize the timing implications and the motivation of the respondents to respond accurately. It may be helpful to tie the posttest responses to a graded assignment.

Our independent coders commented on the length of the coding instrument. Because of the number of responses and the number of questions, the response worksheet grew to twenty-four pages and took thirty to forty minutes to complete. Because this is a first step in developing the pre- and posttest assessment instrument, it is expected that this level of detail in coding would not be needed in the future. As is, the instrument can be used in classes to expand students' awareness of information literacy without the use of independent coders. One question administered did not present itself well due to unambiguous results. Question 7 on the instrument was thrown out in the analysis phase. The students needed to answer too many questions; eflections will be needed to identify which are the most important elements to pre-and posttest. The instrument was only performed on one class. Further testing would reveal data validity.

Conclusion

The results of this project are encouraging insofar as they shed light on how one might go about measuring information literacy in particular classes. It should be noted, however, that this study only included a few IL outcomes chosen specifically to coincide with course objectives. Analysis of coder responses can be used for future course planning to emphasize those elements where higher posttest specificity is warranted.

Use of a pretest/posttest instrument limited the outcomes that can be measured to those of early stage research. For example, a student's ability to combine research into original thought could not be accurately measured before he or she had begun his or her research (Standard 3 Performance Indicator 4: *...compares new knowledge with prior knowledge*).

Reflecting on the collaborative effort of faculty and librarian, we each were exposed to different discipline pedagogy. It is evident that each discipline has its own area of expertise to contribute. From library science we utilized information competencies, citation analysis, steps in the research process, and locating sources for information. From the business discipline we recognized the importance of real-world application, context-specific questioning, and the use of practical research methodology.[1.]

Note

1. Portions of this report were presented at the LOEX of the West Conference, 2002, and published in Reference Services Review (Proceedings of the 2002 LOEX Conference)

Assessment Instrument
Pre-/Posttest

SSM 304 Project Completion Worksheet

Name: ______________________________________

1. Please indicate (%) your status:
   ❑ Freshman ❑ Sophomore ❑ Junior ❑ Senior

2. Place a checkmark next to each entry (%) if you have attended a workshop or lecture on library research:
   ❑ Cal State San Marcos ❑ Palomar College
   ❑ Other (indicate where you attended the workshop or lecture) ___________
   ❑ Took GEL 101 at Cal State San Marcos

3. State, as a question, the organization/management problem you addressed for your research topic in this class. (S1.P1.O5)

4. Describe the information you needed to complete this research.(S1.P1.O5)

5. Books, articles, newspapers, statistics as well as free and fee-based Web sites on the Internet all have a place in business research. From the list of topics below, identify what you think is the best format or media type (e.g., books, newspaper articles, etc.) for locating information on that topic. Explain where you would go to get this type of information, and why you would go there. Where would you find information on¼(S1.P2.O3)

Example:
Recent layoff announcements from across the country
Possible Answer:
Popular press magazines (Time, Newsweek, BusinessWeek)

a. Current examples of industry-specific practices
Answer:

b. Company/Organization press releases
Answer:

c. Employment laws and regulations
Answer:

d. Background reading, commentary on a specific topic
Answer:

6. Consider that you are searching an online index or electronic database to locate journal or magazine articles for your topic. Fill in the box below just as if you were searching that index. Construct your search to get the most useful and accurate results. Include any keywords, operators or truncations you would you use, such as (AND, OR, NOT etc.) to get optimal results. Refer to your answer in question 1 above to help you construct your search. Fill in key words here: (S2.P2.O2)

7. Describe advantages and disadvantages of searching the free World Wide Web on the Internet for research on your particular project. (S1.P2.O5, S2.P1.O3)

Advantages: **Disadvantages:**

8. Study the following citation to an article, and in your own words describe if and how the citation approaches the criteria listed below:(S3.P2.O1)

> Levy, Elliot S., Patricia M Flynn, Diane M Kellog. 1999 Balancing professional and personal lives: The mantra for the next millennium. *CPA Journal* 69 (10): 70–73.

Is this a reliable or trustworthy source? Why or why not?

Is this a valid or reputable study? Why or why not?

Would you say this source is likely to be accurate? Why or why not?

Can you construe the authority of the authors? How or how not?

Is this a timely source? Why or why not?

What would the likelihood of bias be, if any, with a source such as this? Why or why not?

Chapter 15: Using Rubrics to Assess Information Literacy Attainment in a Community College Education Class

Dana Franks

Institution Description

Highline Community College is a public, suburban community college about fifteen miles south of Seattle, Washington. We have a diverse student body in terms of both ethnicity and academic pursuit. In a typical quarter, we serve approximately 9,000 students (5,000 FTE) taking academic transfer (44%), vocational (23%), basic skills (22%), and developmental (10%) classes. Highline's library has an active and growing program of information literacy (IL) instruction, supported by the college administration. In the past decade, our staff of full-time faculty librarians has quadrupled in size (from one to four), and the numbers of classes we regularly teach has tripled. Highline also has a history of encouraging collaboration, including faculty–librarian collaboration. Librarians work closely with faculty to design instruction tailored to course outcomes and assignments, and faculty in the disciplines are becoming accustomed to our asking questions about their learning outcomes at the time they schedule instruction.

Highline also is committed to student learning assessment. We have an assessment committee, with representatives from each division plus the library, and each academic department (including the library) has published outcomes. One of the functions of this committee is to promote assessment activities at the course and department levels, supported in part with an annual influx of state funds. The college is currently involved in the accreditation process and has included significant discussion of the library's IL program in both Standard 2 (Instructional Program) and Standard 5 (Library) of its self-study. In this environment, it was actually quite easy to find partners and support for an information literacy assessment project.

Project Participants

The participants in this project were myself as the lead instruction librarian and a member of our education faculty. We worked with Education 110, Introduction to Education. The class focus is on the major educational philosophies and theories, historical events, and curriculum models that influence American education, with a practical focus on how these are manifested locally in Washington State. The class includes a research component, with students making an end-or-quarter group presentation exploring a significant education issue of their own choosing.

Project Description

I met with my partner, the education instructor, over the summer of 2001. We began by examining course outcomes and assignments for Education 110. After doing so, we decided to focus on providing students with the IL skills they would need to complete the course's major assignment: an end-of-quarter group presentation, accompanied by a brief summarizing essay and bibliography. To identify the necessary skills, I gave the instructor a brief version of our IL outcomes (which are based on the ACRL standards) and asked her to identify those she thought the students would need to complete this assignment. There was fruitful discussion surrounding this activity during which I learned more about her discipline, her class, and past student performance on the assignment. The instructor had several questions, too. Specifically, she needed clarification on some of the outcomes and wanted to know who I thought was responsible for the instruction and assessment. My answer to the latter was that it was up to us to decide that, within the context of this course, but I supposed we would each have a share of that responsibility. Happily, we agreed on that point. In the end, we were also in complete agreement on the selection of IL outcomes to address.

Planning the Assessment

Despite the fact that we had not yet developed specific learning objectives, we decided to examine potential assessment instruments next. With our selected outcomes in hand, we examined the assignments already used in Education 110 to determine the extent to which they could serve our needs. We found that there were two assignments that would work well for several of the outcomes. I developed a third instrument (an annotated bibliography). We believed that, taken together, these three instruments would address all the outcomes.

With the outcomes and the assignments laid out in front of me, I completed a Planning for Assessment table with the following columns:

Information literacy standard	Performance indicator	Outcome	Objective	Instrument and method	Criteria
(3)	(2)	(1)	(4)	(5)	(6)

I began by inserting the outcomes we had selected (1), listing them according to the order in which they appear in the ACRL standards. I then filled in the columns to the left—the corresponding Performance Indicators (2) and Information Literacy Standards (3), again from the ACRL Standards. Using these and the assignments as guides, I then wrote specific student learning Objectives (4). It was relatively simple then to plug in the assignment name and section that would be used to assess that objective. These were our Instruments and Methods (5). When it appeared that the assignment was inadequate, we modified it to meet the need. Finally, I wrote Criteria for assessing student performance on that piece of the assignment/instrument (6). This task presented us with the dilemma of ascertaining the degree of competence we expected of our students.

Education 110 is an introductory course offered during the fall quarter, so it attracts a number of students who are new to the college. For that reason, we decided that we should approach the students as novices to the IL field and assess these skills at a basic level. Consider, for instance, an advanced or upper-division student applying "critical thinking and problem-solving skills to analyze and evaluate information" (one of our outcomes). That student might be asked to do more extensive research or apply previously acquired subject expertise in evaluating a source. A novice student, on the other hand, might simply be asked to identify clues to the reliability of a source, or examine and communicate his or her own thinking process about evaluating it. It is in this way that we decided that we would teach to, and assess for, an introductory level of IL competency.

Developing the Assessment Instrument

Given the assessment tools we were using, we determined that grading rubrics would make the assessment phase of our project easier and more reliable. To develop the rubrics, I went back to the Planning for Assessment table and clipped the "Objective" and "Criteria" columns. The objective became what I was assessing. The criteria became the highest-evel performance criteria (see below).

What was left was to define lower levels of competence. I experimented with various numbers of columns (up to five) and various terms to describe the levels of competence but found that I was splitting hairs when I had more than three. The rubric that emerged had the following columns:

objective	criteria		
objective	exemplary	competent	emergent

The Assessment Instrument

Two of our assessment instruments were assignments, with corresponding rubrics. The other instrument was the group presentation itself for which the instructor had designed a grading rubric based on the education objectives. Even though there was overlap between the education and information literacy objectives for this assignment, they did not match up the way we would have liked. So I created a rubric that piggybacked on the first, for assessing the IL objectives. As it turned out, this was unworkable because the first rubric did not provide enough information to reliably complete the second. Furthermore, the two are redundant and confusing to the students. My goal before fall quarter 2002, then, is to work with the instructor to integrate these instruments. (For instruments, see the end of this chapter.)

Analyzing the Results

When grading, I attach a copy of the grading rubric to each student's assignment. I make my comments right on the rubric with references to their work. The rubric saves my having to repeat comments about common errors from one paper to the next, leaving me more time to add comments tailored to their performance. The more specific the criteria are, the more successful this will be as both a reliable assessment tool and a communication device for the student.

Results

The students' achievement in this class was somewhat disappointing. IL instruction had been provided to this class in previous years, and though it had not been assessed, we were trying to address perceived shortcomings. We made several changes in how we worked with the students, informing them of the IL expectations and modifying both assignments and pedagogy. Based on our first quarter's results, though, we do not appear to have made a significant difference in student performance. With the data in hand, though, we will be able to track our progress from here on out.

Following are the objectives for which the *majority* of the students scored at an "exemplary" level:

1. Students will select one each: a background source, a vocabulary source, a statistical source, and a current events source related to their topic.

2. Students will cite four sources using APA citation style.

Following are the objectives for which *half* of the students scored at an "exemplary" level:

1. Students will identify five concepts, implicit in the main topic, for further investigation.

Following are the objectives for which *no students* scored at an "exemplary" level:

1. Students will meet with group members to refine topic (Section 1).

2. Students can draw tentative conclusions about the topic based on preliminary research.

3. Students can express these conclusions in a clear statement.

4. Students will identify at least one source that substantially increases their vocabulary surrounding their topics.

5. Students will be able to describe the process they used to evaluate the reliability, validity, accuracy, authority, timeliness, and point of view or bias for each of these sources.

Following are the objectives for which the *majority* of the students scored at a "competent" level:

1. Students can draw tentative conclusions about the topic based on preliminary research.

2. Students can express these conclusions in a clear statement.

Following are the objectives for which *half* of the students scored at a "competent" level:

1. Students will meet with group members to refine topic (Section 1).

2. Students will clearly articulate a focused research topic (Section 3).

Following are the objectives for which the *majority* of the students scored at an "emergent" level:

1. Students will identify at least one source that substantially increases their vocabulary surrounding their topics.

2. Students will be able to describe the process they used to evaluate the reliability, validity, accuracy, authority, timeliness, and point of view or bias for each of these sources.

Following are the objectives for which *half* of the students scored at an "emergent" level:

1. Students will meet with group members to refine topic (Section 1).

2. Students will be able to describe how each of their four sources provided the information they needed.

Challenges

We faced various challenges in this process. For instance, writing the criteria without examples of student work was tricky because the degree of specificity we sought was difficult to imagine. As student work did start to come in, we found that their performance was not as strong as we had hoped it would be. Ideally, the rubrics would have been distributed to the students at the time they received their assignments. We just had not developed them in time to do that this year. Another approach we may consider is to add a self-assessment step to the process, requiring students to apply the rubric to their own work before turning it in. In the end, we decided to use this year as a time to experiment with and fine-tune all the materials we developed—the outcomes, the objectives, the assignments, and the rubrics—and apply these new strategies in 2002–2003.

Conclusion

It is tempting to fall into the mind-set that the problem rests with the students: "I taught it to them yesterday; they just didn't learn it!" Of course, that will not work. So instead, we need to look at what changes we need to make to improve student success. One way of looking at assessment—what it is and why we do it—was articulated beautifully by Debra Gilchrist at a presentation to the Immersion class of 2000. The purpose of assessment, she says, is:

1. Knowing what you are doing.
2. Knowing why you are doing it.
3. Knowing what students are learning as a result.
4. Changing because of the information.[1]

That last is now the focus of our efforts. It is clear from our results that changes need to be made in several areas if we are to improve student learning. Some approaches we will examine are:

1. integrating our assessment instruments;
2. polishing the rubrics, using this year's student performance as guidelines to make them clearer and more reflective of our expectations;
3. distributing the rubrics to the students along with the assignment(s);
4. give students a sample copy of a completed assignment as an example of what is expected;
5. introducing a self-assessment requirement, using the rubrics;
6. requiring a one-on-one consult with a librarian to review work before submitting it;
7. providing interim feedback midquarter so students may make corrections.

Updates to this information will be posted at http://flightline.highline.ctc.edu/dfranks/imls_assessment_project.htm.

Note

1. Gilchrist, Debra. Presentation at *Immersion '00*, Seattle, Wash., Aug. 2000.

Preliminary preparation for the GROUP PRESENTATION

Topic: ______________________________

Names and duties of group members:

Names	Specific duties
______________	______________
______________	______________
______________	______________
______________	______________

Why is this topic important?

____

____

Put your topic into a question:

____

____

Complete the "Great Finds" assignment

List five main concepts that you are finding out (state in complete sentence):

____

____

____

____

____

What are your tentative conclusions as a result of your research thus far?

____

____

____

List two or three methods you will use to present your information:

____

____

____

This form is to be submitted by <date>

Rubric for Scoring: *Preliminary Preparation Sheet* Education 110

Criteria for Evaluation	3 – Exemplary	2 – Competent	1-Emergent
Students will meet with group members to refine topic (Section 1).	Group members duties are described on the *Preliminary Preparation* sheet in a way that is reflects group process and planning.	Group members names are listed, and a brief description is given of their research responsibilities.	Students names may or may not be listed, but specific duties are not addressed.
Students will clearly articulate a focused research topic (Section 3).	Topic is stated in terms of a focused question that identifies a claim or argument to explore and clearly suggests what information is needed.	Topic is stated in terms of a question that is a complete sentence but does not identify a claim or argument to explore or does not clearly suggest what information is needed.	Topic is not in the form of a question or is described in a short phrase or string of keywords or is not described at all.
Students will identify 5 concepts, implicit in the main topic, for further investigation	The concepts are implicit in the main topic, demonstrate a clear understanding of its depth and breadth, and clearly suggest what information is needed.	At least three concepts are listed and they are related to the main topic. They do not develop the depth and breadth of the topic.	Two or fewer concepts are listed or more are listed but they don't develop the main topic beyond what is stated in the main topic question.
Student can draw tentative conclusions about the topic based on preliminary research.	Tentative conclusion statement reflects comprehension and synthesis of the previously identified main concepts.	Tentative conclusion summarizes one or two sources but does not synthesize the information.	Tentative conclusion is reflective of only one source or is unsubstantiated.
Student can express these conclusions in a clear statement.	Tentative conclusion statement makes a claim and is a complete thought, clearly expressed.	Tentative conclusion summarizes one or more points but does not make a claim, or it makes a claim but does not communicate it clearly.	Tentative conclusion is inconclusive or expressed in short phrases or is missing altogether.

Great Finds

You are doing research to find information for your group presentations. Now you get to show us how well you can do this. Specifically, we'd like to see that you can:

- *Identify appropriate sources* of information for your research projects. ("Sources" means specific reference books, electronic databases, or books or videos from the library's collection.)
- *Find information* using both print and electronic searching.
- *Evaluate and analyze* information critically so you can select the best of what you found.
- *Cite your sources* using APA format.

Your Assignment

As a group you will assemble an annotated list of four "Great Finds." You may work individually or combine resources, but all members must contribute. This list should contain one of each of the following:

- ***Background source:*** Choose the background information source that gave you the clearest grounding in the issues surrounding your topic.
- ***Vocabulary source:*** Choose the source that provided you with relevant vocabulary or terminology related to your topic. This may be a dictionary or encyclopedia, but it doesn't need to be. Any source (including a Web page or periodical article) could be relevant as long as it introduced you to new terms related to your topic and explained them.
- ***Current events source:*** Choose an excellent current events source that illustrates how your topic is reflected in events that are going on today.
- ***Statistical source:*** Choose the source that provided you with relevant statistics that support some aspect of the information you will present.

Cite each of your sources correctly using APA format (refer to reference sheet or online guide: http://flightline.highline.ctc.edu/reference/Userguides/ug_apastyle.htm).

For each one, write a brief annotation stating:

- how it provided what you needed
- how you judged its reliability/accuracy
- how you judged its timeliness
- how you judged its point or view and/or bias

Criteria for assessment :

- All four types of sources are listed.
- Annotations clearly state how the sources provided the required information.

• Students clearly describe the evaluative process they used in judging the reliability, validity, accuracy, authority, timeliness, and point of view or bias for each of these sources.
• Sources are cited correctly using APA citation style.

Rubric for Scoring: *Great Finds Assignment*
Education 110

Criteria for Evaluation	3 – Exemplary	2 – Competent	1-Emergent
Students will identify at least one source that substantially increases their vocabulary surrounding their topics.	The selected vocabulary source and its annotation clearly demonstrate a substantial increase in vocabulary useful for further research on the topic.	The selected vocabulary source provides some terminology pertinent to the topic, but the annotation does not demonstrate that it substantially increases vocabulary useful for further research on the topic.	The annotation does not indicate how the source provided relevant vocabulary useful for subsequent searches.
Students will select one each: a background source, a vocabulary source, a statistical source, and a current events source related to their topic.	All four types of sources are listed and they fall under the four assigned categories.	Two or three sources are listed, and they fall under the assigned categories, or four sources are listed and they don't all fall under the assigned categories.	One or fewer sources are listed, or more are listed but they don't fall under the assigned categories.
Students will identify at least four library resources, in at least two formats, that, taken together, provide substantial treatment of their topic.	Resources are in at least two formats and, taken together, they provide substantial treatment of the topic and concepts articulated on the *Preliminary Preparation* sheet, number 5.	Resources are all in one format, or they provide essentially the same information as one another though they do treat the main topic.	There are fewer than four resources, or they are only marginally relevant to the topic.

Students will be able to describe how each of their four sources provided the information they needed.	Annotations clearly state how the sources provided the required information.	Annotations describe the sources but don't sufficiently relate them to the assigned categories.	Assignment is not annotated or annotations are limited to short, vague phrases.
Students will be able to describe the process they used to evaluate the reliability, validity, accuracy, authority, timeliness, and point of view or bias for each of these sources.	Students clearly describe the evaluative process they used in judging the reliability, validity, accuracy, authority, timeliness, and point of view or bias for each of their four sources.	Students give opinions about the reliability, validity, accuracy, authority, timeliness, and point of view or bias for each of their four sources but don't describe the evaluative process they used.	Students do not evaluate the sources.
Students will cite four sources using APA citation style.	Sources are cited correctly using APA citation style.	For each citation, three or more of the following— author, title, journal title, volume, date, pages or URL —are provided, but they are not correctly formatted.	Fewer than three elements of any citation are provided and they are not correctly formatted.

Intro to Education **Name** ______________________

Evaluation for Group Presentation

The following elements will be considered in evaluating the group presentations. **You will complete Section 4** (required) **and the Comments** (opt.) and submit this form on the day of your presentation. Criteria will be rated according to the scale of:

5 = "WOW" 4=solid, substantial 3=met expectations 2=needs help 1=poorly done

	Scored by instructor
1. Elements of presentation	
• ***Quality of presentation:*** clear and audible speech, interesting minimal reliance on notes, eye contact, attitude, appropriate attire	5 4 3 2 1
• ***Content/knowledge of subject:*** thorough presentation of information, obvious research done, synthesis and application of information	5 4 3 2 1
• ***Organization/structure:*** introduction, main points presented, "flow" of presentation, closure, keeping within allotted time	5 4 3 2 1
• ***Presentation/style:*** uniqueness, creativity	5 4 3 2 1
• ***Fair/factual:*** balanced presentation of views and comparisons, use of reliable facts and statistics	5 4 3 2 1
2. Paper	
• ***Overview of presentation:*** coverage of main points	5 4 3 2 1
• ***Organization:*** citing of sources, SPG	5 4 3 2 1
3. Handout	
• ***Content:*** information relevant to and representative of presentation	5 4 3 2 1
• ***Organization:*** format, professional appearance, SPG	5 4 3 2 1
Each student will complete this portion for each member of the group (+ self) **4. Peer evaluation**	
• See rubric below to determine the peer scores you will give for this section. Final peer grade for each student will be determined from group score averages.	
Name (self) ______________________	5 4 3 2 1
Name ______________________	5 4 3 2 1
Name ______________________	5 4 3 2 1
Name ______________________	5 4 3 2 1

Criteria for peer group grading:

5 points	4 points	3 points	2 points	1 point
Attended all workdays with a "wow" level of • Significant contributions • Cooperation • Skills in compromise and negotiation • Shared responsibility • Resourcefulness • Enthusiasm	Missed no more than one workday plus a high level of the items in the first column	Missed no more than two workdays plus a moderate amount and level of the items in the first column	Missed two work- days and/or contributed at a low level of the items in the first column and/or/ negatively impacted the group	Significant absence on workdays and/ or lack of participation and/or negatively impacted the group.

Rubric for Scoring: *Evaluation for Group Presentation*
Education 110

Criteria for Evaluation	3 – Exemplary	2 – Competent	1-Emergent
Students will meet with group members to refine topic (section 4 – self and peer evaluations).	Student attended all workdays, made unique or exceptional contributions to project, provided leadership, cooperated, demonstrated skills in compromise and negotiation, shared responsibility and resourcefulness, and participated with enthusiasm.	Student missed no more than one workday, participated in project, cooperated, negotiated, shared responsibility for final product.	Student missed two or more workdays, failed to participate and/or negatively impacted the group.
Presentation has a central thesis, supported by valid evidence (section 1 – organization/structure).	Presentation has an obvious main thesis, and connections are clearly drawn between valid supporting evidence and the thesis.	Presentation has a thesis but it is not presentated in a clear statement – or – cited evidence is incomplete in its scope, or incompletely supports the thesis, or comes from questionable sources.	Presentation has no central thesis or has several theses or indicates a thesis and doesn't follow through, and/or evidence is minimal (2 or fewer sources), unreliable, or only marginally supports the topic.
Student synthesizes information and applies it in a cohesive presentation (section 1 – content/knowledge).	Reference to research sources is evident in the presentation, and information that has been obtained from multiple sources is synthesized and applied in a thorough treatment of the topic.	Reference is made to sources of information, but they are either not diverse to begin with or are not synthesized and/or the relationship between the research and the topic is not clearly drawn by the presenter.	No reference is made to sources of information or no connection is drawn among the information sources or between the information and the thesis.

Student's presentation explores multiple facets of the topic (section 1 – fair/factual).	Presenters demonstrate that they have challenged themselves by seeking out and accurately presenting diverse concepts or points of view and attempting to reconcile them.	Presenters explore at least two facets of the topic but do not identify or explore the more difficult or challenging arguments and/or do not reconcile them or make a well-supported case for one over another.	Presenters offer a one-sided or one-dimensional exploration of the topic.
Student will be able to present information orally to an audience familiar with the field of education, but not necessarily with their specific topic (section 1 – quality of presentation).	Presentation is clear and audible, there is minimal reliance on notes, presenter makes eye contact with audience, has an enthusiastic attitude and appropriate attire, and uses of the language of the education field, but without reliance on jargon.	Presentation volume or articulation are uneven or gestures or posture is stiff, thus distracting from message; presenter tries to make eye contact but not with each member of the audience or occasionally reads notes.	Presentation was either unclear or inaudible or gestures or posture was distracting, no little or no eye contact is made or read significant portions of the speech.

Chapter 16: Assessing Information Literacy in an English Composition Class

Marcia Freyman

Institution Description

Lexington Community College (LCC) is a two-year institution with an enrollment of approximately 7,500 students and 160 full-time faculty. Half of the students are enrolled in technical programs, and the other half will transfer to either the University of Kentucky or one of the other undergraduate public universities in the state. In the eight years I have been doing bibliographic instruction (BI) here, I have experienced a gradual increase in the number of classes reached and the growing interest of our faculty. Currently, there is no wording in our college's mission statement about the commitment to information literacy (IL) as a goal in the education of all of our students. Assessment of IL only began with the initiation of this grant project and is still in the formative stages as far as an institutional commitment. During the past year, our faculty General Education Committee has been working to facilitate the incorporation of course objectives and outcomes for all classes that fall into this category. Some of these in the English area are including outcomes based on the use of library databases and information literacy.

Project Participants

I have been working with eight instructors in the area of English composition who teach both English 101 and English 102. Both of these courses are required for all of our students as part of their graduation requirements. English 101 requires one paper at the end of the course, with a research component. In English 102, students write five papers, all of which require some aspect of library research. The instructors and I decided on those aspects of information literacy that students finishing these two courses should be able to master. At the end of the semester, after working with the classes in their research for their papers, and after the students had written their papers, students completed a multiple-choice test consisting of questions about specific databases, Boolean searching, and other relevant aspects of IL.

Project Description

In this project, I was interested in reaching our students at the beginning stages of doing research and learning to incorporate IL into their class assignments early in their college education. I also realized the importance of expanding this critical thinking training into their larger world beyond a specific class assignment. Because most of our students take English 101 and 102 in their freshman year and these classes require some research component, I chose to work with instructors in this area. However, the limitation was in reaching the majority of the students in these courses when literally only two librarians on our campus are doing bibliographic instruction.

Planning for Assessment

I met with the participating faculty to decide what it was we wanted the students to learn from this method of incorporating aspects of IL into their research for specific paper assignments. I also worked with the faculty to make sure the differences or expected course outcomes of English 101 and 102 were realized. The syllabus in ENG101 requires that a research component be introduced only at the end of the semester into the students' last assignment. This may be in the form of a survey or something the student saw in the newspaper, or in some cases, the use of library materials and databases for sources. In ENG102 all writing assignments require the use and incorporation of library resources. The instruction from the librarians and the assessment tools had to reflect these differences in the course objectives.

Developing the Assessment Instruments

The tests for English 101 and English 102 differed quite a bit, based on the types of assignments given and the expected course objectives for the two courses. They both took the form of multiple-choice questions. The test for ENG102 consisted of questions that went into much more depth and expected a better understanding of library resources and IL than the test for ENG101 did. The tests were administered in the last two weeks of the semester after students had completed their research assignment and handed in their papers. Both tests are included at the end of this chapter.

Analyzing the Results

Mostly, I was interested in determining if the differences in the tests between English 101 and 102 were accurately differentiated. In other words, should the student completing English 101 be expected to know the answers to the questions asked? The same question was true for students in English 102.

Results

English 101

There were four general findings. First, students generally scored weaker on questions relating to the Internet, citation format, and types of library sources (e.g., general encyclopedias as opposed to more specific scholarly journals). Second, students scored the best on interpreting areas of a book entry from the library online catalog, InfoKat (e.g., author, subject, publication date). Third, students seemed somewhat unclear (partially correct responses) about what InfoKat includes. And finally, students were somewhat unclear about the full-text coverage of articles appearing in online databases such as InfoTrac. (See table 16-1.)

English 102

In English 102, the students generally scored weaker generally on: (1) questions about the coverage of full-text articles in online databases such as InfoTrac; (2) recognizing the differences between professional (scholarly) journals and magazines; (3) locating other books on their topic after they had found at least one; and (4) how to locate the full text of an article if it is not available through the online database.

Students scored best on: (1) which database to search for full-text articles;(2) limiting and expanding their searches in InfoTrac to find either more or fewer articles as needed; (3) limiting their search in InfoKat to find only those items in LCC's library; and (4) using the proxy server to access dababases from home. (See table 16-2.)

Challenges

First, I had to decide if the level of questions on the two tests was correct. In other words, should the students in each class really be expected to know what I had asked? I looked at the questions the students missed most often and asked myself the following questions:

1. Was it the wording of the question, or was it that students didn't know the correct answer? I realized early on that I was not trained in the art of good ques-

Table 16-1. English 101 Student Experiences (N=85)

	Correct	Incorrect	Partially Correct
1. Which order of sources describes those from more general to more specific?	47.1%	52.9%	NA
2. Documenting a source is important only when you are using a direct quote from it.	74.2	25.8	NA
3. For books in LCC Library, the first letter of the call number is always the first letter of the author's last name.	37.7	62.3	NA
4. The Internet provides the same information as electronic periodical indexes plus more.	55.3	44.7	NA
5. You can use InfoKat to find:	19.9	9.4	70.7
6. You can use InfoTrac to find:	9.4	9.4	81.2
7. Information on the Internet is screened by professionals for relevancy, accuracy, and currency.	83.4	16.6	NA
8. This book is shelved:	87.1	12.9	NA
9. This book was published in:	100.0	0.0	NA
10. How many people wrote this book?	68.3	0.0	31.7
11. This book is about:	85.9	14.1	NA
12. This book has:	73.0	NA	27.0
13. The title of this book is:	95.3	4.7	NA
14. Which of the following represent secondary source materials?	21.2	28.8	50.0
15. It is a good idea to consult a librarian when:	93.0	NA	7.0
16. Where can I find the bibliographic citation information from the online InfoTrac database?	47.1	52.9	NA

Table 16-2. English 102 Student Experiences (N=66)

	Correct	Incorrect	Partially Correct
1. What is the best place to look for full text magazine articles by topic	94.5%	4.5%	NA
2. When using InfoTrac to find articles, you would use AND between two search terms	86.4	13.6	NA
3. What is the best method of searching InfoKat for **only** those items in LCC's library (and not at UK)	83.4	16.6	NA
4. If your electronic search for magazine articles produces **too many results**, how could you narrow it?	Question worded unclearly		
5. If your electronic search for magazine articles produces **too few results**, how could you find more	97.0	NA	3.0
6. If your electronic search for magazine articles produces **no results**, what could you do	95.5	NA	4.5
7. Electronic periodical indexes include citations for **all articles ever published** in the periodicals they cover	45.5	54.5	NA
8. I would document in MLA style an article from the InfoTrac database the **same** way as one in paper format	80.3	19.7	NA
9. Some sources about Lexington or Kentucky	66.7	0.0	33.3
10. Features of **professional journals**	39.3	0.0	60.7
11. If any article was **not available full text** through the InfoTrac online database, how would I find it?	40.9	0.0	59.1
12. UK's proxy server must be connected to view the full text of articles in online databases.	97.0	3.0	NA
13. You can use **InfoKat** to find	56.2	6.0	37.8
14. Some of the ways to **evaluate internet web sites**	74.2	0.0	25.8

Table 16-2. English 102 Student Experiences (cont.)

15. If you find a book in the library catalog about your topic, what is a good way to **find others?**	37.8	0.0	62.2
16. The title of the article is:	78.8	21.2	NA
17. Feb 13, 2002 represents	77.3	22.7	NA

tion writing. After giving the first draft of my test to several students as an experiment, I realized that I was going to need help from our college's Institutional Research people.

2. Were students missing questions because, in fact, the information had not been covered in any of the BI sessions or wasn't necessary for that particular assignment? Part of the differences in results, I found, was the array of assignments given by the instructors, which allowed for various kinds of resources.

3. Was the format of the question unclear or one that students weren't used to (e.g., when more than one choice was correct in a multiple-choice question)? In discussing this with other faculty, we came to the conclusion that students are used to a certain kind of multiple-choice test in which only a single answer is correct. If given the choice of several answers where more than one is correct, the student will generally try to choose only the "best one." Part of my thought process with regard to coming up with questions on the tests for both courses was to continue the students' learning process by taking the test. In other words, answers to several of the questions were constructed in such a way as to make the student understand more clearly the process of using a particular database or search technique.

4. Was too much library "lingo" used in the questions? Again, after giving the experimental first drafts of the tests to several students and receiving feedback from them on this point, I reworded the questions to substitute more recognizable terms in place of the lingo.

In the fall semester, I was working with only two faculty members as an experiment and found the results of the tests quite disappointing. I realized that perhaps the students were not taking it seriously because they were not being graded on it. So in the spring semester, I suggested to participating faculty members that they tell their students that the test would be counted as a quiz and computed into their final grade. This seemed to solve the problem.

Conclusion

It was obvious from the English 101 class that:

1. More instruction is needed on recognizing differences between Internet

sites and library databases and how to evaluate Internet sites for quality. Librarians at the reference desk will direct students to encyclopedias when appropriate and assist students in finding scholarly journals in our collection.

2. Librarians need to continue to assist students using InfoKat and the library classification system for finding books relating to their topics.

3. Because students probably use books less often than articles for research for this class, librarians need to work with students who use the online catalog in the library for other purposes.

4. Librarians will assist students in finding articles that are not available full text in any of the online databases.

From the English 102 class, we learned that:

1. Librarians need to assist students in finding full-text articles in paper format and other online methods.

2. Students need to be directed to scholarly journals by topic in LCC's LRC.

3. Assistance should be available in the LRC for students to locate topic areas by classification number.

4. Librarians need to assist students in the methods of locating full-text articles not available through InfoTrac and the use of interlibrary loan.

This project is a work in progress. The goal is to expand it to include all of the students in English 101 and English 102 classes here at LCC, with the outcome that what students are learning about information literacy in a freshmen-level course will carry into upper-division courses. Some revision of the instruments will be necessary as more results are analyzed.

Assessment Instrument
INFORMATION SKILLS TEST
English 101

Name ____________________
Instructor ____________________ Course ____________________

1. If your teacher tells you to start your paper research by looking at **more general works before more specific works**, in which order would you look at the sources below?
   a. encyclopedias, books, research articles
   b. books, research articles, encyclopedias
   c. research articles, books, encyclopedias
   d. research articles, encyclopedias, books

2. Citing a source in a bibliography or works-cited page is important **only** when you are using a direct quotation from it.
   a. True
   b. False

3. The first letter of the call number on books in LCC's library is always the first letter of the author's last name.
   a. True
   b. False

4. The Internet provides the **same information** as electronic periodical indexes plus more.
   a. True
   b. False

5. You can use **InfoKat** (LCC's library catalog) to find:
   a. articles in magazines owned by the LCC library
   b. any book, video, periodical title, or music CD owned by the LCC library
   c. what textbooks are being used for courses at LCC

6. You can use **InfoTrac** to find:
   a. electronic full text of encyclopedia articles
   b. magazine and journal article citations
   c. full text of some Lexington Herald Leader articles

7. Information on the Internet is screened by professionals for relevancy, accuracy, and currency.
   a. True
   b. False

Use this record from InfoKat to answer questions 8–13.

Main Author: Nieves, Luis R.
Title: Coping in college: successful strategies / by Luis R. Nieves ; with contributions from Jacquelyn J. Schecter, Carol J. Turner.
Publisher: Princeton, N.J.: Educational Testing Service, 1984.
Subject(s): College students—Psychology. Study skills. College student orientation —Handbooks, manuals, etc.
Notes: Bibliography: pp. 129–33.
Description: 133 p.: ill.; 27 cm.
Database: University of Kentucky Libraries
Location: LCC stacks
Call Number: LB2343.3 .N53 1984
Status: Not charged

8. This book is shelved:
   a. in reference
   b. in the stacks
   c. on reserve
   d. in AVs

9. This book was published in:
   a. 1984
   b. 1952
   c. 1998
   d. This information is not given.

10. How many people were involved in writing this book?
   a. one
   b. two
   b. at least three
   d. This information is not given.

11. This book is about:
   a. how students in the United States choose a college
   b. study skills
   c. why students in the United States go to college
   d. This information is not given.

12. This book has:
   a. more than 100 pages
   b. a bibliography
   c. illustrations
   d. all of the above

13. The title of this book is:
   a. College students—Psychology.
   b. Student development in college: Theory, research, and practice
   c. Coping in college: Successful strategies
   d. This information is not given.

14. Which of the following is an example of a **primary source material?**
  a. interviews
  b. magazine articles
  c. books

15. It is a good idea to **consult a librarian** when:
  a. you don't know where to start looking for information or you need more information on a subject
  b. you want to be sure you have used the best sources for your research
  c. you need help using the internet for research
  d. all of these

16. Where can I find the bibliographic citation information to use for my works-cited page when I use an article from the online InfoTrac database?
  a. All the citation information is at the top of every article.
  b. All the citation information is at the bottom of every article.
  c. I have to go back to the original screen listing all the articles about my topic to find the bibliographic information.

INFORMATION SKILLS TEST
English 102

Name ______________________________
Instructor __________________________ Course _______________

1. Which of the following is the **best place** to look for some full-text magazine articles by topic?
   a. Periodicals titles notebook
   b. InfoTrac (Expanded Academic ASAP)
   c. Lexis-Nexis
   d. Courier Journal

2. When using an online database (like InfoTrac) to find articles, you would use AND between two search terms to:
   a. make sure that at least one of the terms is present in the search results
   b. make sure that both terms are present in the search results
   c. make sure that only the first term is present in the search results

3. What is the best method of searching InfoKat for **only** those items in LCC's library (and not at UK)?
   a. Make sure the limits are set to Lexington Community College.
   b. Type in LCC as part of your search with your keywords.
   c. Just type in your keywords and sort through all the results looking for those with an LCC location.

4. If your search for magazine articles in InfoTrac produces **too many results**, how could you narrow it to obtain fewer?
   a. Add another keyword to the search statement.
   b. Narrow the search results to recent publication dates.
   c. Either of these

5. If your search for magazine articles in InfoTrac produces **too few results**, what could you do to find more?
   a. Use different terms for your concepts.
   b. Make your search simpler, with fewer concepts.
   c. Make sure you have spelled all your search terms correctly.
   d. All of these

6. If your search for magazine articles in InfoTrac produces **no results**, what could you do?
   a. Make sure you are spelling all words correctly.
   b. Ask a librarian for help.
   c. Use different keywords or synonyms.
   d. All of these

7. Electronic periodical indexes include citations for **all articles ever published** in the periodicals they cover.
   a. True
   b. False

8. My MLA citation for a *Time* magazine article from InfoTrac would look exactly the **same** as one I found in paper format in the library.
   a. True
   b. False

9. Some sources to look for information about Lexington or Kentucky specifically are: (Circle all that apply.)
   a. Lexington Herald Leader
   b. Courier Journal
   c. New York Times
   d. Time Magazine

10. What are some features of **professional or juried journals** (as opposed to magazines like *Time* or *Newsweek*)? (Circle all that apply.)
   a. list of references at the bottom of the article
   b. at least one, if not more, author's names listed
   c. lots of pictures
   d. length of usually more than 5 pages

11. If any article was **not available full text** through the InfoTrac online database, how would I find it? (Circle all that apply.)
   a. Look up the title of the journal in InfoKat to see if LCC or one of the UK libraries subscribes to it in paper format and then look for it in the library.
   b. Request the article through ILL (interLibrary loan) on the library's Web page.
   c. Go to the Internet and do a search for it using a search engine.
   d. Look to see if it was available full text on the KVL (Kentucky Virtual Library) database.

12. In order to view the full text of articles in the library's electronic resources from home or off campus, students must first connect to UK's proxy server.
   a. True
   b. False

13. You can use **InfoKat** (the library catalog) to find:
   a. articles in magazines owned by the LCC library
   b. any book, video, periodical title, or music CD owned by the LCC library
   c. what textbooks are being used for courses at LCC

14. Some of the ways to **evaluate Internet Web sites** to determine their validity for use as resources in papers include: (Circle all that apply.)
   a. finding out who the author is and his/her credentials
   b. determining when the site was last updated
   c. finding out if there is a bias or slant to the information provided
   d. looking at the URL to see the domain for the site (e.g., gov, org, com)

15. If you find a book in the library catalog (InfoKat) about your topic, what is a good way to **find others related in subject**? (Circle all that apply.)
   a. Go to the call number area of the library to find that book and look at those on either side of it.
   b. Look at the subject heading(s) of that book's record and search for books using those subjects.
   c. Try another keyword search using synonyms and words related to my original seach.
   d. Look in the book on my topic for a bibliography to see if there are some other books listed that pertain to my topic.

The following is a citation from InfoTrac:
   Executing justice. (Second Thoughts on the Death Penalty). (United States)
   John Dart. *The Christian Century* Feb 13, 2002 v119 i4 p6 (1)

16. The title of the article is:
   a. Executing justice
   b. The Christian Century

17. Feb 13, 2002, represents:
   a. the date that the article was published originally in the magazine/journal
   b. the date that you found the article searching InfoTrac

Chapter 17: Webliography Assignment for Lifetime Wellness Class

Nancy Gauss and Kathleen Kinkema

Institution Description

Western State College (WSC) is a public four-year undergraduate institution with approximately 2,120 students and 100 faculty. Public lands offering numerous recreational opportunities surround the campus, located in the rural Rocky Mountains community of Gunnison, Colorado.

WSC faculty and administration are committed to weaving information literacy (IL) instruction into the curriculum. IL is one of the five basic skills taught throughout the general education curriculum. WSC's instruction in information literacy is assignment driven. Librarians provide "one-shot" sessions for classes at all levels and within all disciplines. Each session is tailored to the individual needs of the students based on their assignments.

Over the past two years, the college has focused on assessment in preparation for a comprehensive evaluation and accreditation by the North Central Association of Colleges and Universities in 2002–2003. An institutional self-study, part of the evaluation process, is addressing assessment of programs and learning outcomes.

Project Participants

Dr. Kathleen Kinkema, Associate Professor of Kinesiology, and I collaborated in assessing selected IL skills learned during a Lifetime Wellness class. This was a distance education class taught using WebCT. I approached Dr. Kinkema about collaborating on this project because:

1. Information literacy was a required skill for the class.
2. Dr. Kinkema was interested in redesigning assignments for the online class.
3. One-shot IL sessions were included in previous classes.

Project Description

Lifetime Wellness introduces students to concepts and issues related to health, wellness, disease, and disease prevention. Because it is an introductory course within a popular discipline, Lifetime Wellness usually attracts a high number of freshmen. It also is part of the general education curriculum and has always included an IL module where students learn how to find, evaluate, and cite information. This section of Lifetime Wellness included ten freshmen, three sophomores, and one senior.

Planning for Assessment

At the ACRL Immersion '00 Track 2 workshop, Debra Gilchrist, Pierce College, outlined five questions to be asked when thinking about assessment.

1. What do I want the student to be able to do as a result of this instruction?
2. What does the student need to know in order to do this well?
3. What activity will facilitate the learning?
4. How will the student demonstrate the learning?
5. How will I know the student has done this well?[1]

Dr. Kinkema answered these questions in relation to her Lifetime Wellness class. I identified standards and performance indicators from the Information Literacy Competency Standards for Higher Education that matched her objectives. From the performance indicators identified, three were selected for assessment:

1. Standard I, Performance Indicator 4.2 (describes criteria used to make information decisions and choices)

2. Standard III, Performance Indicator 2.1 (examines and compares information from various sources in order to evaluate reliability, validity, accuracy, authority, timeliness, and point of view or bias)

3. Standard V, Performance Indicator 3.1 (selects an appropriate documentation style and uses it consistently to cite sources)

Developing the Assessment Instrument

We began discussing assignments that might help students develop the skills needed for meeting the performance indicators. From Dr. Kinkema's experience with this class, she knew that many of her students would appreciate investigating a health-related topic that affected them personally. In collaboration, a pathfinder assignment, called a Webliography, was created with worksheets, guides, and progressive due dates for each section to help students keep on target. The sections of the Webliography included:

1. introduction to the topic and description of the audience for the Webliography;
2. criteria for selecting Web sites and articles, including general criteria (i.e., currency, reliability, etc.) and criteria specific to the audience (i.e., appropriate for teenagers);
3. descriptions of databases and search engines selected for finding information;
4. keywords and search statements used;
5. annotated resources selected based on the described criteria and cited in American Psychological Association (APA) format.

To evaluate the entire assignment, we created a rubric that described the components of each section in the Webliography and definitions of performance at the basic, proficient, and advanced levels. The three performance indicators applied to three of the section components. We created the following objectives for these three components:

1. Criteria for selecting articles and Web sites: At least 75 percent of the students will develop at least one criterion for selecting articles or Web sites that is specific to their audience. This converts to performance at the "proficient" level. [Standard I, Performance Indicator 4.2].
2. Criteria for annotated resources: For at least 75 percent of the students, more than 50 percent of the articles and Web sites included in the Webliographies will satisfy the criteria previously described for selecting sources. Each source adds some new information on the topic. This converts to performance at the "proficient" level. [Standard III, Performance Indicator 2.1].
3. Criteria for annotated resources: At least 75 percent of the students will cite all sources in APA format with less than 50 percent containing some errors. This converts to performance at the "proficient" level. [Standard V, Performance Indicator 3.1].

The assignment and grading rubric are included at the end of this chapter.

Analyzing the Results

Because each student required a letter grade for the assignment, Dr. Kinkema assigned a point value to each section component and performance level on the rubric. She developed a key that linked point values to an overall grade for the assignment. For this assessment project, we were interested not in grades, but percentages. She reported the percentage of students who performed at the three levels within each component. For the three performance indicators assessed:

1. Fifty-eight percent achieved Standard I, Performance Indicator 4.2.

2. Thirty-eight percent achieved Standard III, Performance Indicator 2.1.
3. Thirty-eight percent achieved Standard V, Performance Indicator 3.1.

The Results

Using the Webliography Rubric Assessment, we found the proficiencies and problem areas shown in table 17-1.

After the webliographies were graded, we regrouped to discuss what worked well, the problem areas, and, specifically, how we should refine this assignment and rubric for future classes.

What Worked Well

For students who were self-disciplined, the rubric helped them understand expectations for each section. Students also provided positive feedback about the value of the assignment. For example, one student stated that the assignment was "fun." She went on to comment, "I got to learn more about running, and I also learned that there are really great sources of info out there if you take the time to look."

What Did Not Work Well

Although the Webliography and the assessment rubric were explained in a formal class and separate due dates were created for each section of the assignment, many students had difficulty meeting the deadlines. This was characteristic of not only this assignment, but also of other assignments for this class. Some of the assessment results for this project may have been confounded by the fact that the class was Internet based. Students who had trouble with the Webliography also were having trouble with other aspects of the class. Although Dr. Kinkema introduced students to the "Top 10 Behaviors Needed to Survive an Internet Class" and had each student complete a self-assessment of their aptitude for Internet learning, perhaps some did not understand their own behaviors sufficiently to assess whether they were good candidates for this class.

Challenges

Novice college students, particularly freshmen, may lack qualities necessary to succeed in an online environment. Next year, the class will be offered in a traditional format using a similar Webliography assignment. It will be interesting to compare the results.

Students were encouraged to contact us with questions, either in person or by e-mail or phone, but none did. In seven of the ten section components, more than 10 percent of the students scored "inadequate" or did not include a section from the Webliography.

Most of the Webliography sections were due at different dates except the section on databases, search engines, and keywords. In retrospect, we should have

TABLE 17-1. Results of Grading Assignment

Grading Area	Proficiency	Problem Areas
Introduction Topic Description	80% Proficient/Advanced; 20% Basic; 0% Inadequate/Missing	Citations, Supporting evidence for importance of topic
Introduction Audience Description	64% Proficient/Advanced; 18% Basic; 18% Inadequate/ Missing	Audience not mentioned, Relevancy of topic to audience lacking or not developed enough
Introduction Arrangement of Websites	56% Proficient/Advanced; 9% Basic; 35% Inadequate/ Missing	Many did not go back and add this prior to turning in the final project
Search Criteria	29% Advanced; 28% Proficient; 29% Basic; 14% Inadequate/Missing	Clearly defining what the chosen criteria will mean for the topic; not differentiating between article criteria and website criteria
Databases and Search Engines	21% Proficient/Advanced, 64% Basic, 14% Inadequate/Missing	Relying on too few databases or search engines
Key Words, Phrases, and Search Statements	60% Proficient/Advanced, 40% Inadequate/Missing	Not completing this portion of the assignment, not using enough relevant synonyms, search com-mands not specific to the database or search engine.
Annotated Resources 5 articles/5 websites	25% Advanced; 13% Proficient; 37% Basic; 25% Inadequate/ Missing	Some confusion about online articles vs websites (e.g., too many websites, not enough articles); inclusion of sources that didn't meet the previously identified criteria.
APA style	38% Advanced; 0% Proficient; 37% Basic; 25% Inadequate/Missing	Missing information, improper use of APA
Abstracts	25% Advanced; 25% Proficient; 25% Basic; 25% Inadequate/Missing	No evaluative information, too brief, no description of usefulness for audience, no description of how source contributes to topic
Writing	37% Advanced; 50% Proficient; 13% Basic; 0% Inadequate	Various minor writing mistakes: spelling, punctuation, sentence construction, and capitalization.

asked students to turn in this section separately. Forty percent of the students did not include the description of keywords in their final product.

Conclusions

Students did not have difficulty describing the criteria they would use to select sources for this assignment. Applying the criteria, however, was a problem. In many cases, an annotated source did not meet the previously identified criteria. Our typical instruction sessions review the appropriate criteria for "good" Web sites and articles, but this project demonstrates that we need to emphasize applying the criteria perhaps to Web sites and articles.

We also were surprised at the difficulty students had with converting a citation into APA format despite available guides. Perhaps some exercises in this activity would help.

Should the Assignment and Rubric Be Refined for Future Use?

In general, Dr. Kinkema recommended using the Webliography assignment again and perhaps in other classes. The students who kept up with all assignments did well in the Webliography assignment and had positive feedback about the assignment overall.

If the Webliography assignment were added to a traditional classroom course, Dr. Kinkema would schedule some class time to provide an overview of the assignment and some class time to explain each section at the time when students would be expected to begin working on it. Although she suggested that students visit with both of us at least once about their progress on the assignment, few did. Required individual meetings with either a librarian or Dr. Kinkema might help to keep students on track and clear up any misconceptions about the assignment.

The rubric might require some modification to clarify the levels of proficiency expected for each portion of the assignment. Dr. Kinkema suggested that students be required to meet the "basic" level for each step as a minimum prerequisite for moving on to the next section of the Webliography.

Note

1. Debra Gilchrist, Pierce Colleges, Pierce County Washington. *Assessment from the Inside Out* (Workshop for the Library Media Directors Council of Washington, 1999.)

WEBLIOGRAPHY ASSIGNMENT
Overview

What is a Webliography? For purposes of this class, a Webliography is:

An annotated list of resources on a specific topic *and* for a specific audience.

The purpose of the Webliography is to direct people interested in a specific topic to resources that will help them improve their understanding of the topic.
For this assignment, resources will include articles and Web sites. Books are not required. However, if you find an appropriate book, or other type of source like a video, please add it.

Your audience may be any group, as long as you can define the group. Examples of audiences include: teenagers, elderly, college athletes, mountain climbers, or adolescent girls with eating disorders. The components of the Webliography are:

I. Introduction.
The introduction includes:
- Description of the topic and why it is important
- Statement about the intended audience for the Webliography and why the audience would be interested in this topic
- How the annotated resources will be organized and why the organization is important

II. The Criteria for Selecting Resources
Specifically, this portion will address the criteria used to select resources for your Webliography. The criteria should include:
- General criteria that one might use for evaluating any resources on the topic
- Criteria specific to your audience

III. Databases, Search Engines, and Keywords
In this section, you will list the databases and search engines used and the keywords or phrases that were successful in finding relevant information. You should also include a justification for why these databases and search engines were selected. Your databases and search engines may include:
- General databases and search engines that locate sources on all topics
- Databases and search engines specific to health-related issues

IV. The Annotated Sources
Each source must be cited in APA (American Psychological Association) format.
Each annotation will include about 4–6 sentences addressing:

a. A brief summary of the site or article

b. A statement about the credibility or qualifications of the author, the author's organization, and/or the journal in which the article is published

c. A statement about the source's potential value to the audience

The four sections of the Webliography will be due at different times throughout the semester. Toward the end of the semester, you will be asked to put all the sections together to create your webliography. At that time, you may be editing or changing some of the sections as you learn more about the topic and sources.

There are separate instructions for each of the four sections. You will also receive a chart, sometimes called a "rubric," explaining Dr. Kinkema's expectations for "basic," "proficient," and "advanced" performance on this Webliography assignment.

Your Webliography will be placed in the WebCT classroom on the college server for others to critique and use as a resource.

If your webliography is written well and appropriate for your designated audience, we may wish to place it on the web for others to review, with your approval.

Webliography Due Dates/Points Values

What	*When*	*How Much*
Information Literacy Preassessment	Sept. 3	30
Topic Choice/Approval	Sept. 10	20
Topic Narrative/Introduction	Sept. 17–24	40
Search Criteria	Oct. 1	35
Database and Search Engines/Keywords	Oct. 8	25
Annotated Sources (1st four)	Oct. 22	50
Final Revised Webliography	Nov. 19	75

Webliography Assignment
Grading Rubric

Introduction	**Basic***	**Proficient/Advanced**	
Description of the topic to be addressed by the information sources	Instructor approves topic. The topic is similar to one identified in class, or of personal interest. Topic is described for uninformed reader.	Instructor approves topic. The topic is similar to one identified in class, or of personal interest. Topic is described for uninformed reader. Description includes justifications and relevant citations for why topic is timely.	
Description of the intended audience	Audience is broadly described. Statement on why audience would be interested in this webliography is lacking.	Audience is described in specific detail with identifying characteristics relevant to the topic. Includes a statement on why audience would be interested in this webliography.	
Statement on how the articles and web sites are arranged.	Arrangement of sources is described.	Arrangement of sources is described and tied to needs of the audience.	
Criteria	**Basic***	**Proficient**	**Advanced**
Criteria for selecting the articles and web sites	Criteria are general and not tied to the specific audience (e.g., currency, authority of author, generally relevant to topic)	Appropriate general criteria are described, as well as 1 specific criterion relevant to the characteristics of the audience and topic.	Appropriate general criteria are described, as well as at least 2 criteria relevant to the characteristics of the audience and topic.
Databases and Search Engines	**Basic***	**Proficient**	**Advanced**
List of databases and search engines used to find articles & web sites	List includes at least one periodical database and at least one search engine.	Description includes at least 3 databases and search engines selected, with at least one of each.	Description includes at least 3 databases and search engines selected, with at least one of each, and justifications for why these databases and search engines were selected for this topic

Keywords, Phrases, and Search Statements	**Basic***	**Proficient/Advanced**	
Lists keywords and phrases that were successful in finding sources. Databases and search engines are listed along with the specific search statements used in searching each one.	Keywords and phrases used in searching are listed, but relevant synonyms are lacking. Databases and search engines are listed along with the specific search statements used in searching each one.	Keywords, relevant synonyms, and related terms are listed. Databases and search engines are listed along with the specific search statements used in searching each one. Appropriate search commands specific to each database or search engine are indicated.	
Annotated Resources	**Basic***	**Proficient**	**Advanced**
5 articles and 5 web sites are selected based on the established criteria	50% of the sources selected meet the established criteria. Some sources repeat the same information.	Over 50% of the sources selected meet the established criteria. Each source adds some new information on the topic.	All of the sources selected meet the established criteria. Each source adds some new information on the topic.
Sources are cited in APA format.	All citations include information sufficient to identify and locate the sources. APA format is followed but 50% or more contain some errors.	All citations include information sufficient to identify and locate the sources. APA format is followed but less than 50% contain some errors.	All citations include information sufficient to identify and locate the sources. APA format is followed correctly with no error.
Abstracts or summaries	50% of the abstracts include: a brief summary of the article or site, an evaluative statement about the credibility of the author or the author's organization, and a statement about the potential value to the audience.	Over 50% of the abstracts include: a brief summary of the article or site, an evaluative statement about the credibility of the author or the author's organization, and a statement about the potential value to the audience.	All of the abstract includes: a brief summary of the article or site, an evaluative statement about the credibility of the author or the author's organization, and a statement about the potential value to the audience

Writing Proficiency	Over 50% of the abstracts include errors in grammar, mechanics or spelling. Sentences are somewhat mechanical or awkward. Vocabulary could be confusing or inappropriate for the audience.	50% or less of the abstracts include errors in grammar, mechanics or spelling. Sentences are constructed properly. Vocabulary is precise, interesting, and natural.	Abstracts include no errors in grammar, mechanics or spelling. Sentences are constructed properly. Writing style and vocabulary, while precise, interesting, and natural, is appropriate for the audience.

* Anything less that "Basic" will be considered "Inadequate." Absence of any of the portions will be assigned a "0."

Chapter 18: Assessing Student Learning Outcomes in Political Science Classes

Elizabeth O. Hutchins

Institution Description

St. Olaf College, a four-year Lutheran (ELCA) college located in Northfield, Minnesota, offers a strong undergraduate education committed to the liberal arts, rooted in the Christian Gospel, and incorporating a global perspective. Seventy-seven percent of the student body (2,939 FTE) is from the Upper Midwest, with 54 percent from Minnesota. The college has 249 FTE faculty—214 full-time and 104 part-time. Most librarians have faculty status, participate in library and college committees, and have been evaluated according to faculty standards. Although tenure-track hires were the rule in the past, this has changed recently across campus with an increased percentage of faculty hired on term contracts.

The St. Olaf Libraries are "teaching libraries" with a strong course-integrated library instruction program established in 1977 on the Earlham Model with the mentoring of Evan Farber. Supported by a long-standing collaborative relationship with faculty in other disciplines, the library instruction program focuses on the research process and critical thinking, thereby sharing many of the goals of information literacy (IL). Evidence of past support for IL includes an Associated Colleges of the Midwest (ACM) Bibliographic Instruction Conference (1998) organized by St. Olaf; involvement by a reference/instruction librarian in the first

ACRL Immersion Institute on Information Literacy (1999); participation of librarians in NSF, ACM, JSTOR, and ACRL grants; and funding to match the ACRL/IMLS Assessment Grant. In 2000, the Libraries' Information Literacy Action Plan was approved and integrated into the libraries' self-study and long-range plan. Librarians also have been actively involved during 2000–2001 in a number of departmental self-studies, which have included comprehensive reassessments of majors and examination of disciplinary competencies.

Project Participants

The project's primary participants have included a reference/instruction librarian and two political science professors. The project builds on a strong partnership between the library liaison and the social science departments developed over the past six years. Although this report focuses on collaboration with the political science department, the grant also influenced the continued development of a four-section information lab in an introductory experimental psychology lab course where the librarian served as a member of the teaching team. This lab evolved into including pretests, posttests, lab worksheets, and posters. (An evaluation sheet is at the end of the chapter.) The lab manual for this course will be published in the APA's peer-reviewed online *Project Syllabus.*

Political Science 264 (Latin American Politics), the primary focus of this project, had 32 students: 23 women and 9 men. Class makeup included 16 seniors, 5 juniors, 5 sophomores, 3 first-year students, and 3 foreign students at St. Olaf for one year. Political Science 220 (Analyzing Politics and Policy) had 31 students, including primarily sophomores and juniors. The introductory psychology course, mentioned above, had 60 students with 15 in each lab.

Project Description

Both the political science and psychology departments conducted extensive self-studies in 1998–2000 culminating in the redesign of their majors and course sequence. In each case, the library was involved in internal discussions of competencies deemed important by the departments. At the invitation of these departments to focus on sequential "intellectual competencies," it was my intention to align and integrate IL skills and assessment with departmental curricula, thereby affirming and enhancing what already exists. Throughout the project, the political science and psychology curricula were the starting points, with rubrics evolving from already successful assignments. A key goal of the assessment project was to provide guidelines that enable students to understand course expectations and be partners with the faculty in assessing their own learning.

The project included two Level II courses, Latin American Politics 264 and Analyzing Politics and Policy 220. PS 264 placed major emphasis on a developmental research process incorporating literature reviews, an annotated bibliography, and a research paper submitted as a draft and final product. Collaboration on this course assessment included assignment creation, a partnership in evaluating assignments, advanced instruction in sequential research strategies, and mutually high expectations. Before using a rubric in this course, we chose to do preliminary testing of our assumptions in the PS367 Latin American seminar to identify the skills students need to have mastered before enrolling in a Level III course. Simultaneously, close collaboration on PS220 course design, taught by another professor during both semesters I & II, encouraged us to broaden the testing of our assessment instrument in semester II to include that class, as well. PS 220 is the reconfigured required research course for the department with a focus on developing an extensive research portfolio, including an annotated bibliography, data and statistics, and a detailed project proposal, all of which require the use of Endnote 5. The course objectives included:

- the ability to find and evaluate a broad cross section of scholarly resources that provide evidence;
- conceptual arguments and theoretical explanations;
- awareness of diverse modes of inquiry in political science;
- an understanding of the process of scholarly research through the formation of questions;
- design of analytical and methodological approaches, use of evidence, development of theses, and citation of sources.

Planning for Assessment

Planning for this project was at all times based on creating assignments, assessment tools, and instruction that developmentally built on each other. At the outset, the PS264 professor and librarian met several times to identify the goals and objectives of her course. These discussions focused on course content, her expectations, and assignments that would match the learning outcomes she valued. With the hope of testing a variety of learning outcomes, we considered a spectrum of assignments including:

- close examination of scholarly articles;
- literature reviews;
- research journals;
- annotated bibliographies;
- class presentations;
- a lengthy research paper.

After the assignments were selected, we identified the sequence in which they would take place, keeping in mind both the political science perspective with its focus on the students' acquisition of disciplinary content and an IL perspective with its focus on developmental research skills. PS367 students then received advanced research strategy instruction from the librarian in preparation for conducting a literature review and compiling an annotated bibliography. Subsequently, comparing PS367 student thesis statements and annotated bibliographies results with our desired outcomes, we honed the goals and objectives for PS264. The librarian then matched PS264 course goals, expectations, and assignments to selected standards, performance indicators, and outcomes of the *Information Literacy Competency Standards for Higher Education* (http://www.ala.org/acrl/ilstandardlo.html). After reviewing the IL standards encompassed by the course, the PS264 professor and librarian made final decisions on the library assignments to assess during semester II. The goal was to gather multiple indicators of student learning. Finally, objectives included in *Information Literacy Competency Standards* (http://www.ala.org/acrl/guides/objinfolit.html) were matched to the student learning outcomes of PS264 course assignments.

Developing and Implementing Assessment Instruments

In preparing to create a rubric to assist PS264 students in assessing scholarly articles and compiling annotated bibliographies, the professor and librarian developed and outlined criteria based on the PS367 experience. The librarian then created the rubric, Annotated Bibliography Evaluation Guidelines (included at the end of this chapter), which was subsequently revised in collaboration with the PS264 professor. The PS220 professor then adapted the revision to match her research course needs. The research journal assignment was incorporated into the rubric by asking students to note how they found and obtained their sources. At same time, the librarian created a Citation Skeleton (included at the end of this chapter) to be used by students in identifying and evaluating different components of scholarly journal articles. This worksheet adapted a format designed in the 1990s by the psychology department. Early in semester II, a Library Resource Survey (included at the end of this chapter) was conducted in advance of library research instruction. This survey enabled students to identify their comfort level in using specific research tools and databases. PS264 and PS220 students subsequently completed both the Citation Skeleton and their annotated bibliographies using the rubric.

Analyzing the results

Using the rubric's point system, the librarian and PS264 professor independently corrected the annotated bibliography to test for inter-rater reliability. The librarian also established a spreadsheet to assess whether there was a meaningful correlation between the grades earned by students on the annotated bibliography and the use of certain key indexes and databases. In addition, the rubric was useful in explaining results to students who remained challenged by the assignment. The librarian and PS264 professor jointly requested feedback from students on the effectiveness of rubric (see below), at the same time that they discussed with the PS220 professor the effectiveness of rubric from a faculty perspective and ways in which it could be revised.

Results

Without a doubt, this rubric has served as a catalyst for extraordinarily fruitful conversations among library and political science faculty. It provided the opportunity for colleagues in the same department to discuss course design, assignments, and assessment, which proved to be rewarding professional development. Involved faculty were very grateful for the guidance provided by the librarian and the IL standards. The ripple effect of the project is only beginning to become visible. Colleagues in the same department hearing of the project have requested permission to use the rubric in their classes.

In addition to this spin-off, the project has been instrumental in the development of pre- and posttests for an IL lab in Principles of Psychology 122, the qualitative analysis of research journals for Biopsychology 265 and the mentoring of a reference librarian–history professor team on developing assessment instruments for a history research project.

Feedback was solicited directly from students through a class discussion and individual interviews. (See table 18-1.)

Overall, the students who understood the goals and objectives of the annotated bibliography were very positive and did well. The mean grade was 84.5. In finding a close match between the students who found the annotated bibliography and subsequent research paper a challenge, it would appear that having a strong grasp on effective research strategies to find and evaluate relevant scholarly resources had a direct impact on the subsequent success with the paper. By extension, therefore, developing a rubric that helps students write a successful annotated bibliography is deemed to be instrumental in assisting them with the overall

Table 18-1. Feedback

Positive Feedback	Negative Feedback
• Specificity of rubric was helpful • Knew what was expected to reach the exceptional level of achievement • Clear outline with various required components was helpful. • Very useful in helping students to organize their research. • Helpful in highlighting which sources were truly relevant. Students initially collected more sources than were ultimately useful for the topic. • Recording where and how one found the resource was at first difficult but in the end very helpful in teaching the research process.	• Timing was difficult for some students. Hard to evaluate sources when you haven't had time to read them. • Noting where the resource was found and tracking the research process was busy work. • Recording where resource was located required some students to repeat the search, as this step had been forgotten. • Web sites did not give enough information to comply with all the annotation criteria.

research process, including writing the paper. It should be noted, however, that the rubric standards were high, which made it a particular challenge for most of the students for whom English was not a first language.

Requiring students to identify how they found and obtained their resources was extremely useful in informing future library instruction and affirming its value. Virtually all the students used the St. Olaf College Libraries' online catalog and the Web-based research guide for the course.

About 50 percent used Expanded Academic ASAP. The use of scholarly databases is integral to student success in finding and evaluating pivotal refereed sources. With PAIS, Econlit, and Sociological Abstracts serving as some of the key databases for this course, it is noteworthy that of the students (34% of the class) who used the Cambridge Scientific Abstracts (CSA) social sciences databases, through which they can access these resources, 91 percent earned a grade of 88 or above. Also, of particular interest was the heavy use of Lexis-Nexis Academic, which offers access to full-text newspapers. Because use of CSA and Lexis-Nexis Academic virtually split the class between the top 38 percent of the class who earned over 88, none of whom used Lexis-Nexis Academic, and the remaining 62 percent, only 9 percent of whom used CSA, I am inclined to surmise that the students used Lexis-Nexis Academic not only to locate newspapers, but also as a default to finding journal articles through the use of scholarly databases. This assumption needs further research. Finally, the minimal use of the online versions of Hispanic American Periodicals Index and the Handbook of Latin American Studies could indicate either that the other social science databases provided adequate materials or that more instruction is needed in introducing students to these resources.

Challenges

Finding time to meet with faculty members involved in the project was a challenge. Being able to offer grant-supported lunches was very effective and much appreciated. Transforming the outline of criteria compiled by the professors into a multifaceted rubric also took considerable time. However, it was helpful for all three of us (the librarian and the PS 264 and 220 professors) to distinguish the skills that comprised the distinctions between a weak, acceptable, or exceptional annotated bibliography. Initial grading of the bibliographies also was time-consuming, but the rubric enabled a consistent approach from student to student. There is often discussion of the challenge of finding a common language to talk about IL competencies. This was resolved by matching IL competencies and language to political science competencies and disciplinary concepts. It was facilitated by placing priority on the political science perspective. At no point did I expect political science professors to know or use IL language. However, I consistently discovered they appreciated the thoroughness of standards after we matched the IL competencies with the political science desired learning outcomes.

Conclusion

The rubric encouraged faculty to focus on essential criteria and performance levels for individual assignments, which in turn enhanced and empowered student learning by providing students with a rubric that identified expectations. For the most part, the students understood and appreciated the distinctions between weak, average, and exceptional work. The detailed rubric facilitated feedback to the students who continued to be challenged.

POLITICAL SCIENCE 264
LIBRARY RESOURCES SURVEY

Please indicate below with which of the following aspects of bibliographic searching you are familiar and how comfortable you are with the resources (scale of 1 to 5, with 1 being not at all comfortable and 5 being extremely comfortable). Also please indicate in which classes you have used them.

	Comfort index (1–5)	**Instruction was given in … (Identify the course)**
Expanded Academic Index		
Cambridge Scientific Abstracts (CSA)		
PAIS		
Historical Abstracts		
Handbook of Latin American Studies (HLAS)		
Hispanic American Periodical Index (HAPI)		
JSTOR		
World News Connection		
Lexis-Nexis Academic		
Proquest National Newspaper Database		
World Cat		
Boolean Logic; i.e. use of AND, OR, NOT		
Subject vs. Keyword Searching		

Year of graduation __________

Your feedback will help us structure the PS264 research session.

Annotated Bibliography Evaluation Guidelines

Criteria	Weak	Acceptable	Exceptional
<u>Annotations</u> • Author(s)' credentials • Summary of content • Source's intended audience • Research methodology/design and theory/conclusions (when appropriate to source) • Usefulness and/or limitations for topic • Accuracy and reliability • How you found and obtained source	[2] Significant inconsistent inclusion of specified categories of evaluation. Location of where you found the source not included with *majority* of sources.	[6] Inconsistent inclusion of specified categories of evaluation. Location of where you found the source not included with *each* annotation.	[10] Inclusion of all specified categories of evaluation in each annotation. Notation of where you found the source i.e. in which catalog, index, bibliography etc.
<u>Types of Resources</u> • Emphasis on scholarly journal articles, books, and chapters • Government documents • Human rights sources • Newspaper articles • Balance of primary and secondary sources	[1] Few scholarly articles, books or chapters. Poor balance of types of resources, relying inappropriately on popular sources. Inclusion of encyclopedia articles not specifically relevant to topic. Poor balance of primary and secondary sources.	[3] Good balance of types of resources. Inclusion of some scholarly articles, books, and chapters, with a majority of popular sources. Lack of some primary or secondary sources.	[5] Strong representation of scholarly articles, books and chapters, supported by a balance of types of resources appropriate to the project. Balanced inclusion of both primary and secondary sources.

Criteria	Weak	Acceptable	Exceptional
<u>Appropriateness of Sources</u> • Relevance of sources to research topic • Pivotal scholarly sources representing a political science perspective or other disciplines where relevant to research topic.	[1] Many sources are overly broad or not specifically relevant to topic. Several pivotal sources missing. Few respected political science journals and publications, or other scholarly journals and publications, appropriate to topic.	[3] Some sources are overly broad or not specifically relevant to topic. Missing pivotal sources. Political science journals and publications, or other scholarly journals and publications underrepresented.	[5] All citations accurately conform to citation style. Complete bibliographic information. Entire bibliography follows formatting requirements as specified in assignment.
<u>Currency</u> • A balance of publication dates appropriate to the project • All projects need some current sources • Historical projects are expected to include earlier sources	[1] Nearly all sources published more than 8 years ago, with no recent sources.	[3] Few significant recent sources, with majority of sources published 6-8 years ago.	[5] Includes significant sources published in last 5 years, plus earlier sources when appropriate.
<u>Quantity of Sources</u>	[1] 4–6	[3] 7-10	[5] 10 or more

Criteria	Weak	Acceptable	Exceptional
Bibliographic Format • Citations conform to APSA style or other acceptable style guide. See Rolvaag Library home page for guidelines: **http://www.stolaf.edu/library/instruction/styles.html** • Annotated bibliography as a whole follows formatting requirements specified in assignment.	[1] Persistent errors in chosen citation style. Incomplete bibliographic information. Significant flaws in formatting of entire bibliography.	[3] Some errors in chosen citation style. Complete bibliographic information. Minor flaws in formatting of entire bibliography.	[5] IAll sources are specifically relevant to the topic. Inclusion of pivotal sources considered key to the topic (i.e., cited frequently by other scholars or recommended by professor.) Strong representation of political science journals and publications, or other scholarly journals and publications, appropriate to topic.

Optional Extra Credit:
Summarize your research process: Which resources, indexes, and/or databases did you consult? Which ones were/were not useful to you, and why? What keywords and search strategies did you find most effective? If you were to repeat the research process you have just completed, what would you do the same and what would you change? What advice would you give students just starting out on their research for this paper? Your feedback will help future students in this course.

Annotated Bibliography Evaluation Guidelines designed by reference librarian Elizabeth Hutchins in consultation with Kris Thalhammer and Sheri Breen.

Citation Skeleton for Political Science 264

Your Name ____________________ Date ____________

Full citation of article (Use APSA style):

Institutional affiliation or credentials of first author. For a review article, what do you know about the expertise of the authors' reviewed?

Type of article: (e.g., scholarly article, literature review, popular press article)

Goal of article: (What are they trying to do?)

Who is the audience of the article?

Summarize thesis of the article:

Evidence supporting the thesis:

List terms defined conceptually:

Conclusions suggested by the article: (What does the author assert?)

Criticisms or limitations of the article: (What might have been done better?What limitations exist in the analysis?)

Why is this resource useful for your research project?

So what next? (Give some ideas for further research that could be done. What would you like to see investigated further?)

Political Science Citation Skeleton was adapted by Elizabeth Hutchins and Kris Thalhammer from a model created by the St. Olaf College Psychology Department.

PRINCIPLES OF PSYCHOLOGY 122: EXPERIMENTAL FOUNDATIONS WITH LAB

POSTER EVALUATION FORM

Students____
Lab Section___________________________

CRITERION	POINTS POSSIBLE	POINTS	COMMENT
Title	2		
Contributors	2		
Class	1		
College	1		
Topic Description	5		
Research Summary	5		
Hypothesis	5		
Operational Definition	5		
Subjects	6		
Materials	4		
Procedure	10		
Means	2		
Standard Deviations	2		
Range	2		
Bar Chart	5		
Second Graph	5		
Description of Results	4		
Summary/Conclusion	5		
Link to Intro	5		
Limitations	5		
Future Research	5		
REFERENCES	10 (2 @5)		
Neatness	1		
Readability @ 3'	1		
Balance	1		
Aesthetics	1		
TOTAL POINTS	100		

Compiled by the St. Olaf College Psychology 122 team.

Chapter 19: Montana State University: Information Literacy Assessment Project

Ken Kempcke

Institution Description

Montana State University (MSU) has a student enrollment of 11,700. Of the total student body, 8 percent are working on master' and doctoral degrees, 88 percent are working toward a first bachelor'degree, and 4 percent are continuing their studies beyond the first bachelor's. Students represent all fifty states and seventy-six foreign countries. Montana residents comprise 73 percent of the student population, and 23 percent are over twenty-five years of age. MSU currently offers bachelor's degrees in fifty fields with many diverse options, the master's degree in forty-seven fields, and the doctorate in seventeen.

All librarians at MSU have faculty status, participate in library and university committees, and must meet expectations for research/creative activity and service/outreach for promotion and tenure. Each faculty position within the MSU Libraries requires a second subject master's degree. Librarians contribute to the teaching/learning enterprise of the university by being involved as instructors in a number of programs. Library faculty have taught in the University Honors Program (UHP), the Department of History and Philosophy, the Education Department, the General Studies program, and the College of Letters and Science.

Two library faculty members have affiliate appointments in other colleges, and librarians also serve on graduate committees. Several librarians have been actively involved in the Reinventing the Core project. In 1999, a group of faculty, administrators, and students began working on a project to improve the core curriculum. Supported by a grant from the William and Flora Hewitt Foundation and by funding from MSU, the Reinventing the Core project has involved several hundred members of the campus community in an attempt to enrich the educational experience of all of MSU's undergraduates. Information literacy (IL) is a stated objective of the "new core."

In addition to this ACRL assessment project, librarians have always been encouraged to consult with other faculty following the delivery of a class or the completion of an assignment, and some formal assessment is conducted in classes that lend themselves to reliable and insightful evaluation of information literacy.

Project Participants

Project participants included all faculty involved with the development of the new core curriculum. One of the core classes, General Studies (GS) 101 (a freshmen seminar), was specifically targeted for study. In cooperation with the GS faculty, I helped design two research assignments for this class. One of the goals of this project was to assess the effectiveness of these assignments in teaching information literacy skills.

Project Description

Because IL is a stated objective of the new core, my project focused on how well the new curriculum succeeds at achieving this objective. Assessment focused on how well the overall model for the new core builds IL skills and how well the GS course, in particular, increases students' abilities to locate information, evaluate information, and use information effectively to accomplish a specific purpose (ACRL Competency Standards Two, Three, and Four). In the pilot phase of this project, assessment efforts switched the original focus from the New Core program as a whole to the GP course as an element of the program that includes significant IL components and learning outcomes.

Planning for Assessment

I had one primary objective for this assessment project: *I wanted the results to be reliable, meaningful, and useful.* I wanted to be able to confidently communicate my findings to the new core faculty, GS instructors, and the campus community to reveal the success of initiatives (so that they might be marketed and replicated) and/or point out weak areas that could be targeted for improvement. It also was my intention that colleagues could use the instruments I developed to evaluate their own instructional efforts. I determined that the only way to gather reliable results was not to rely on one assessment method or tool. Many learning outcomes cannot be measured by one simple survey instrument. Skills must be tested, observed, or otherwise demonstrated by students.

Developing the Assessment Instrument

Therefore, I designed a multifaceted approach to my project:

1. I drafted a survey for faculty instrumental in shaping the new core to explore their views on how well the new core addresses the teaching of information literacy.
2. I developed a survey designed to collect feedback from students as to the quality and value of library classroom instruction.
3. I created a rubric by which I would evaluate student IL skills while observing their group presentations.
4. I designed a survey instrument to gather comments from GS students as to how well the library instruction, handouts, assignments, and presentations improved their IL skills.
5. Finally, I developed another survey that asked GS instructors and upper-division peers to assess how well their students performed in their assignments and presentations, and the quality of the bibliographies the students turned in.

This approach allowed for verification of results on multiple levels from a variety of sources and assessment instruments. The assessment tools did not require much time to complete and by attending classes and observing presentations, I was able to build a rapport with students in the three GS sections so that the evaluation did not seem too intrusive.

The pre- and postsurvey, Survey on Library Research Skills, grading rubric, and Questions for GS Peers and Instructions are included at the end of this chapter.

Analyzing the Results

The Survey on Information Literacy was distributed (via an e-mail pointing respondents to a Web form with radio buttons for responses and text boxes for comments, a form currently still available deom: http://www.lib.montana.edu/instruct/krksurvey.html) to colleagues across campus in October, 2001. I compiled the results by listing each response as a percentage of total responses. For example, here are some of the more illuminating replies:

1. Ninety-six percent of respondents "Agreed" or "Strongly Agreed" that "Incoming freshmen do not have the necessary skills to use a research library."
2. Fully 100 percent of respondents "Agreed" or "Strongly Agreed" that "All MSU students should be taught information literacy skills early in their academic career."
3. Eighty-eight percent of respondents "Disagreed," "Strongly Disagreed," or were "Undecided" with the statement: "I believe the New Core (as it exists now) adequately addresses the teaching of information literacy skills."

4. Ninety-two percent of respondents "Agreed" or "Strongly Agreed" with the statement: "I would like to see my students receive more formal instruction on information literacy."

The rest of the survey and empirical work was conducted late in spring semester 2002 and results are not available as of this writing.

Results

I observed and evaluated a total of twelve student (group) presentations. Other surveys were not distributed until the last week of spring semester classes. Results of my presentation evaluations and surveys are not available at the time of this writing. When compiled, I will post results of the evaluations and surveys to http://www.lib.montana.edu/~kempcke/acrlgrant.html.

Conclusions

Listed below are some of my thoughts on the assessment project as it nears conclusion:

- Just the act of assessment has the potential to improve instruction by forcing one to think deeply about pedagogy, teaching, learning outcomes, presentation structure/style, etc.
- Don't set expectations too high. Do what's doable and, most of all, what's meaningful.
- Your determination of what to assess and why has a huge impact on the vocabulary used in the survey instrument(s) (important vocabulary is unconsciously, if not consciously, developed during the planning stage) and the design of the instrument(s).
- Don't dismiss informal feedback (e.g., talking to students or instructors after class) just because it is difficult to document/quantify.
- Don't rely too heavily on one approach (e.g., surveys). Multiple approaches/instruments allow for verification of findings.
- Often empirical/qualitative studies are the only way to assess the comprehension or demonstration of skills (such as those in ACRL Standard Four).

Library Instruction Session
Presurvey

1. Do you feel that you know a lot about how to use MSU library's information resources (both print resources and electronic resources)?
   A. I know a lot about the library's information resources.
   B. I know a little about the library's information resources.
   C. I know very little about the library's information resources.

2. How comfortable or skilled do you feel in being able to locate high-quality information resources in the library for any given assignment?
   A. Very comfortable/very skilled
   B. Somewhat comfortable/somewhat skilled
   C. Not very comfortable/not very skilled

3. Which of the following material can you find by searching the library catalog?
   A. Government documents
   B. Encyclopedias
   C. Magazine articles
   D. Videos
   E. Newspaper articles
   F. All of the above

4. Have you used library databases to find journal articles?
   A. No
   B. Yes. Which database(s) have you used? ______________________________

Library Instruction Session
Postsurvey

What are the most important things you learned during this session?

What questions do you still have about using library resources or conducting research?

Would you like additional instruction on how to effectively and efficiently locate and evaluate information resources? *Please circle.*

1. Yes
2. No

Overall, the presentation on library resources was: *Please circle.*

1. Very helpful
2. Somewhat helpful
3. Not helpful at all

THANK YOU FOR YOUR INPUT!

Survey on Library Research Skills
(Post Assignment Evaluation - Students)

Please circle the appropriate response:

1. How comfortable or skilled do you feel in being able to locate high-quality information resources in the library for any given assignment?
   A. very comfortable/very skilled
   B. somewhat comfortable/somewhat skilled
   C. not comfortable/not skilled

2. Do you feel that you know a lot about how to use MSU library's information resources (both print resources and electronic resources)?
   A. I know a lot about the library's information resources.
   B. I know a little about the library's information resources.
   C. I know very little about the library's information resources.

3. Would you like to receive more instruction on how to use the MSU library's information resources effectively and efficiently?
   A. Yes
   B. No

4. Do you feel that the Persuasive Speech ("Pro/Con") Assignment and Group Presentation Assignment improved your ability to find and evaluate information resources?
   A. Yes
   B. No

5. *(Short answer)* What were the greatest benefits of these two assignments? What problems did you encounter?

   How would you change the assignments to improve learning how to do research?

6. *(Short answer)* What questions do you still have about library research?

Questions for GS Peers and Instructors:
(Post Assignment)

1. Do you feel that the Persuasive Speech ("Pro/Con") and Group Presentation Assignments improved your students' abilities to use library resources?

2. Did the students successfully incorporate their research into their presentations?

3. Did the lists of references turned in by your students include appropriate, high-uality materials?

4. How would you improve the two assignments?

For web-based survey form distributed to "new core" faculty, see: http://www.lib.montana.edu/instruct/krksurvey.html.

Rubric for Evaluating Student Presentations

INFORMATION LITERACY STANDARD	EVALUATION CRITERIA USED TO JUDGE PRESENTATIONS
3.1.B: "Restates textual concepts in his/her own words and selects data accurately" 3.1.C: "Identifies verbatim material that can be then appropriately quoted" 2.B: "Analyzes the structure and logic of supporting arguments or methods" 3.4.C: "Draws conclusions based upon information gathered" 3.4.G: "Selects information that provides evidence for the topic" 4.1.C: "Integrates the new and prior information, including quotations and paraphrasings, in a manner that supports the purposes of the product or performance" 4.3.D: "Communicates clearly and with a style that supports the purposes of the	1. Cites specific print or electronic resources 2. Cites author, speaker, organization (e.g. Sierra Club), etc. 3. Describes the credentials of author, speaker, organization, etc. 4. Provides definition(s) of terms or concepts 5. Uses direct quotes 6. Provides statistics, surveys, or studies 7. Provides evaluation of resources and/or arguments 8. Presents in a clear and persuasive manner 9. Provides a summation/conclusion

Chapter 20: Institutionalizing a Graduation Requirement

Andy Kivel

Institution Description

Diablo Valley College (DVC), located twenty-five miles east of San Francisco, is a two-year community college with an enrollment of more than 22,000 students. DVC is one of 108 California community colleges serving 2.5 million students at campuses throughout the state. This project developed as policy initiatives to establish information competency as a graduation requirement are being pursued at the state (system) level, at DVC, and at several other colleges in the system.

The board of governors of the California Community Colleges highlighted the importance of information competency in its New Basic Agenda (1996), and the state chancellor's office has funded a feasibility study and pilot projects to develop curriculum and instructional program models. In addition, the state Academic Senate for the California Community Colleges, the faculty body with primary responsibility for curriculum and degree matters, has recommended that information competency be a graduation requirement for the AA degree. At DVC, the faculty reviewed general education requirements and in May 2000 adopted information competency as a new area of required study for earning an AA or AS degree.

Project Participants

This project has focused on both programmatic and institutional levels of activity as well as the development of a specific assessment instrument. Consequently, the participants have included: (1) the statewide activities of the Academic Senate of the California Community Colleges and the Chancellor's Office Consultation Council Information Competency Task Force; (2) the Diablo Valley College Information Competency Task Force, composed of two library faculty, five classroom faculty, the curriculum committee chair, and the assistant dean of instruction; and (3) a regional group of library faculty who have developed the assessment instrument described below.

Project Description

The assessment instrument central to this project is a two-part proficiency exam designed to measure whether students have mastered the overall information competency learning abilities expected of an AA and AS degree. It is not keyed to a specific course or curriculum but, rather, is designed to be utilized in a variety of ways at different institutions. For example, the exam may be used: (1) as a pre- and postassessment for specific courses to inform curriculum development and assess student learning outcomes; (2) to compare learning achievements resulting from different curriculum and teaching/learning activities; and (3) to provide a mechanism for students who wish to satisfy an information competency graduation requirement by earning the "credit by exam." In other words, the primary goal of this proficiency exam is to assess how information competent a student is and whether he or she has reached a level of information skills deemed appropriate for a two-year college degree, whatever his or her learning path might have been.

Planning for Assessment

The two-year project to create the assessment instrument began with a group of library faculty from several institutions developing learner outcomes that realistically describe the abilities expected of someone with a two-year college degree. This effort has run parallel to institutional policy developments at the state chancellor's office and at DVC. Each of these policy recommendations has defined information competency learning outcomes at varying degrees of specificity. Taken as a whole, these statements provide a structure for institutional implementation of an information competency program. Listed hierarchically they include:

- **Title 5, California Code of Regulations:** Draft language to include information competency as a degree requirement for the California community colleges. This text was written by the Chancellor's Office Consultation Council Information Competency Task Force, a group representing all constituencies of the community college system.

- **Diablo Valley College GE Area VII—Information Competency Catalog Statement:** This brief description of the new general education requirement will be included in the 2003–2004 college catalog. It was adopted by DVC faculty in May 2000 and approved for implementation by the college administration and board of governors in August 2002.
- **Area VII Learning Outcomes, DVC Information Competency Task Force:** This document expands the seven-point catalog definition mentioned above with detailed descriptions of student learning outcomes.
- **Information Competency Standards, Performance Indicators and Learning Outcomes:** This document, developed by the Bay Area Regional Assessment Group of Community College library faculty, describes the overall information literacy (IL) learning outcomes expected of a two-year college degree. An edited version adapted from the ACRL IL standards, the document describes the learning outcomes to be measured by the proficiency exam. The library faculty group met several times and communicated via e-mail over two years to examine the complete the standards and draft a document to be used for curriculum development, policy formulation, and assessment. While this work progressed, a variety of instruction models were pursued at each campus.

Developing an Assessment Instrument

When we had a good working document of the standards, we began to develop a two-part assessment instrument designed to measure each learner outcome. Part A is a cognitive exam of forty-five questions, and Part B is a performance-based assessment. We examined each outcome and keyed it to specific exam questions (multiple choice, true/false, short answer) in Part A and/or performance activities in Part B. A chart was developed mapping the learning outcomes to each specific test item (assessment method).

Both exam components were pilot-tested with approximately twenty-five students in April 2002. The results of the first field test were examined by someone with expertise in educational tests and measurements who provided feedback on test format, individual question language, and overall structure. With this help and the responses from the test takers, the two exam parts were revised to prepare for a second field test scheduled for fall 2002.

In addition to revising the proficiency exam questions and activities, test feedback was utilized to develop an answer key for the cognitive component and a scoring rubric for the performance component. If the test questions and activities were the method by which students would demonstrate their abilities, an evaluation method also was needed to determine how well, or to what extent or degree, the students had achieved each learning outcome. However, the rubric was developed only to determine whether an exam response meets the criteria of information competence and it doesn't provide a system for determining what degree of satisfactory answer has been provided. A sample page of the scoring rubric is included at the end of the chapter.

The second field test will include scoring exams by multiple scorers to determine whether the rubric can be used successfully to measure the qualitative nature of the performance activities with an acceptable inter-rater reliability.

The Assessment Instrument

After the exam is finalized, it will be used to assess student learning in a one-unit information competency course at DVC as well as provide the challenge method by which students will satisfy the new graduation requirement without taking a course. As other curriculum models are developed, the exam will be utilized to compare the effectiveness of various curricula.

Results

As this goes to press, most aspects of the project have not yet been concluded. At the institutional level, the board of governors of the California Community Colleges considered the proposed Title 5 language establishing a graduation requirement on information competency at their July 2002 meeting. The issue was then placed on the consent agenda for the board's September meeting. However, just days before this meeting, the State of California Department of Finance issued a letter to the chancellor's office stating that the proposed change to Title 5 regulations amounted to an "unfunded mandate" and could not move forward for approval. Responding to this action is now in the hands of the chancellor's office staff and the Academic Senate.

Challenges

There have been numerous challenges to the success of this project. In terms of establishing DVC institutional policy on information competency, the primary challenge has been collaborating with nonlibrary faculty and college administrators to formulate policy recommendations. Although it has been easy to garner general support for the importance of information skills for student success, getting agreement on student learning outcomes and curriculum models with the substance necessary to ensure success has been problematic. It took a gradual approach of introducing people to key literature on the subject and then a willingness to let different constituencies find the learning outcomes language that makes sense to them. By focusing on learning outcomes rather than any particular curriculum model, DVC has laid an institutional foundation for an information competency program without getting stuck on finding the one method that everyone might agree to pursue.

The biggest challenge in developing the assessment instrument has been the difficulty of creating a scoring rubric to measure the qualitative responses of the performance activities. Deconstructing each activity into discreet and describable criteria and then determining the level of correctness needed to reach the bar of information competent was particularly difficult. A scoring manual has been written to assist evaluators with additional content and guidelines for interpreting the rubric.

Conclusion

At Diablo Valley College, students entering in fall 2003 will be required to satisfy a new graduation requirement on information competency. Student learning outcomes have been approved to guide curriculum development. At this time, a one-unit library course, Information Competency and Research Skills, has been approved to meet the requirement. The college's Information Competency Task Force will continue meeting to encourage the development of additional collegewide curriculum models. This effort is the result of a broad-based collaboration among librarians, faculty, and administrators

The assessment instrument and scoring rubrics will be revised again after the results of the second field test. After that, it will be used to assess learner outcomes achieved from actual curriculum and teaching/learning experiences. The development team is confident that the assessment is built on careful linking of learning outcomes to evaluation methods, but key questions remain. Does this assessment accurately measure a level of information competence across the breadth of the ACRL standards appropriate to a two-year college degree? Are students who "pass" this proficiency exam ready to succeed as a transfer student entering a four-year institution prepared to do upper-division work? Does the rubric measuring the qualitative aspects of a performance-based assessment result in an acceptable level of consistency in scoring? Additional collaboration among community college librarians and our peers at four-year institutions will be required to begin answering these questions.

Special thanks to Topsy Smalley, Instruction Librarian extraordinaire at Cabrillo Community College, my primary collaborator on the performance component of the assessment tool.

Assessment Instrument

Draft instrument reprinted with permission of The Bay Area Community Colleges Information Competency Assessment Project.

Bay Area Community Colleges Information Competency Assessment Project
Information Competency Proficiency Exam—Part B: Performance Component
Draft Version VII

Directions: Type your responses into the boxes provided. You must keep this form open while taking the exam. Open a new browser window to use the Web as required by the exercises. When you are finished filling out this form, click on the Submit button at the bottom.

<u>EXERCISE I</u>
Your instructor has given you the broad subject of civil rights in America and an assignment to write a 3–5 page research paper on some aspect of this topic.

Narrow this subject to a manageable topic for the assignment.

1. Narrowed topic: (B.1.a.)
In two or three sentences, describe the steps you took to develop your narrowed topic. (B.1.b.)

Next, take your narrowed topic and pose it as a research question you might address in this 3–5 page writing assignment.

2. Research question: (B.2.)

<u>EXERCISE II</u>
You've been given the assignment to write a 3–5 page research paper on the following topic: Should colleges be allowed to restrict student speech?

3. Name the three key concepts represented by the topic, and name alternate terms and synonyms that you would use in searching for information on this topic.

Key concept 1: (B.3.a.1)	Key concept 2: (B.3.b.1)	Key concept 3: (B.3.c.1)
Synonym (B.3.a.2)	Synonym (B.3.b.2)	Synonym (B.3.c.2)
Synonym (B.3.a.3)	Synonym (B.3.b.3)	Synonym (B.3.c.3)

4. Identify three relevant sources for this topic:

- one book
- one periodical article
- one Web site

Carefully select your sources based on standard evaluation criteria for college research papers.

For each source, you will

a) Write a complete bibliographic citation using a standard citation format
b) Describe how you found the source
c) Explain why you chose the source

What citation format will you be using (e.g., MLA, APA, CBE)? B.4.*

Source 1
a. Write a complete bibliographic citation for the source using the citation format you noted above. Use an underscore (_) before and after bibliographic elements that are underlined. Because this form on the Web does not accommodate indentation, proper indentation will not be part of the scoring. (B.4.a.1)

b. How did you find this source? In two or three sentences, describe you steps. (B.4.a.2)

c. Why did you choose this particular source? In two or three sentences explain your reasons. (B.4.a.3)

Source 2
a. Write a complete bibliographic citation for the source using the citation format you noted above. Use an underscore (_) before and after bibliographic elements that are underlined. Because this form on the Web does not accommodate indentation, proper indentation will not be part of the scoring. (B.4.a.1)

b. How did you find this source? In two or three sentences, describe you steps. (B.4.a.2)

c. Why did you choose this particular source? In two or three sentences explain your reasons. (B.4.a.3)

Source 3
a. Write a complete bibliographic citation for the source using the citation format you noted above. Use an underscore (_) before and after bibliographic elements that are underlined. Because this form on the Web does not accommodate indentation, proper indentation will not be part of the scoring. (B.4.a.1)

b. How did you find this source? In two or three sentences, describe you steps. (B.4.a.2)

c. Why did you choose this particular source? In two or three sentences explain your reasons. (B.4.a.3)

5. In addition to the three sources above, describe in two or three sentences what additional research steps you might take to adequately address the research question. (B.5)

<u>EXERCISE III</u>

6. Imagine that you are researching melatonin and find the three Web pages listed below. Visit each site. Then pick two of them and in two or three sentences evaluate each according to standard evaluation criteria. Be as specific as possible.

URL http://www.priory.com/mel.htm

URL http://www.fda.gov/fdac/features/1998/498_sleep.html

URL http://www.aafp.org/afp/971001ap/cupp.html

Evaluation of site 1 (B.6.a)
Identify the Web site:
Your evaluation:

Evaluation of site 2 (B.6.b)
Identify the Web site:
Your evaluation:

7. Using information found in one of the Web sites you evaluated, describe in two or three sentences the uses of melatonin *in your own words.* (B.7)
Identify the Web site:
Uses of melatonin:

Information Competency Proficiency Exam – Performance Component
SCORING RUBRIC WITH MAPPING OF LEARNER OUTCOMES
Version 2.3—Page 1

Outcome	Test item	Criteria to apply	What constitutes competent
1.1.4 Modifies the information need or research question to achieve a manageable focus.	B.1.a Your instructor has given you the broad subject *civil rights in America* and an assignment to write a 3- to 5-page research paper on some aspect of this topic. Narrow this subject to a manageable topic for the assignment.	B.1.a 1. Topic is narrowed by specifying time frame, or persons, or organization or group, or location, or event or incident, or some combination of these, or other similar, appropriate limiter(s) is (are) applied. AND 2. Narrowed topic is within subject assigned. AND 3. Narrowed topic is appropriate to a 3-5 page research paper.	B.1.a At least one of the narrowing techniques has been applied to the subject. AND The other two criteria are met.
1.1.3 Effectively uses background information sources to increase familiarity with the topic.	B.1.b In two or three sentences, describe the steps you took to develop your narrowed topic.	B.1.b The student describes the process used to 1. Consult additional resources, such as back-ground information sources, to develop a narrowed topic. AND/OR 2. Implement his/her own prior knowledge to develop a narrowed topic.	B.1.b What the student writes indicates that the process used meets Criterion 1 AND/OR Criterion 2
1.1.2 Formulates appropriate question(s) based on information need or research topic.	B.2 Next, take your narrowed topic and pose it as a research question you might address in this 3- to 5-page writing assignment.	B.2 1. The student composes a research question that contains a subject. AND 2. The question is a recognizable *type* of question (such as a question of fact; a posited hypothesis; some topic for comparing/contrasting; or it is a probing or investigative question; etc.). AND 3. The research question is within the narrowed topic. AND 4. The research question is appropriate to the assignment.	B.2 The research question meets all four of the criteria.

Chapter 21: Assessing Student Learning through the Analysis of Research Papers

Lorrie A. Knight

Institution Description

University of the Pacific, located in Stockton, California, is an institution of 3,233 undergraduate and 506 graduate students. There are 375 faculty members. The university's mission is "to provide a superior, student-centered learning environment integrating liberal arts and professional education" (General Catalog, 2001–2002). The largest school is the College of the Pacific, which has a focus on the liberal arts. In addition, there are professional schools in education, business, engineering, pharmacy, physical therapy, and international studies (SIS), as well as a conservatory of music. Recently, the university received reaccreditation from the Western Association of Schools and Colleges following a two-year self-study, the theme of which was student learning assessment. The university has retained this focus on outcomes assessment based on learning objectives. Through collaboration with faculty in many disciplines, the library hopes to link information competencies to departmental learning objectives.

Project Participants

The participants in the study are students in the School of International Studies (SIS) and the professor who teaches their capstone senior seminar. The mission of the SIS is to create a "global" learning environment in every sense of the word. The students are required to study the languages, economics, and political and environmental issues of countries of the world, as well as spend at least one semester abroad. The school has defined learning objectives, several of which emphasize the skills needed to locate, evaluate, and synthesize information. One measure of the students' achievement of these objectives is the successful completion of a senior capstone course. The course requires a lengthy research paper that includes a literature review and statistical analysis.

Project Description

SIS students are expected to accomplish progressively more demanding research throughout their academic careers, culminating in the final paper. The majority of the students have participated in library workshops as components of their first year dean's seminar and later in a required course called Contemporary World Issues. Because of the sophisticated and unique subject matter of the final papers, they are encouraged to make individual appointments for research assistance. Many do. The librarian's assessment of the literature reviews and bibliographies submitted with the capstone papers is one way to measure the integration of information literacy (IL) standards into the students' conceptual learning.

Planning the Assessment

An initial step in planning the assessment was to meet with the faculty member to discuss shared learning objectives. We decided to gather "benchmark" data in the spring of 2001 to test the objectives and the assessment instrument. Final data will be collected following the spring 2002 semester.

The objectives for the library research component of the paper are as follows:

1. The students will demonstrate their ability to locate information through the use of print and online sources and will know how these materials can be acquired.

2. The students will demonstrate their understanding of scholarly sources of information, how it is organized, and how the "world of information" surpasses the holdings of the of the university library.

3. The students' final papers will indicate that the information sources cited were critically evaluated for authorship, credibility, and pertinence to the topic.

4. The students' final papers will demonstrate their understanding of the importance of recognizing the path of scholarship through the use of appropriate citations.

The second step in the assessment planning involved mapping the learning objectives to the *ACRL Information Literacy Competency Standards for Higher Education* and identifying performance indicators and learning outcomes. After making the links between the standards, the learning objectives, and indicators, I developed a checklist or rubric to evaluate the students' literature reviews and bibliographies (included at the end of this chapter). The rubric was revised several times after testing with the spring 2001 bibliographies.

Analyzing the Results

At this time, I have only preliminary data. However, my plan is to develop a numeric rating for each student researcher, based on evaluation of the individual citations in the bibliography and the literature review. From this rating, students will be classified as beginner, intermediate, or experienced in their research skills.

Preliminary Results

My findings are based on evaluation of papers submitted by the spring of 2001 and the fall of 2001 sections of the senior seminar. The two groups were very different. The group in the spring semester (12) had very standard topics, such as the effect of the media on political participation. The group in the fall semester (6) had much more "contemporary" topics, such as the effect of the Internet on the use of the English language. It is not surprising that the balance of Web to print sources was much greater in the fall. Despite greater use of freely available Web sources, I was able to retain many attributes of the original rubric, including use of scholarly sources. Although the number of papers was small, the majority of the students compiled lengthy literature reviews and bibliographies. For the groups as a whole, the average number of citations per paper was twenty-one and approximately 60 percent of the sources were found in the university library. My final data analysis will be based on examination of the spring 2002 capstone papers. This group should provide excellent data, as there are more than twenty students. Table 21-1 represents the results of the compilation of scores on the rubric.

Challenges

The major challenges for a project of this nature lie in trying to elicit the needed information without adding to the workload woes of the students! It would be helpful if they could be asked to keep a research journal, but that is not realistic on our campus. It also would be helpful if the students strictly followed the bibliographic guidelines for citing electronic sources. However, this was not the case with the first papers; hopefully subsequent groups will be more attentive to this issue. To rate the preliminary data, I looked up many of the citations myself to attempt to replicate the research path the students followed.

Conclusion

Analyzing students' research papers is one way to measure their learning of research skills. This also provides insights into the ways that students use the library

Table 21-1. Frequency of Scores on Information Literacy Standards

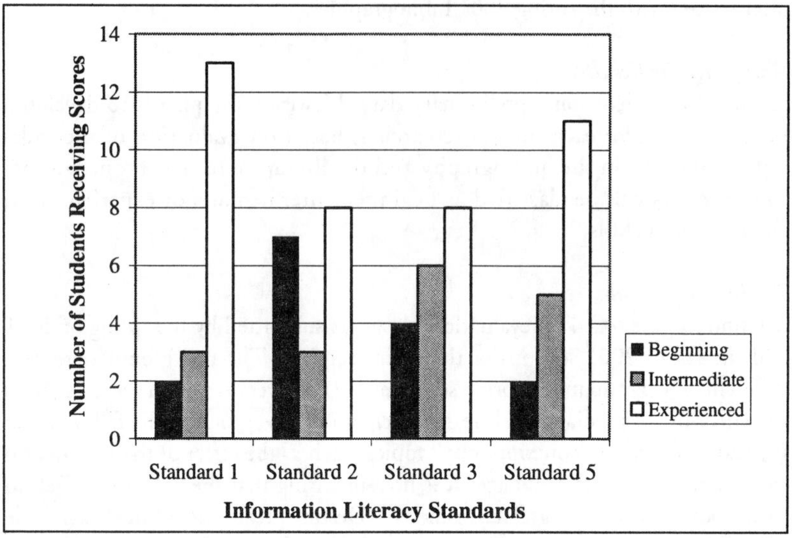

and its bibliographic tools. One important outgrowth of my project to date is an "assessment of the assessment." My project would be improved by a comparison of groups with and without library instruction. A second strategy for improvement would be a requirement for research journals or focus groups that inform us of the students' search strategies.

Assessment Rubric

The standards, performance indicators, and outcomes are based on *Information Literacy Competency Standards for Higher Education*, Association of College and Research Libraries, January 2000.

Categories: Beginner = 1 Intermediate = 2 Experienced = 3

Standard 1: The information-literate student determines the nature and extent of the information needed.

Performance Indicator: The information-literate student identifies a variety of types and formats of potential information sources.

• **Outcomes:** Identifies the value of resources in a variety of formats (books, journals, Web sites) and for different purposes (scholarly, popular)

o **Experienced:** At least one half of the sources will be from books published by academic presses or from scholarly journals.

o **Intermediate:** At least one third of the sources will be from books published by academic presses or from scholarly journals.

o **Beginner:** Fewer than three of the sources will be from books published by academic presses or from scholarly journals.

Standard 2: The information-literate student accesses information effectively and efficiently.

Performance Indicator: The information-literate student retrieves information online or in person using a variety of methods and understands that the universe of information is larger than that of the institution's library.

• **Outcomes:** Uses specialized online or in-person services available to retrieve information, such as ILL, full-text databases, and document delivery.

o **Experienced:** At least 20% of the sources were retrieved from sources other than the host library resources.

o **Intermediate:** At least one source was retrieved from a source other than the host library resources.

o **Beginner:** All sources were retrieved from the host library

Standard 3: The information-literate student critically evaluates information and its sources and incorporates selected information in his or her knowledge base.

Performance Indicator: The information-literate student summarizes the main ideas from the information gathered and compares new knowledge with prior knowledge to determine value added or contradictions.

• **Outcomes:** Identifies verbatim material that can be quoted and determines if the information satisfies the information need.

o **Experienced:** In the literature review, the student discusses the major authors/ theories of the field of study.

o **Intermediate:** In the literature review, the student explains why sources were used.

o **Beginner:** In the literature review, the student mentions sources without evaluation of why they were selected.

Standard 4: The information-literate student accesses and uses information ethically and legally.

Performance Indicator: The information-literate student acknowledges the use of information sources in communicating the product or performance.

• **Outcomes:** Selects an appropriate documentation style and uses it consistently to cite sources.

o **Experienced:** The student distinguishes between online and print sources in accordance with current style sheets.

o **Intermediate:** The student cites sources in a consistent manner.

o **Beginner:** The student fails to cite sources or does so in a haphazard manner.

Example of Scoring Instrument

Student #	Std. 1 Score	Std. 2 Score	Std. 3 Score	Std. 4 Score	Total Score

Chapter 22: Information Literacy in Community College Communications Courses

Barbara Kobritz

Institution Description

Tompkins Cortland Community College (TC3) serves two counties in rural upstate New York. Our 2,800 FTE students comprise a typical community college mix—every age and level of academic preparation, with more emphasis on international students than the typical community college. We offer thirty degree programs, both terminal degrees in applied sciences (e.g., hotel and restaurant management, nursing, early childhood) and transfer degrees in arts and sciences (social sciences, electrical engineering). Information literacy (IL) is one of our eleven general education requirements. We expect to meet that requirement by infusing IL into each program's course of study.

My job is to consult with faculty in each degree program to help them infuse IL into their curriculum and to certify to the dean of academic affairs that the program is meeting an acceptable standard of IL education. In addition to the dean's direct support, our accrediting agency, Middle States, has announced that in future accreditations IL will play a central role and that the responsibility for IL education will rest with the faculty, not the library. Expectations set by the dean and Middle States allow me to position myself as a consultant who can help faculty meet demands from higher authorities, rather than trying to persuade them to work on IL because it is a good thing to do.

Project Participants

I began with the Communications and Media Arts program and am having a great time working with the chair of the program. The chair is the only full-time regular faculty person for the program. She came to TC3 directly from the work market, so she speaks with authority. Moreover, she is an incredibly energetic person who gives her students 110 percent. Therefore, she has a lot of legitimacy when she asks for the same in return. She has the same students in many classes as they move through their degree. They get used to her style, which is to set high expectations and give the students all the support they need to meet them. Her motto for the program is, Don't tell me what you can't do. Show me what you *can* do.

The class we focused on was COMM225: Communication Law and Ethics. COMM225 functions almost as a capstone course because it is typically one of the last courses taken before graduation; it is taken by all students in all six tracks within the program; and its subject matter provides the students with plenty of interesting research topics.

Because our long-term goal is to assess our success in the program as a whole, rather than in one or two classes, COMM225 was the ideal place to start. It allows us to look at our students on their way out the door, focus on the objectives we think are most important, and see which ones are unmet by the program overall. Then we can go back and look for opportunities to improve the instruction of key objectives in COMM225 and in other required courses earlier in the program tracks.

Project Description

Planning for Assessment

I chose to collaborate with the communications program because it is one of the easier programs to do. I have a good working relationship with the faculty, and the content of the program lends itself well to IL concerns. My strategy for the whole college is to go from easiest programs to hardest. As I get to the harder ones midway down the list, I will have a carrot (the toolkit of assessment instruments already developed by early adopters) and a stick (pressure to conform as this process becomes the norm for programs rather than the exception).

Because I was doing a programwide assessment, I collected every syllabus, course outline, and assignment from the communications program I could get my hands on.

Our goal is to look at just as many of the learning outcomes as we possibly can. We do not need separate assignments and assessments for each one. One assignment can easily address twenty objectives. I went through the standards one by one and, for every outcome that I felt was assessable, wrote a learning objective using the formula:

A = Audience B = Behavior C = Conditions D = Degree

Developing the Assessment Instrument

Our current instrument does not address the entire list of objectives. The long-term plan is to start with a selected set of objectives, look at student success, and adjust the instruction until we are happy with the results, then move on to another set, perhaps with a break of a year or two in between. Eventually, we will come back to the objectives in the original assessment and validate that we are still OK (or not!). One key concern is to avoid faculty burnout. Assessment is a burning issue at our institution. I have to keep in mind that faculty, most of whom know very little about formal assessment, are being asked to assess their success on specific program goals as well as ten other Gen Ed goals, in addition to IL. Therefore, we will probably develop a long-term strategy of choosing what seems most important to assess every second or third year and doing an assessment, adjusting the instruction, and redoing the assessment each semester until we're satisfied—for the time being!

Every method has advantages and disadvantages. I wanted to go in the direction of qualitative assessment (performance, portfolio, writing) because we are evaluating higher-order skills, evaluation and synthesis, which do not work well with objective testing. For database searching skills (button-pushing as I've come to call it), I might try something more objective. Gathering qualitative information is difficult, but I think it's worth the effort.

For me, at least in this particular implementation, the selection of the objectives and method and the creation of the instrument were not sequential. It was more of a dialectical process. Generally, I knew I wanted something that would speak to the issue of the quality of sources students select. I developed something that did that (Source Evaluation Sheet is included at the end of this chapter) and then went back to see which specific objectives it addresses. The clarity of the objectives helped me sharpen the instrument. In the future, I may work this way again or I may start from specific objectives and work in a more linear way with them. I think it depends on what you're trying to accomplish. You may already have an assessment/assignment you're using, which you can analyze to see which objectives it addresses, as I did. You may want to add a few other points in light of the ACRL standards, as I did. Or you may want to start from scratch and ask yourself which objectives are absolutely key for you and develop your instrument accordingly. Either way can work.

The Assessment Instrument

Our assessment instrument is performance based. The students are being asked to select resources and tell us why they are reliable. This type of qualitative data requires a rubric to convert it into reportable numbers (included at the end of this chapter). The rubric establishes four categories of progress: mastery, good progress, minimally acceptable, and needs further instruction. The categories are applied to four different sets of learning objectives. I grouped the learning objectives in this way to make the data more meaningful and more manageable. Each student—not each source—will be placed on the rubric somewhere. We are trying to answer questions such as, How many of our students can use evaluation skills to select a reasonable group of resources that address a specific research topic?

As part of a large semester-long research project, students were required to fill out the source evaluation sheets. The professor graded the students according to the rubric I developed. As she graded, the professor unfortunately had to add a fifth category to the rubric: no evidence. Note: We are assessing the instruction, not the students. If the professor can use this as a grading tool, that is a by-product.

Results

The results for our first assessment showed that the more mechanical the skill, the better the students scored. The higher-order skills, synthesis and evaluation, scored lower. (See table 22-1.)

Challenges

The biggest challenge I face is how to map the assessment of an entire program (essential in this institution) to something that is doable. We are responding to

Table 22-1. Mastery of Learning Objectives

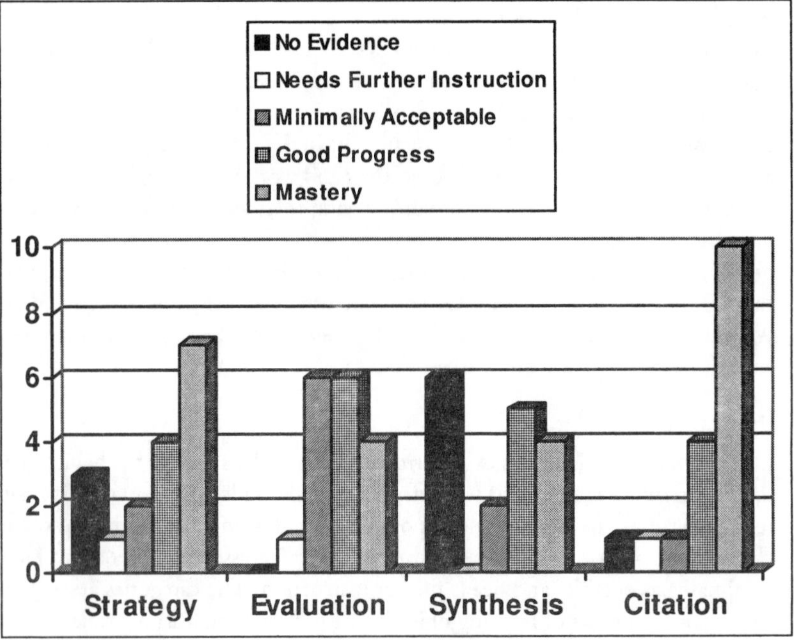

that challenge by slowing down and assessing just a few things at a time. Although I didn't realize it at first, I do not need data from every student on every ACRL standard every semester.

Conclusion

Thus far, I have not mentioned curriculum. The first goal of this project was to assess what was already happening. After seeing these results, we brainstormed the following list of possible changes for this class:

1. Integrate the Il rubric into the overall grading sheet for the project to reduce the load on faculty.
2. Distribute grading rubrics ahead of deadlines so that students understand what we are looking for.
3. Give more credit for the rough draft to encourage students to take advantage of the feedback opportunity.
4. Maybe hand out a model assignment.
5. Add a library instruction session focused on the idea of synthesis.
6. Give more support through the process of resource selection
7. Require students in the communications program to take the one-credit IL course offered on campus.
8. Give similar assignments earlier in the program.

We are now requiring the IL course, and the first cohort is going through that. Changes in the communications law course itself will have to wait until the next time it's offered in spring 2003.

SOURCE EVALUATION

DIRECTIONS: Submit one form for each source you use in your project. Fill the form out completely, using the back side if necessary. Your goal is not to get the form filled out; your goal is to evaluate the worth of the sources you are citing.

Citation:

Would you describe this source as:
Scholarly Professional Serious Popular

Is the content: Primary research Secondary research Other (describe below)

What assertions does the author make about your topic?

What evidence does the author give to support those claims?

What evidence can you find on the book jacket or in an author ID about the author's credentials in this field? How extensively has the author published in this area?

What key ideas make this piece useful for your research?

Evaluation of Student Research Process

OBJECTIVE	NEEDS FURTHER INSTRUCTION	MINIMALLY ACCEPTABLE	GOOD PROGRESS	MASTERY
STRATEGY I.4.1 Midway through the research project(C) students (A) will submit a written description of information gathered and information still needed. (B) III.6.3 As part of the research project (C) students (A) will confer with experts (B).	Research summary lacks cohesion; sources do not address the same aspect of the topic; *and/or* Research shows a lack of persistence in trying varying search strategies; *and/or* Research summary does not include at least one human expert; *and/or* Research summary indicates a lack of understanding of knowledge gaps.	Research summary lists a variety of types of sources, *and* Sources selected are mostly or completely focused on the same aspect of the topic; *and* Research summary includes at least one human expert; *and* Research summary proposes at least one strategy for continuing the search.	Research summary includes a variety of opinions focused on the same aspect of the issue; *and* Research summary demonstrates persistence in following clues from one source to another; *and* Research summary includes at least one human expert; *and* Research summary lists some further strategies for continuing the search.	Research summary demonstrates substantial effort put forth to find the seminal sources and experts on the topic; *and* Research summary demonstrates that the student has a grasp of the contours of the issue and the major organizations and experts involved; *and* Research summary demonstrates that the student understands remaining gaps in his or her knowledge and has a plan for closing those gaps.

EVALUATION I.2.5 As part of the research project (C) students (A) will describe each source used as primary research, secondary research or some other type of information which they can describe (B). I.4.2 As part of the research project (C) students (A) will submit a source sheet for each resource used with a written description of how sources were chosen and strengths and weaknesses of each. (B) III.2.1 III.5.1 As part of the research project (C) students (A) will submit a well-rounded selection of resources that reflect concern for accuracy, objectivity and timeliness. (B)	Source evaluations indicate substantial confusion as to the description of particular sources, *and/or* Source evaluations indicate substantial confusion about authors' theses and evidence, *and/or* Source evaluations indicate an inability to verify authors' credentials.	Source evaluations are inconsistent in describing types of material; *and/ or* Source evaluations are inconsistent in explaining authors' arguments and supporting evidence; *and/or* Source evaluations ignore the author's credentials.	Any errors in describing sources are minor; *and* Student clearly grasps the concept of analyzing the argument and evidence; *and/or* Student uses any obvious external clues to reliability, such as author identification, included in the source	Source evaluations accurately describe each source; *and* Source evaluations display concern for the internal logic of each piece; *and* Source evaluations clearly demonstrate the usefulness of each source in the present context; *and* Student uses any obvious external clues to reliability, such as author identification, included in the source.

SYNTHESIS III.1.1 Students (A) will use source sheets (C) to demonstrate an understanding of each source's main ideas. (B)	Research summary shows a lack of understanding of the authors' main points; *and/or* Research summary shows a lack of direct connection between sources and the student's thesis.	Source evaluations accurately summarize each author's main points; *but* Source evaluations do not demonstrate a clear connection between the authors' purposes and the student's thesis; *and/or* Sources selected are on the same general topic but lack a cohesive point.	Sources are all related to the student's thesis. Source descriptions show a good understanding of the authors' purposes.	Sources comprise a cohesive body of research which show a clear theme running from one source to another; *and* Descriptions show a clear understanding of what each author was trying to accomplish; *and* Sources do not make identical points but support and challenge the student's thesis with various congruent arguments.
CITATION II.5.3 V.3.1 On research project source sheets (C) students (A) will use an assigned citation format to create complete and accurate citations for sources used. (B)	Citations give the reader insufficient information to locate the original source.	Citations show substantial errors in format but would not prevent the reader from locating the source.	Citations have only minor errors in form, such as misplaced punctuation, that would not prevent the reader from locating the source.	Citations are consistently accurate in both content and form for sources in various formats.

KEY

Numbers for each objective refer to ACRL Standards
Objectives are developed using the A-B-C-D method:
A=Audience being assesses
B=Behavior to be performed.
C=Conditions underwhich behavior will be performed
D=Degree to which behavior will be performed, defined by the rubric

Chapter 23: Integrated Information Literacy Impact Study

Patrick McCarthy and Gregory Heald

Institutional Description

The University of Northern Colorado is a general baccalaureate and specialized graduate research university serving a student population of 11,000. As the primary institution for undergraduate and graduate teacher education in Colorado, the university takes pride in its leadership role in professional education instruction and research. In the fall of 2000, the North Central Association of Colleges and Schools recognized the university for its outstanding efforts in "defining learning outcomes, developing assessment measures, using these measures to gage students' acquisition of knowledge and skills, and using the results to make appropriate changes in curricula and services." Moreover, the university's provost has identified information literacy (IL) as a top priority and has allocated special university funds to support the library's teaching mission. The university libraries participates fully in the institution's assessment efforts by conducting regular IL analyses. This approach makes the University of Northern Colorado uniquely qualified to provide longitudinal comparisons.

Project Participants

Patrick McCarthy was the manager of library instruction and assistant professor of library science at the University of Northern Colorado, and Gregory Heald is the instruction librarian and assistant professor of library science there. Two additional librarians instruct undergraduate students in the composition and organization of collegiate research papers through the university's Center for Human Enrichment (CHE). The CHE is a comprehensive student support program of academic advising, general education instruction, tutorial services, technological resources, and scholarship opportunities for the university's diversified student population.

Project Description

Our course-integrated instruction program is centered on the library's Core Library Instruction Program (CLIP), a three-tiered program designed to introduce freshmen to resources and services available from an academic library. Faculty from the English department brought their students into the library for one or more workshops over the course of one to two weeks. Students were issued the pretest by the collaborating English faculty during their English class one to two days prior to instruction. They then received two separate fifty-minute IL training sessions taught by librarians over the course of several days. Within two weeks after the instruction, the students were issued the posttest by the English faculty during English class.

Our credit course is an eight-week, one-credit IL program taught by librarians. During the length of the course, students are exposed to sixteen fifty-minute sessions. The pretest was issued at the beginning of the first class session. The posttest questions were integrated into the final exam and then extracted later for analysis. Many of the students in the course participate in the university's learning communities. Our course was offered as part of a multicourse learning community. The students are part of a coordinated cohort that enrolls in an English composition course and the library's research course. In addition, the course syllabi are coordinated and linked. We have regular contact and collaboration with the other learning community faculty through regular workshops and planning sessions. Because some sections of our course were linked with collaborating faculty and some were not, we were able to assess the impact of the collaboration as well as the IL instruction. To avoid sampling bias, we assessed every student that enrolled in the course.

Planning for Assessment

The purpose of our project was to assess the impact of both course-integrated and credit course IL instruction on student acquisition and retention of Information Literacy Competency Standards. We already had active and well-developed relationships with departmental faculty at our campus, so collaboration was not an obstacle. Our methodology included the delivery of a pre- and posttest survey to determine the students' knowledge of library resources and services prior to instruction and shortly after the conclusion of instruction.

Developing the Assessment Instrument

The assessment instrument was developed through a two-part process. The first part involved an analysis of existing publications on assessing students' IL skills. This provided a framework of questions. The second part was an analysis of our existing curriculum. We tuned the questions to core aspects of the curriculum content and then issued the instrument to test groups to identify ambiguities and question weakness. Several questions required substantial revision to both the wording and multiple-choice answers.

Analyzing the Results

The results were analyzed with the help of statistical management software. Information about the course section, instructor, year, term, learning community participation, and pre- or posttest were keyed into a spreadsheet along with the answers. The data then were imported into the Statistical Package for the Social Sciences (SPSS) for cross-tabulation. Our primary focus was to compare performance on the posttest to that of the pretest. However, we also examined differences between instructors and learning community collaboration.

Results

The final results are still being analyzed, but some preliminary conclusion can be drawn. First, students taking the credit course improved their scores on the posttest dramatically. For example, one of the most basic questions asked students to identify how books were arranged in the library. On the pretest, only 45 students correctly answered by Library of Congress classification number. However, on the posttest, 250 students answered correctly. Other questions had similar results. Only 23 students knew to use the Library of Congress Subject Headings (LCSH) guide to look up terms for catalog searching. On the posttest, 242 students correctly identified the LCSH guide. Although many students still struggled with the content of the course, we are confident that many more are improving their IL skills.

When we broke down our analysis by level of collaboration, we also saw an interesting result. We worked with a total of three learning communities: the CHE mentioned earlier, the Academic Advantage, and the Class Act, which is limited to students seeking K–12 teacher certification. Sixty percent of the students assessed in our study enrolled as part of a learning community where we had strong collaborative connections with departmental faculty outside the library. The remaining 40 percent enrolled in open sections that involved no library–department collaboration.

For the above question on the arrangement of books in the library, the students who were not part of a learning community improved their performance by 62 percent. However, those in the Academic Advantage learning community improved by 73 percent. The CHE students improved by 75 percent and the

Class Act students by 76 percent. Similar results were found for the other questions. These results confirm our belief that collaborating with faculty outside the library by linking curriculum and pedagogy reinforces the course content and its value to the student.

Challenges

The primary challenge for the assessment program was time. We did not receive release time from existing work responsibilities, so we were forced to limit our commitment. Moreover, we had to devote many evening and weekend hours to completing each phase of the project. In the last part of 2001, we received one FTE support staff member to assist with data entry. Without this help, it is unlikely we would have been able to complete the project. Collaboration was not a problem because we built on existing relationships. Every English faculty member we requested assistance from agreed to help without hesitation.

Conclusion

Students taking the course-integrated workshops did not improve their skills as dramatically as did students enrolled in the eight-week course. This was not surprising because they received only two hours of instruction, whereas the credit course students received sixteen hours of instruction. However, they did improve their IL skill enough to justify continuing the program. At the time of this publication, we have not merged the two data sets to make specific cross-comparisons. We hope to make these relationships clearer in the future and to provide access electronically.

Assessment Instrument

Please take a few minutes to answer the following questions as accurately as possible. The information is used for research purposes only and THE RESULTS WILL NOT AFFECT YOUR GRADE.

How are magazines and journals arranged in the Michener Library?
- a. Numerically by Library of Congress classification number
- b. Numerically by Dewey Decimal classification number
- c. Numerically by Superintendent of Documents classification number
- d. Alphabetically by title
- e. Don't know

How are books arranged in the Michener Library?
- a. Numerically by Library of Congress classification number
- b. Numerically by Dewey Decimal classification number
- c. Numerically by Superintendent of Documents classification number
- d. Alphabetically by title
- e. Don't know

Which statement BEST describes a periodical index?
- a. A list of magazines and journals in a library
- b. A list of magazine and journal articles grouped by subject
- c. A directory of where magazines and journals are located in a library
- d. A directory of magazines and journals held on reserve
- e. Don't know

What is the BEST procedure to follow if UNC Libraries does not own a magazine or journal article that you need?
- a. Go to another library
- b. Ask the library to purchase a subscription to the item
- c. Request a copy of the article through interlibrary loan
- d. Search for the article on the Internet
- e. Don't know

What resource should you consult to determine if UNC Libraries owns a particular book?
- a. InfoTrac
- b. Books in Print
- c. The Source online catalog
- d. WorldCat
- e. Don't know

What resource should you consult to determine if UNC Libraries owns a particular issue of a journal?

a. InfoTrac
b. Books in Print
c. The Source online catalog
d. WorldCat
e. Don't know

When searching for books in the Michener Library, how can you determine the official subject heading(s) for your topic?

a. Consult the Michener Library Subject Headings guide
b. Consult the Library of Congress Subject Headings guide
c. Consult the online subject heading thesaurus
d. Consult the UNC Libraries serials list
e. Don't know

What is the best type of search to perform when no adequate subject heading exists for your topic?

a. Word
b. Title
c. Author
d. Subject
e. Don't know

Which resource is the BEST place to look for information on an actor's recent arrest for handgun possession?

a. Social Sciences Index
b. Britannica Online
c. WorldCat
d. Academic Universe (Lexis-Nexis)
e. Don't know

Which is a characteristic of Expanded Academic Index?

a. A "for fee" database available by subscription
b. A restricted database available only in the libraries
c. A free Internet site open to everyone
d. A free database available only in the libraries
e. Don't know

Which is a characteristic of Expanded Academic Index?

a. Contains only full text
b. Contains no full text
c. Contains some full text
d. Contains only bibliographic citations
e. Don't know

Which is an advantage of subject heading searches?
  a. Results are grouped by topical division.
  b. Results are arranged chronologically.
  c. Abstracts (summaries) of records are searched.
  d. Controlled vocabulary terms are not used.
  e. Don't know

What is the undergraduate loan period for books and government publications from the Michener Library?
  a. 2 weeks
  b. 4 weeks
  c. 8 weeks
  d. 12 weeks
  e. Don't know

What is the undergraduate loan period for periodicals from the Michener Library?
  a. 1 hour
  b. 2 hours
  c. 1 day
  d. 3 days
  e. Don't know

Which of the following is an example of a scholarly journal?
  a. Wall Street Journal
  b. Men's Journal
  c. Ladies Home Journal
  d. New England Journal of Medicine
  e. Don't know

Have you ever attended an instruction session on how to use library resources at UNC?
  Yes
  No

Which of the following is the BEST resource to use to locate U.S. government statistical publications?
  a. American Statistical Publications
  b. WorldCat
  c. SuDoc
  d. Congressional Universe
  e. Statistical Universe

Chapter 24: Assessing Information Literacy in Community College Human Services Courses

Robert Schroeder

Institution Description

Spokane Falls Community College (SFCC) is one of two community colleges in Spokane, Washington, with approximately 8,500 FTES and a head count of 17,484 students. There are 320 full-time equivalent faculty at SFCC, four full-time librarians, and two part-time librarians.

An information literacy (IL) component is *not* required of students graduating from SFCC, so most IL skills are taught through the library's library instruction program, which consists of the traditional one-hour BI sessions. One or two credits of a library research class are usually offered once a year in conjunction with other classes ("paired classes" or "learning communities"). A two-credit Internet issues class also is offered each quarter and is required of students in the Internet networking, graphic design, and library technician programs. One way that IL is promoted to the college is via our Outcomes and Assessment Committee. One of our collegewide outcomes is Analysis, Problem Solving, and Information Literacy.[1] Within the outcomes and assessment group, the assessment of IL skills is promoted, but involvement in these abilities is voluntary and thus does not rise to the level of a mandatory campuswide initiative.

Project Participants

For this project, I worked with two faculty members in the Human Services Department. One instructor is Judith Noel, who teaches Introduction to Education (ED 201). Because this is an exploratory class for students in education, the students are introduced to research in ERIC, ProQuest, and the Internet. The other instructor was Polly McMahon, who teaches Death, Grief, and Loss (DGL250) paired with an English composition class.

Project Description

I solicited faculty collaborators by sending out an invitation to faculty to work with me to incorporate IL into their classes. I also announced the opportunity in our Outcomes and Assessment Committee.

Planning for Assessment

I started the planning process by asking the instructors for copies of their syllabi and the specific assignment to which I would be teaching. I noted in the assignment where IL skills were already incorporated. I circled the IL components and added suggestions of my own that would "ratchet up" the IL quotient of the assignment (such as not only requiring an Internet site for a paper, but also including a rubric for critically evaluating the site that would be handed in). In addition, I made other suggestions around the assignment that would only require minimal or no change or work for the instructor. I sent the revised assignments back to the instructors, and after I received them back with their acceptance, I cross-referenced the IL teaching points to the ACRL standards. In this manner, I "back-filled" the 5-column Assessment Planning Grid, starting in the middle "Outcomes" column and then filling in with the appropriate "Standard" and "Performance" indicator columns. (See appendix A for a sample of the Assessment Planning Grid.)

Developing the Assessment Instruments

I already had the first three columns of the Assessment Planning Grid filled in, and I knew what I wanted to teach the students (and how I would teach them). Starting with each outcome, I devised a specific objective that would indicate its successful completion. I tried to use assessments that the instructor already had the students performing, such as writing a list of works cited or the paper itself. I also adjusted an Internet evaluation page that would help me assess some of my objectives. For each of my objectives, I had to decide what would indicate a "successful level of completion." For example, if the objective were that "the student will correctly use the APA Web citation format," I had to decide how many correct elements in the citation would show "success" and even how many Web citations were needed to meet this level. The answers to these kinds of questions were what informed my assessment rubrics.

Analyzing the Results

I had the instructor return a copy of the list of works cited and other supplemental pages I had requested for analysis. With a copy of my rubric in hand, I assigned points to each student's work. I then put the individual scores to each of the rubric questions in an EXCEL spreadsheet so that I could see how each individual did (in the rows). I also could see how the group did on the different objectives (in the columns). From this kind of spreadsheet analysis, I could ascertain patterns. Often a few students missed all of the points (which made me wonder if I needed to try another teaching style or perhaps talk with the instructor to determine what might work for that student). Other times, the whole group would miss an objective, which definitely gave me cause for reflection on the way the point was taught and the length of time I might devote to it in the future. (A same spreadsheet is provided at the end of chapter).

Results

ED 201 Results Analysis

Table 24-1 shows that approximately two-thirds of this class understood 100 percent of the topics taught. Of the three topics shown in table 24-2, the least well understood was the correct use of APA format for ProQuest and the Web (69% adequate understand to 31% inadequate), with the Web page format being the least understood (66% from table 24-3).

DGL 250 Results Analysis

Table 24-4 shows that 63 percent of the students understood less than 50 percent of the material assessed. Table 24-5 shows that only 32 percent of the students

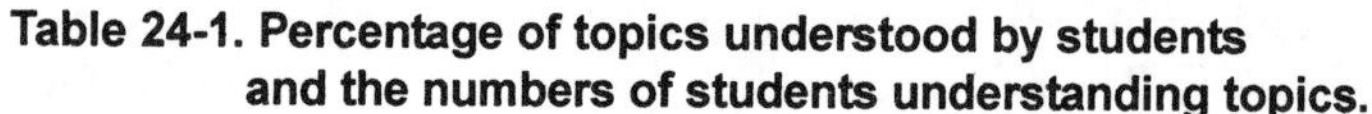
Table 24-1. Percentage of topics understood by students and the numbers of students understanding topics.

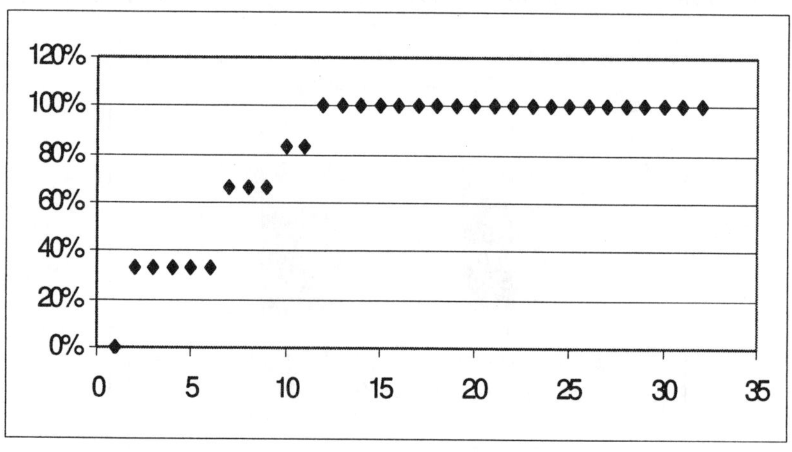

Table 24-2. Adequate or inadequate understanding of concepts or skills assessed.

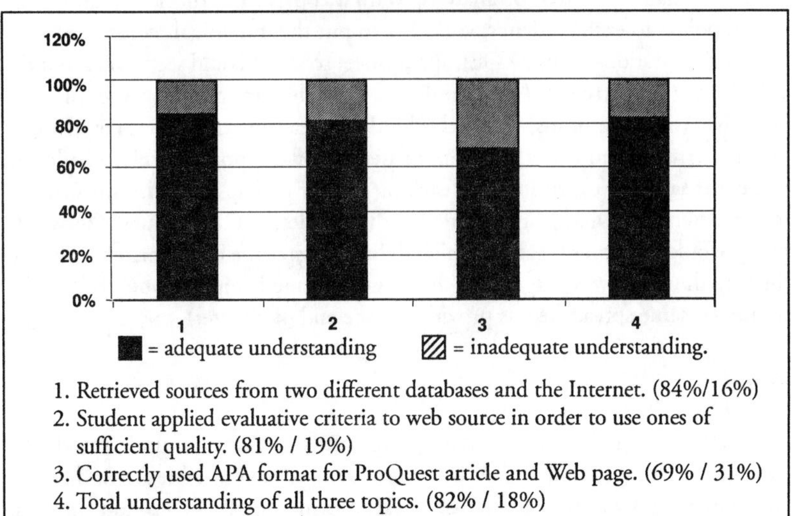

1. Retrieved sources from two different databases and the Internet. (84%/16%)
2. Student applied evaluative criteria to web source in order to use ones of sufficient quality. (81% / 19%)
3. Correctly used APA format for ProQuest article and Web page. (69% / 31%)
4. Total understanding of all three topics. (82% / 18%)

recognized a professional or scholarly journal, and only 56 percent recognized a "quality" Web site.

Challenges

It was easy to find faculty to partner with in that many faculty members at SFCC see the need to incorporate more IL concepts and skill into their classes. The challenge is how to reach the uninspired faculty, especially because IL is not mandated at SFCC. The reference librarians are currently working on a Web page that will allow instructors to click on an ARCL IL standard that would link to

Table 24-3. Adequate/Inadequate use of APA citation formats.

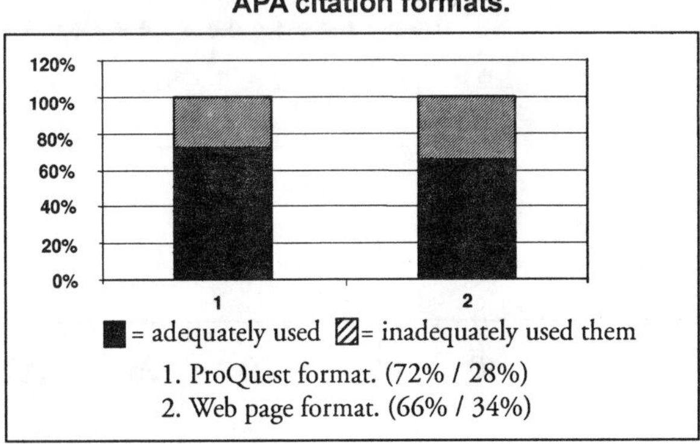

1. ProQuest format. (72% / 28%)
2. Web page format. (66% / 34%)

Table 24-4. Percentage of topics understood by students and the numbers of students understanding the topics.

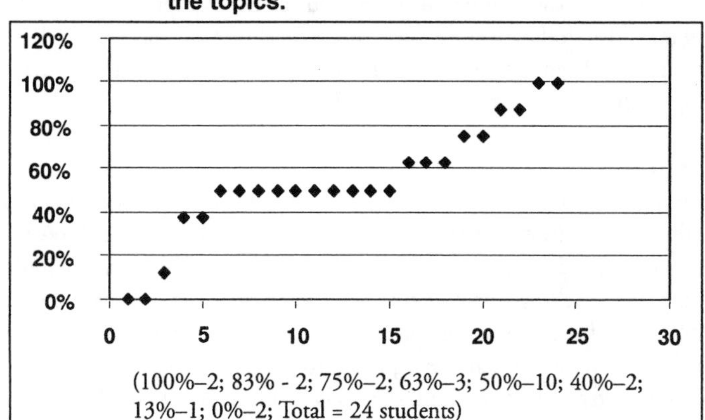

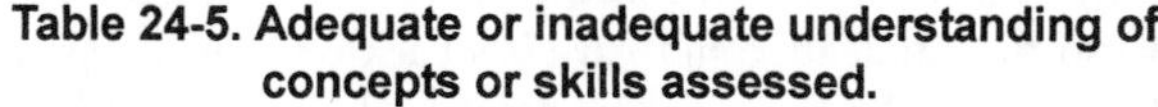

(100%–2; 83% - 2; 75%–2; 63%–3; 50%–10; 40%–2; 13%–1; 0%–2; Total = 24 students)

Table 24-5. Adequate or inadequate understanding of concepts or skills assessed.

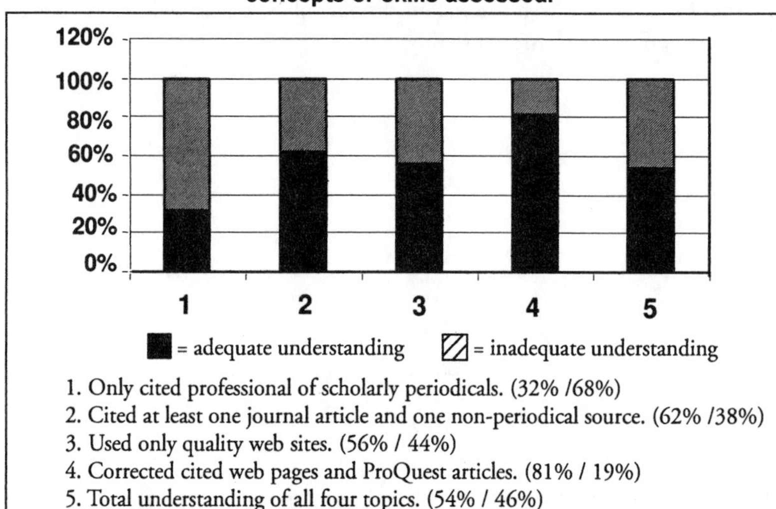

1. Only cited professional of scholarly periodicals. (32% /68%)
2. Cited at least one journal article and one non-periodical source. (62% /38%)
3. Used only quality web sites. (56% / 44%)
4. Corrected cited web pages and ProQuest articles. (81% / 19%)
5. Total understanding of all four topics. (54% / 46%)

suggested ways of teaching that skill. They also would be able to link to sample assessments and rubrics related to the standard and the suggested assignments.

No matter how often I analyzed the assessment instrument and the rubrics, it seemed I could never anticipate all the possible ways a question could be answered. I highly recommend doing a pilot test of a small group before giving the assignments to a whole class. In this way, one could adjust the rubric to reflect the full range of results.

Another challenge, somewhat outside the issue of this study, is how to get IL made a mandatory requirement for graduation. In a sense, this study may hold the answer in that partnering with interested faculty is a great place to begin. Building up a loyal following of IL supporters on campus through these kinds of partnerships could generate the necessary critical mass that would allow IL move to the top of the college's agenda.

Conclusion

After looking over the results that indicated many students failed at understanding certain concepts (such as proper APA citation formats or the need to evaluate Web pages or periodicals), my first inclination was to work to devise better ways of teaching and reaching the students. However, when I looked at the number and complexity of subjects being taught, I came to a different conclusion (probably not new to many): We are being asked to pack too much information into our traditional fifty-minute sessions! One way to alleviate this "info-crunch" may be to have parts of the learning take place outside the classroom, either before or after the fifty-minute session. Assignments could be made (that would need to be handed in) so that students could have feedback on their progress. Using the Internet for an online Web tutorial on various subjects also could take some of the burden off of the classroom setting.

Assessment Instrument

The following is a sample assessment tool (I also used the students' list of works cited pages):

Web Page Evaluation Checklist

Your Name:________________________

Address of the site you are evaluating: ____________________________________

What search engine did you use? ______________________________________

What was the search that you entered into the search textbox to find this Web page?
____

Accuracy ***Your analysis here:***
What's the aim, intent?
Is the publisher/sponsor identified?
Hint: Check the sidebar and bottom
Is it meant to inform with facts and data?
Explain? Persuade? Sell/entice? Share?

Authority.
What type of domain is it?
Who wrote it? Credentials?
Hint: Look at the URL first: .com/.org/.net
.gov/.mil/.us./.edu.
In Google search: link all or part of URL
Who links to it?

Objectivity .
Is it designed to sway opinion?
Is there advertising on the page?
Who links to it?
Hint: Truncate back the URL if you cannot find a sponsor
Why was it written? What is the viewpoint?

Currency
Is it dated?
Are all pages the same date?
Are links still viable?

Sample Assessment Planning Grid

Assessment Planning Grid—ED201 Winter 2002

Information Literacy Standard	Performance Indicator	Outcomes	Objective	Instrument & Method
II. The ILS accesses needed information effectively and efficiently.	2.The ILS constructs and implements effectively designed search strategies.	d. Constructs a search strategy using appropriate commands for the information retrieval system selected...	The student will be able to construct an appropriate Internet search strategy at a search engine.	A student will indicate on a checklist the name of the search engine used and the strategy used to find their web site.
II. The ILS accesses needed information effectively and efficiently.	2.The ILS constructs and implements effectively designed search strategies.	e. Implements the search strategy in various information retrieval systems using different user interfaces and search engines with different command languages, protocols, and search parameters.	The student will be able to retrieve sources from two different databases and the Internet.	The student will turn in a reference list comprised of four resources from four different categories – two web pages (one retrieved via a search engines, the other via a subject guide); one ProQuest article; and one ERIC document abstract.
III. The ILS evaluates information and its sources critically and incorporates selected information into his of her knowledge base and value system.	2. The ILS articulates and applies initial criteria for evaluating both the information and its sources.	a. Examines and compares information form various sources in order to evaluate reliability, validity, accuracy, authority, timeliness, and point of view or bias.	The student will apply evaluative criteria to web sources in order to only use ones of sufficient quality.	A Web page will be evaluated by the student with the help of a four -point checklist. The student's responses on the checklist will indicate their understanding of the evaluative criteria, in that they will accurately describe the web page. A rubric will be used giving 0 points for less that 2 of the 4 points being accurate reflections; 1 point for 2 of 4; and 2 points for 3 or more of 4.
V. The ILS understands many of the economic, legal, and social issues surrounding the use of information and accesses and uses information ethically and legally.	3. The ILS acknowledges the use of information sources in communicating the product or performance.	a. Selects an appropriate documentation style and uses it consistently to cite sources.	The student will correctly use the APA Web citation format for Web pages and ProQuest articles.	The list of works cited will be evaluated for correct citation formats. A rubric will be developed in which 0 will be given for no proper citations; 1 will be given for mostly proper citations; and 2 will be given for all proper citations.

Sample Spreadsheet for Data Analysis

ED 201 Winter 2002 AM Group

Objective II.2.e Types	Objective III.2.a Evaluate	Objective V.3.a Pro+Web	@ Student Total	@ Student Potential Total	@ Student Percent Successful	@ Student Percent Unsuccessful
2	2	2	6	6	100%	0%
2	2	2	6	6	100%	0%
0	2	1	4	6	67%	33%
2	2	2	6	6	100%	0%
2	2	0	6	6	100%	0%
2	2	2	6	6	100%	0%
2	2	2	6	6	100%	0%
2	0	0	2	6	33%	67%
2	0	0	2	6	33%	67%
1	2	0	5	6	83%	17%
1	2	0	5	6	83%	17%
2	2	2	6	6	100%	0%
2	2	1	6	6	100%	0%
2	2	2	6	6	100%	0%
2	2	2	6	6	100%	0%
2	2	2	6	6	100%	0%
2	2	2	6	6	100%	0%
0	2	0	4	6	67%	33%
2	2	2	6	6	100%	0%
2	2	1	6	6	100%	0%
0	0	0	0	6	0%	100%
2	0	2	2	6	33%	67%
2	0	1	2	6	33%	67%
2	0	2	2	6	33%	67%
2	2	2	6	6	100%	0%
2	2	1	6	6	100%	0%
2	2	1	6	6	100%	0%
2	2	2	6	6	100%	0%
0	2	2	4	6	67%	33%
2	2	2	6	6	100%	0%
2	2	2	6	6	100%	0%
2	2	2	6	6	100%	0%
Total Class						
54	52	44	158	192	82%	18%
Potential Total						
64	64	64	192			
Percent Successful						
84%	81%	69%	82%			
Percent Unsuccessful						
16%	19%	31%	18%			

Chapter 25: Assessment of Student Learning in ENGL 101 Composition

Risë L. Smith

Institution Description

Dakota State University is a four-year, public university (Baccalaureate II) that recently added two master's programs. With an FTE enrollment of 1,600 and a head count of just over 2,000, the university specializes in programs in computer management, computer information systems, and other related undergraduate and graduate programs. There are eighty-eight faculty members. A special emphasis is the preparation of elementary and secondary teachers with expertise in the use of computer technology and information processing in the teaching and learning process. The library has emphasized information literacy (IL) formally in the strategic plan for the past few years by making it one of the library's four strategic initiatives. The university has not formally adopted a definition of IL, but the library's definition has been so thoroughly accepted over several years that it appears in various university documents, including general education goals and student outcomes. Each of the three categories of general education requirements—systemwide general education requirements (shared with other public higher education institutions in South Dakota), institutional requirements, and information technology literacy requirements—addresses IL in some way in its goals or student outcomes.

Project Participants

The goal of this project was to assess IL student learning in ENGL 101, the basic composition course. The course description for ENGL 101 is: "Practice in the skills, research, and documentation needed for effective academic writing. Analysis of a variety of academic and nonacademic texts, critical thinking, and audience awareness will be included." Project collaborators included two English professors and two librarians responsible for instruction.

Project Description

The project addressed our desire to assess student learning of IL in ENGL 101 composition. Librarians had worked collaboratively for some time with English faculty to integrate basic IL into ENGL 101. Because of the course's content, because most students had to take it, and because students took it early in their academic careers, ENGL 101 was a good course in which to develop basic information literacy.

Planning for Assessment

The collaborators first met during the summer of 2001 and began by reviewing the process for designing an assessment that was presented to IMLS grant participants in June 2001 in San Francisco. We defined the scope of our project as assessing student learning outcomes in ENGL 101 related to information literacy—a class-level (as opposed to a program-level) assessment. We discussed our goals, what we ultimately wanted to gain from the assessment. Our goals were to measure student learning and to use those results to improve instruction. We developed a timeline that included piloting the assessment in fall 2001 and administering it in spring 2002. The five-column Planning the Assessment chart, introduced to grant participants during training, was used to develop the assessment instrument in late summer and early fall.

Developing the Assessment Instrument

We used the Planning the Assessment chart to identify standards we wanted to address, to select performance indicators and outcomes, to articulate objectives, and to determine an instrument and method. First, we reviewed the *ACRL Information Literacy Competency Standards for Higher Education* to identify those we thought were—or should be—addressed in ENGL 101. During this process, we selected the specific standards, performance indicators, and outcomes in the standards that we wanted to address with the assessment. We chose to measure standards 1, 2, and 3, and we selected four performance standards (two in standard 1 and one each in standards 2 and 3). Within those performance standards we selected a total of six outcomes. Second, we wrote objectives for each of the outcomes selected. Finally, we developed an instrument and method for testing the objectives. During our discussions about objectives and instruments/methods, we decided to use a pretest and posttest to measure student learning before instruction and at the end of the semester. We also wanted to have a test that was performance based, one that asked students to think and do tasks typically required to find and evaluate information. In this context, performance-based assessment meant that the assessment elicited performance of thoughts and actions that a student would typically carry out in doing his or her work. These questions were not "authentic" because they were fantasized scenarios for assessment purposes; however, they were realistic scenarios. As a result of this approach, many of the questions were open ended.

Analyzing the Results

By spring 2002, the two teaching faculty working on this project were each teaching only one section of ENGL 101, and one of these was a very small Internet section. The pretest was administered in January 2002; the posttest was administered in May. For both the pretest and the posttest, a percent correct was calculated for each student, and an average student score for each course section was obtained from these scores. Pre- and posttest scores were compared to assess how much improvement occurred during the semester. In addition, we examined performance on each individual question to see whether specific questions remained problematic for students at the end of the semester. This information was used to identify where instructional content and methods might need improvement. We identified *quantitatively* the questions on which students performed well and those on which they performed poorly (and/or showed least improvement between the pre- and posttests), and we examined their responses *qualitatively* for common errors and patterns of error.

Results and Discussion

The average student score in course section A, the Internet section, was 50percent (30 out of 60 points; n=5) for the pretest and 65 percent (39/60; n=5) for the posttest. On average, students in this section gained 15 percentage points overall. The average student score in section B was 24 percent (14.67 out of 60 points; n=15) for the pretest and 52 percent (31.23/60; n=13) for the posttest, an average gain of 28 percentage points overall. As expected, student learning did occur between the pre- and post-assessment and was demonstrated by improvement in the average score. The higher average score in section A was explained when we discovered that some of these students had accessed the Web-based information literacy tutorial while they were taking the pretest. Figure 25-1 displays average scores for course section A. In the posttest, on average, students in section A obtained their lowest posttest scores on questions 3 (5 points out of 10; 50%), 4 (6.6 points out of 13; 51%), and 5 (13.2 points out of 20; 66%). They performed best on questions 1 (1.4 points out of 2; 70%), 2 (5.6 point out of 6; 93%), and 6 (7.2 points out of 9; 80%). Their greatest improvement was made in

Figure 25-1. Section A

POINTS:	2	6	10	13	20	9	60
Question:	**Q1**	**Q2**	**Q3**	**Q4**	**Q5**	**Q6**	**Total Pts**
pretest (n=5)							
avg points	1.60	5.20	4.20	4.40	9.20	5.40	30.00
avg %	80%	87%	42%	34%	46%	60%	50%
posttest (n=5)							
avg points	1.40	5.60	5.00	6.60	13.20	7.20	39.00
avg %	70%	93%	50%	51%	66%	80%	65%
difference							
avg points	-0.20	0.40	0.80	2.20	4.00	1.80	9.00
avg %	-10%	7%	8%	17%	20%	20%	15%

questions 5 (increasing from 9.2 correct to 13.2 correct out of 20) and 6 (increasing from 5.4 to 7.2 correct out of 9). While recognizing that using percentages with such few observations is problematic, the average scores for questions 5 and 6 increased 20 percentage points (46 to 66% in question 5; 60 to 80% in 6). Question 4 gained 17 percentage points (34 to 51%), and improvement in question 3 between pre- and posttests was 8 percentage points (42 to 50%). Pretest scores were high for questions 1 and 2, and posttest scores were up only 7 percentage points for question 2 and down 10 for question 1.

Figure 25-2 displays average scores for course section B. Section B students performed best on the posttest on questions 2 (5.54 points out of 6; 76%) and 6 (6.15 points out of 9; 68%), and exhibited the greatest improvement on question 6 with an average increase of 3.88 points (from 25% to 68% correct; an increase of 43 percentage points). They performed the worst on questions 3 (4.31 out of 10 points; 43%) and 5 (8.23 out of 20; 41%). However, between the pre- and

Figure 25-2. Section B

POINTS:	2	6	10	13	20	9	60
QUESTION:	Q1	Q2	Q3	Q4	Q5	Q6	Total Pts
pretest: (n=15)							
avg points	0.60	4.00	0.40	5.67	1.73	2.27	14.67
avg %	30%	67%	4%	44%	9%	25%	24%
posttest: (n=13)							
avg points	1.08	4.54	4.31	6.92	8.23	6.15	31.23
avg %	54%	76%	43%	53%	41%	68%	52%
difference:							
avg points	0.48	0.54	3.91	1.25	6.5	3.88	16.56
avg %	24%	9%	39%	10%	32%	43%	28%

posttests, their scores went up 39 percentage points on question 3 and 32 percentage points on question 5. They made the least improvement on question 2 (9 percentage points) where they had the highest score and on question 4 (10 percentage points) where they scored 53 percent. Pretest questions on which students performed well should reveal areas where learning need not be reinforced in ENGL 101 Neither section scored in the 90th percentile on any of the pre-test questions, so no areas were identified for elimination. However, scores for question 2 were higher than those for many of the other questions, so time allocated to that instructional area could be reduced and spent on areas causing more difficulty. Questions on which students performed poorly in the pretest and on which little improvement was made in the posttest served to identify instructional areas where more emphasis or different instructional approaches were needed. Students in Section A improved less than 10 percentage points on questions 1 through 3. Questions 1 and 2 were among their highest scoring questions, so the low differential was unimportant. However, question 3 was their lowest scoring question in the posttest, so the small differential between pre- and posttests suggested that this instructional area needed to be examined for improvement. Section B students improved 10 or less percentage points on questions 2 and 4, but question 2 was their highest scoring question. Question 4 was the fourth highest or third lowest score, so this instructional area needed to be examined, also, for improvements in content or method of instruction. The quantitative data directed us to where we needed to improve student learning to a greater degree. We also examined the posttests qualitatively to help us identify specific problem areas on which to focus. Looking more closely at answers to question 4 by students in Section B, we found (and were surprised) that students had trouble distinguishing full-text articles from abstracts. Examining Section A answers to question 3 revealed that student ability to successfully translate a research topic into a search command using Boolean and other search techniques was weak. In both sections, the lowest posttest scores were for questions 3, 4, and 5. Examining their answers to question 5 revealed that their ability to evaluate the objectivity of articles was limited; an "objective" article seemed to be one that matched their beliefs. On the other hand, when evaluating Web page content in question 6, they recognized when someone was trying to sell them something and were aware of the value of knowing the author's credentials. By examining answers qualitatively, we were able to get a clearer understanding of areas where students were having difficulty and areas where they were demonstrating greater information competency.

Challenges

A major challenge was in writing the questions. The decision to make questions performance based, that is, to use realistic scenarios or activities, made certain kinds of questions more appropriate than others. This focus helped by reducing the number of question types and making our choices more manageable. Even so, writing well-phrased questions that would elicit what they were intended to elicit was not easy. Finding the appropriate level of difficulty for questions was also challenging. We piloted the posttest in fall 2001 and, as a result, made major changes in one question and minor corrections in other. Even after obtaining the pre/posttest results and drawing some conclusions about areas for improvement, a concern remained. Did poor student performance on a question reflect a lack of learning or a poorly constructed question? Another challenge was determining how similar the pre- and posttest should be to each other, but ultimately we used the same test for both in order to have comparable results.

Conclusion

Using the five-column Planning the Assessment chart to work from the ACRL standards to instrument/method made the process of developing the assessment much more manageable and directed. This directed approach helped facilitate collaboration within the development team. It also made choosing assessment questions easier because each was the direct result of a specific objective (tied to a specific outcome). Analyzing quantitative and qualitative data helped us to identify areas of learning that were problematic and suggested specific areas on which to focus to improve our instruction and student learning.

Assessment Instrument
Spring 2001—ENGL 101 Information Literacy Assessment Posttest

1. Imagine that you have found two articles about "hating America" (about the topic of anti-U.S. feelings around the world). Both articles contain the information you need for your paper. One of the articles was professionally peer reviewed and published in a journal. The other article was found on someone's personal Web pages.
Based on this information, what preliminary conclusions can you draw about the quality of the information provided in each of these two articles? Why?

2. Imagine that you need to find the type of information or type of source given in 2-1 through 2-6 below. Select the tool on the right that is the **best** source for finding the information needed on the left. Write the letter of the correct answer in the blank provided.

Types of information needed:	**Information tools:**
____ 2-1. journal article	a. biography
____ 2-2. general definition	b. book/monograph
____ 2-3. brief overview of broad topic	c. dictionary
____ 2-4. current information on a topic	d. directory
____ 2-5 book/monograph	e. encyclopedia
____ 2-6. geographical location	f. journal article
	g. periodical index
	h. library catalog
	i. atlas

3. Use Boolean operators, phrase searching, and truncation to translate the search topics in 3-1 through 3-5 into search commands for Infotrac Expanded Academic Index. **[Note: In Infotrac, the Boolean operators are AND/OR/NOT. The truncation wild card is the asterisk (*). Phrases are created by using the W1 connector.]**

3-1. statistics on teen pregnancy

____

3-2. defaults on student loans

____

3-3. racial profiling by police

____

3-4. effects of irrigation on the Colorado River

____

3-5. stem cells in the treatment of diseases

____

4. Imagine that you have been assigned to research and write about the topic described in the paragraph below.

> Title IX was enacted 20 years ago to ensure equality between men's and women's sports programs in federally funded high schools and colleges. What impact has Title IX had on sports programs?

4-1. What are the **key concepts** in the paragraph that you would use in your search for information about this topic? ______________________________

4-2. Translate the search topic into a search command for a Proquest database. [Note: In Proquest, the Boolean operators are AND/OR/AND NOT. The truncation wild card is the question mark (?). Two-word phrases need no special marking; phrases of three or more words are surrounded by quotation marks.]

Search command in Proquest: ______________________________

4-3. Use **Proquest *Research Library*** to find a **full-text article** about the topic. Fill in the following information that would be needed for a citation:
Author(s) of article: ______________________________
Article title: ______________________________
Title of Magazine/Journal: ______________________________
Volume and Issue (if provided): volume __________ issue __________
Date of Publication: ______________________________
Page(s): ______________

5. Select an appropriate database (**not** Onefile) in **Infotrac** to search for **full-text** journal (or magazine) articles to support your argument that **racial profiling by police is a complex issue.**
Select **two** full-text articles:

1) one that you **would use** as evidence for your argument and
2) one that you **would NOT use** as evidence

5-1. Describe article 1 by filling in the following information needed for a citation:

Database used in Infotrac: ______________________________
Author(s) of article: ______________________________
Article title: ______________________________
Title of Magazine/Journal:______________________________
Volume and Issue (if provided): volume __________ issue __________
Date of Publication: ______________________________
Page(s): ______________

5-2. Explain **why** article 1 would be a **good** source for your argument.

5-3. Describe article 2 by filling in the following information needed for a citation:

Database used in Infotrac: ______________________________

Author(s) of article: ______________________________
Article title: ______________________________
Title of Magazine/Journal: ______________________________
Volume and Issue (if provided): volume ________ issue ________
Date of Publication: ______________________________
Page(s): ________________

5-4. Explain **why** article 2 would **not** be a good source for your argument.

6. Imagine that you are researching "melatonin" and find the three Web pages listed below in 6-1 through 6-3. Evaluate each of the Web pages in terms of each of the five evaluation criteria (accuracy, authority, objectivity, currency, and coverage).

- To review the five evaluation criteria, see http://www.departments.dsu.edu/library/courseuse/evalcrit.html.
- A blank line is provided for each criterion on which you should make notes about the quality of the Web page relative to the criterion.
- To save typing each URL, links to all three Web pages may be found at: http://www.departments.dsu.edu/library/courseuse/q6links.htm.

After evaluating each Web page,

a) indicate whether you consider the page to be good evidence for a paper in ENGL 101 by indicating whether you would use the Web page (yes or no), and

b) explain why or why not (**based on the evaluation criteria**).

6-1. Go to http://www.melatonin.com/, click on "Melatonin" in the left border, and evaluate that page.
Accuracy ______________________________
Authority ______________________________
Objectivity ______________________________
Currency ______________________________
Coverage ______________________________

6-1-a. Would you use this web page? ¨ yes ¨ no
6-1-b. Use your notes from above to explain why or why not.

____

6-2. Evaluate http://www.nia.nih.gov/news/pr/1999/11%2D05.htm.
Accuracy ______________________________
Authority ______________________________
Objectivity ______________________________
Currency ______________________________
Coverage ______________________________

6-2-a. Would you use this Web page? ¨ yes ¨ no
6-2-b. Use your notes from above to explain why or why not.

____

6-3. Evaluate http://www.aafp.org/afp/971001ap/cupp.html.

Accuracy ____
Authority ____
Objectivity ____
Currency ____
Coverage ____

6-3-a. Would you use this Web page? ¨ yes ¨ no
6-3-b. Use your notes from above to explain why or why not.
____

Chapter 26: Information Literacy Assessment for Introduction to Music Course

Ann Viles

Institution Description

Appalachian State University is a comprehensive university located in Boone, North Carolina, in the Appalachian Mountains. It has an enrollment of almost 13,000 students and employs 633 full-time faculty. Librarians have faculty status and serve on a number of significant university committees. Increasing its impact on student learning and development of information literacy (IL) abilities is a strategic goal of Appalachian's library. Measuring the academic skills of freshmen and monitoring students' gains in skills across the college years is a concern of the Appalachian Assessment Office and the faculty. IL goals are an integral part of the goals for undergraduate and graduate education at Appalachian. An IL assessment program was implemented on the campus in 1999 when 1,951 students, or 95 percent of the freshman class, completed an IL test during Fall Focus Day in September. This test, developed by the library and administered by the Assessment Office, was designed to establish a benchmark for entering freshmen. The results of the test will be used to determine changes in students' skills when they are tested again as second semester sophomores and seniors. The second phase of this assessment was completed in January 2001 when more than two hundred students completed a more extensive assessment test using WebCT, and the remainder of the cohort repeated the original test administered in fall 1999. The last phase will involve extensive collaboration with teaching faculty in as many academic departments as possible to develop discipline-based assessment tools to be administered during the cohort's senior year.

Project Participants

The principal participants in the project included the author, Ann Viles; six librarians; and a faculty member from the School of Music. Student participants were enrolled in an Introduction to Music (MUS 2011), a "non-technical course for students with little or no musical background. Emphasis is placed on the style and form of music as perceived by the listener" (Appalachian State University General Bulletin, 1999–2001).

Project Description

The project used the ACRL *Information Literacy Competency Standards for Higher Education* (*ILCSHE*) to identify the basic IL goals and objectives of the core humanities course Introduction to Music (MUS 2011) and collected data to document student achievement of those goals and objectives.

Planning for Assessment

Beginning with a relatively small class during the summer 2000 semester, library faculty in collaboration with music faculty began developing an IL module for the course. The basis of the module is an annotated bibliography assignment requiring the students to locate and use a variety of music materials in several formats. Librarians participated in the design of the assignment and contribute to the evaluation of the final project, which comprises 25 percent of the course grade. A team of librarians teaches at least two sessions of each of the multiple sections of the course, and the students are encouraged to make appointments with library faculty for one-to-one consultations following the class sessions. The final evaluation of the project is the responsibility of the music faculty, but librarians give feedback on the appropriateness of sources and check the citations and annotations for completeness and form. An evaluation of the project by the student is one of the required elements of the assignment, and the quality of the completed annotated bibliographies serves as an indicator of student achievement of specific IL goals and objectives.

Developing the Assessment Instrument

Brief pre- and posttests were developed during the summer semester of 2001. At the beginning of the first session of library instruction and at the end of the second session, each student answers three open-ended questions to demonstrate his or her understanding of the terms *bibliographic citation* and *annotation* and the concept of scholarly versus popular periodicals. After grading was begun, a checklist of the elements considered essential for each type of annotation also has been helpful in achieving equity in the grading.

All components of the assessment were pilot-tested during the fall semester of 2001, but the results of the pre- and posttests had to be thrown out for two sections of the class because the students accidentally received handouts with definitions for the terms in the pretest before taking it.

Analyzing the Results

Content analysis is used to organize the results of the students' open-ended evaluations of the project and to analyze responses to the questions in the pre- and posttests. Both of these components of the assessment have already been used to make adjustments to the library instruction sessions and to the study guides provided for the students. Numerical data from the librarian's evaluation checklist are being used to analyze progress in the quality of the students' work from semester to semester. Feedback from the music faculty member already has indicated a perceived improvement in the final projects since the project began.

Results

The assessment was conducted with two sections of the Introduction to Music course with a total enrollment of 112 students during spring 2002. Twelve students did not complete either the pre- or posttest and were not included in the analysis of those data. Thirteen students did not complete the final project in time for inclusion in the assessment, but their pre- and posttest data are included.

Students demonstrated the ability to identify "the value and differences of potential resources in a variety of formats" (ACRL *Information Literacy Competency Standards for Higher Education)* by successfully completing an annotated bibliography, which contained one article from a music reference source, one book, two sound recording tracks, one Web site, and two periodical articles. Only 12 percent of the students correctly defined the term *annotation* in the pretest, compared to 78 percent in the posttest.

Seventy-two percent of the students demonstrated an understanding of the "purpose and audience of potential resources" *(ILCSHE)* by correctly indicating in their final projects whether two articles were from popular magazines or scholarly journals. Fifty-eight percent of the students taking the pretest and 89 percent taking the posttest correctly described at least one characteristic of a scholarly journal that distinguishes it from a popular magazine.

All of the students used "various search systems to retrieve information in a variety of formats" *(ILCSHE)*. All but five of the ninety-six students whose final projects were evaluated located and annotated at least one article from a music encyclopedia, one book and one recording located in an online catalog, one Web site using either a Web directory or a search engine, and two periodicals using an index to music periodicals either online or in print.

Most of the students demonstrated the ability to differentiate "between the types of sources cited" and an understanding of "the elements and correct syntax of a citation for a wide range of resources" *(ILCSHE)* by completing citations in MLA style for five different types of resources. Forty-two percent completed all seven citations with 0-1 minor errors. Eighteen percent completed six citations with 0-1 minor errors. Fourteen percent completed five citations with 0-1 minor errors. Twenty-six percent completed only four or fewer with 0-1 minor errors.

Overall, 81 percent of the students who completed both the pre- and posttest performed better on the posttest, 18 percent showed no change, and 1 percent actually did worse on the posttest. Because they were not anonymous, most of the project evaluations were not surprisingly extremely positive. However, a number of students commented that the library sessions were too simplistic and redundant and that the handouts repeated too much information from the project's Web site. Almost half the students indicated that they had learned more about library resources and services, and many of them commented that they had learned more about their music topics than they had expected.

Challenges

One of the biggest challenges throughout this project has been finding time to evaluate fairly and consistently the work of up to 240 students per semester. Even with a team of four librarians working together, the burnout rate for those involved is high. In an effort to reduce the amount of time required for grading, the number of annotations required has been reduced by half to a total of only seven items. Achieving consistency in the evaluations also has been an illusive goal. Because the team of librarians is not the same each semester, it is necessary to meet after the completed projects have been received to begin the process of evaluation together. After a couple of hours of thinking out loud and consulting with each other as we grade, we begin to come to a consensus about the marking and can work separately with only occasional consultations.

Conclusion

This team effort has added a great deal of student contact as well as an expanded IL component to the library's instruction program. It has generated goodwill and opened the door to even more collaboration with the music faculty. As a side effect of the project, use of the music databases RILM and IIMP has more than quadrupled since the project began.

Assessment Instrument
Pre-test and post-test

Music 2011: Introduction to Music.
Annotated Bibliography Research Project, Spring 2002

Your Name: ________________ E-mail address: ____________________

Please circle your classification: Freshman Sophomore Junior Senior

1. What is a bibliographic citation?

2. What is an annotation?

3. Describe one characteristic of a scholarly journal that distinguishes it from a popular magazine.

Assignment (evaluated by librarians)

Annotated Bibliography Research Project

Annotations
- 1 Biographical or background sketch from a reference source
- 1 Book (or chapter from a book)
- 2 Tracks from a Music Library CD
- 1 High quality Web site
- 2 Articles

Evaluation of the Project
(Directions for the evaluation: A well-written evaluation of your project should be included. This evaluation should explain how this exercise has benefitted you and include suggestions on how you might have enhanced your work. Please include an evaluation of the library sessions, handouts, and Web site. This is an important aspect of the project.)

LIBRARIANS' CHECKLIST FOR PROJECT EVALUATION

Student: ____________________ Date: ___________

Elements of the Annotated Bibliography (See Project Guidelines for form.)	Excellent	Good	Fair
Cover page format (maximum points: 8/8 = 1)	1	0.5	0

__ Student's name __ Consulting Librarian's name
__ Project title __ Student's e-mail address
__ MUS 2011 and section number
__ Student's phone number
__ Professor's name __ Date of submission

	Excellent	Good	Fair
Biographical sketch or background sketch (maximum points: 6/2 = 3)	3	2	1

Citation in MLA style:
__ Information __ Format
__ Punctuation

__ Resource appropriate
__ Annotation addresses topic
__ Source of full text indicated

	Excellent	Good	Fair
Book annotation (maximum points: 6/2 = 3)	3	2	1

__ Entire book or chapter
__ Source of full text indicated
__ Annotation addresses topic

Citation in MLA style:
__ Information __ Format
__ Punctuation

	Excellent	Good	Fair
Discography annotation of track no. 1 (maximum points: 8/2 = 4)	4	3	2

__ Recording from Music Library
__ Location of recording statement
Citation in MLA style:
__ Information
__ Punctuation
__ Format

Annotation includes 3+ of the following:
__ Performers and/or instruments
__ When recorded or special circumstances
__ Description of music
__ Reasons for liking (or not liking) music
__ Why representative of topic

	Excellent	Good	Fair
Discography annotation of track no. 2 x (maximum points: 8/2 = 4)	4	3	2

__ Recording from Music Library
__ Location of recording statement
Citation in MLA style:
__ Information
__ Punctuation
__ Format

Annotation includes 3+ of the following:
__ Performers and/or instruments
__ When recorded or special circumstances
__ Description of music
__ Reasons for liking (or not liking) music
__ Why representative of topic

Web Site Annotation 3 2 1
(maximum points: 6/2 = 3)
__ 1st page printout
Citation in MLA style:
__ Information __ Format
__ Punctuation

Annotation includes 2+ of the following:
__ Relevance to topic __ Design & usability
__ Authority __ Currency
__ Content & coverage

Article annotation no. 1 (maximum points: 6/2 = 3) 3 2 1
__ Citation in MLA style
__ Source of citation indicated
__ Resource appropriate

Annotation includes:
__ Distinctive feature/s
__ Critical evaluation
__ Indication of scholarly or popular

Article annotation no. 2 (maximum points: 6/2 = 3) 3 2 1
__ Citation in MLA style
__ Source of citation indicated
__ Resource appropriate

Annotation includes:
__ Distinctive feature/s
__ Critical evaluation
__ Indication of scholarly or popular

Student's evaluation of the project 1 1 1
(included = 1, not included = 0)

TOTAL POINTS: ______________

Chapter 27: Assessing Abilities of Freshmen to Reconcile New Knowledge with Prior Knowledge

Marjorie M. Warmkessel

Institution Description

Millersville University of Pennsylvania is a comprehensive public institution with an enrollment of approximately 6,600 undergraduate and 950 graduate FTE students. The 440 faculty members offer a wide range of degree programs in the liberal arts and professional areas. The information literacy (IL) program at Millersville University emphasizes course-integrated library instruction. Each session is tailored to meet the needs of a particular course, usually geared toward specific course assignments. In the spring semester of 1999, the university's Faculty Senate approved a set of assessable objectives for the existing general education curriculum. Inquiry/information literacy is included as one of six objectives within the fundamental skills. Within this document, IL, paired with inquiry rather than communications technology literacy, which is a separate objective, is defined as students being able to: (1) generate research questions/pose problems; (2) recognize when they have a need for information;)3) find reliable sources; (4) evaluate information found and select relevant information; and (5) make effective use of information, including being able to integrate what they have learned into a final product. In January 2001, a coordinator of general education was appointed to serve as an advocate for general education issues and to facilitate assessment of the university's general education program.

Project Participants

Project participants are Marjorie Warmkessel, humanities librarian and library instruction coordinator, and a professor of English. Students participating in the project were from one section of freshman composition in the fall 2001 semester and two sections of freshman composition in the spring 2002 semester. Student participation was voluntary.

Project Description

Library instruction has been an integral part of the professor's freshman composition classes for years. She has been particularly interested in finding ways to help freshmen improve their ability to discriminate among resources and to integrate secondary sources smoothly with their own ideas and sees library instruction with an emphasis on critical thinking skills as one way to accomplish her goal. I have worked very closely with her for several years, meeting with her classes during their regular class period twice during the semester. The first library instruction section has emphasized finding information and the second has emphasized evaluating various information sources.

Planning the Assessment

In designing this project, we decided to maintain our usual methods of providing library and IL instruction so that we could determine whether what we have been doing is really as effective as we hope it is. Having developed an informed consent form, which was approved by Millersville University's Human Research Review Committee, we introduced our project to the students and invited them to participate. For the fall semester, twelve of eighteen students chose to participate. I assume that a comparable percentage of students will choose to participate in the spring semester as well.

In addition to in-class free-writes and other informal writing assignments, students work on three major essays throughout the semester, the second of which requires them to use secondary source materials to support their own arguments. The second assigned essay—the research essay—became the focus of our IL assessment project. We began the project by asking the following two questions: How do first-year students use reading and writing to actively reconcile new knowledge with prior knowledge? And through these interactions with the ideas of others, how do students make decisions about how they might reshape their value systems? By reviewing various drafts of an assigned research essay, we hoped to be able to answer these questions in terms of students' IL skills.

Developing the Assessment Instrument

Focusing on standard 3 of the *Information Literacy Competency Standards for Higher Education,* "The information literate student evaluates information and its sources critically and incorporates selected information into his or her knowledge base and value system," we developed an assessment rubric that we could use in evaluating multiple drafts of each student's research essay. The IL assessment rubric was adapted from the grading rubric that the course instructor has been using with her freshman composition classes for several years. Although the grading rubric did incorporate certain aspects of information literacy, it includes other skills pertinent to writing as well; however, the assessment rubric we developed for this project addresses IL skills exclusively. Because our goal throughout the project was to assess ourselves, to determine whether what we were doing was having the impact we hoped, and because we did not want to confuse students by introducing two distinct assessment rubrics, we did not distribute the IL assessment rubrics with the participating students.

Analyzing the Results

At the end of the fall semester, the professor shared with me the writing portfolios of all students who had volunteered to participate in the project. Each student included between four and eight drafts of his or her research essay in the portfolio along with a reflective essay—responses to specific questions—that described the student's perception of the process of writing a research essay. I reviewed the various drafts of each student's research essay and reflective essay looking for evidence of those aspects of information literacy spelled out in our assessment rubric. I developed a grid to show evidence of IL competencies, comparing students' early drafts with the final draft of their research essays. I expect to follow the same process for analyzing the drafts of students' research essays at the conclusion of the spring semester.

Results

Using an assessment rubric, I analyzed various drafts of twelve students' research essays as well as a reflective essay—responses to specific questions—on the process of writing a research essay. Table 27-1 shows the placement within the assessment rubric of the various drafts of each student's research essay and reflective essay.

All students made progress through the various drafts of their research essays, and most exhibited through their reflective essays an understanding of the need to find current and authoritative sources to be integrated into their essays.

Of the seven students whose early drafts fell into the "emergent" category, five fell squarely into the "gaining control" category by the final draft, one was moving toward the "gaining control" category, and one exceeded the "gaining control" category, moving toward "strong." The student whose early drafts fell be-

Table 27-1. Progress of students at various stages of the assignment

Student	Early Drafts	Final Draft	Reflective Essay
#1	Gaining /Strong	Strong/Distinguished	Strong
#2	Emergent	Gaining	Emergent/Gaining
#3	Emergent	Gaining	Gaining/Strong
#4	Emergent	Emergent/Gaining	Emergent/Gaining
#5	Emergent	Gaining/Strong	Gaining/Strong
#6	Gaining/Strong	Strong/Distinguished	Strong
#7	Emergent/Gaining	Gaining/Strong	Emergent/Gaining
#8	Gaining	Strong/Distinguished	Strong/Distinguished
#9	Emergent	Gaining	Gaining
#10	Gaining	Strong	Strong
#11	Emergent	Gaining	Gaining
#12	Emergent	Gaining	Emergent/Gaining

tween the "emergent" and "gaining control" categories moved beyond "gaining control" toward "strong" by the final draft. One of the two students whose early drafts fell into the "gaining control" category moved squarely into the "strong" category by the final draft; the other exceeded the "strong" category and was moving toward "distinguished." The two students whose early drafts fell between "gaining control" and "strong" exceeded the "strong" category by the final draft and were moving toward "distinguished."

Challenges

The primary challenge we struggled with was in determining how we could actually assess the extent to which students had evaluated information sources, incorporated information sources into their essays, and integrated them with their own ideas. We worked through several versions of the assessment rubric before deciding on the one we used.

Conclusion

Using an assessment rubric has proved to be an effective way of assessing students' abilities to evaluate information resources and integrate them with their own ideas. Although the process of analyzing students' research essays is both subjective and time-consuming, it revealed certain trends that point to progress in students' development of IL skills, probably directly attributable to the instruction and guidance they received from me and from the professor. The analysis also brought to our attention certain areas of confusion or misunderstanding on the part of students of which we had previously been unaware. Recognizing these problems has enabled us to shift the emphasis of our instruction so that we can try to avoid these kinds of misunderstandings in the future. In addition to using the assessment rubric with future sections of freshman composition, I hope to apply the same assessment rubric to an analysis of early and final drafts of research essays written by students in our junior-level advanced composition classes.

Assessment Rubric

Distinguished

Evidence from essay

- Very strong support. Offers a lot of information and an in-depth, well-developed view into topic. Contains much detail/evidence, many examples. Sufficient in support of thesis. Secondary sources cited are current and relevant.
- Information found through various sources is well integrated into a unified argument in essay. Develops new ideas and hypotheses through the integration of existing information. Develops original ideas based on existing information. Develops original analysis of topic.
- Compares new information with own knowledge and other sources considered authoritative to determine if conclusions are reasonable.
- Compares different points of view with one another.
- Develops different perspectives into/ways of looking at topic; clearly develops one (writer's own) as central.

Evidence from response to questions about the process of writing the essay

- Reveals careful reflection and analysis about whether or not information retrieved is sufficiently current for the information need.
- Reveals careful reflection and a thorough understanding that other sources may provide additional information to either confirm or question point of view or bias.
- Reveals careful reflection and a thorough understanding that some information sources may present a one-sided view and may express opinions rather than facts and that some information sources may be designed to trigger emotions, conjure stereotypes, or promote support for a particular viewpoint or group.
- Reveals a thorough understanding of the relationship between new information and previous information or knowledge.
- Reveals a thorough understanding of the process for deciding whether or not to accept a particular point of view.

Strong

Evidence from essay

- Strong support. Contains much information, though not fully developed in one or two spots. Contains much detail and many examples generally sufficient in support of ideas.
- Information found through various sources is integrated into the essay. Begins to develop new ideas and hypotheses through the integration of existing information. Begins to develop original ideas based on existing information. Begins to develop an original analysis of topic.

- Compares new information with own knowledge and other sources considered authoritative.
- Compares two different points of view.
- Describes different perspectives into/ways of looking at topic and describes one (writer's own) as central.

Evidence from response to questions about the process of writing the essay

- Reveals an understanding of the need to find current information and some analysis about whether or not information retrieved is sufficiently current for the information need.
- Reveals a thorough understanding that other sources may provide additional information to either confirm or question point of view or bias.
- Reveals an understanding that some information sources may present a one-sided view and may express opinions rather than facts and that some information sources may be designed to trigger emotions, conjure stereotypes, or promote support for a particular viewpoint or group.
- Reveals awareness that there is a relationship between new information and previous information or knowledge.
- Reveals some understanding of the process for deciding whether or not to accept a particular point of view.

Gaining Control

Evidence from essay

- Contains some support. Evidence and examples fill out the essay somewhat, but these are insufficient in amount or depth. Writer may overgeneralize.
- Some information found through various sources is integrated into the essay. Suggests a new idea or hypothesis or original idea through the integration of existing information.
- Presents new information along with own knowledge and other sources considered authoritative.
- Presents at least two different points of view.
- Describes different perspectives into/ways of looking at topic and identifies one (writer's own) as central.

Evidence from response to questions about the process of writing the essay

- Reveals an understanding of the need to find current information.
- Reveals some understanding that other sources may provide additional information to either confirm or question point of view or bias.
- Reveals some understanding that some information sources may present a one-sided view and may express opinions rather than facts and that some information sources may be designed to trigger emotions, conjure stereotypes, or promote support for a particular viewpoint or group.

- Reveals some awareness that there is a relationship between new information and previous information or knowledge.
- Reveals an awareness of the process for deciding whether or not to accept a particular point of view.

Emergent

Evidence from essay

- Support is weak. Evidence and examples are offered, but these are insufficient in amount or depth. Writer may overgeneralize or seem close-minded. Essay may be too one-sided; it may include others' opinions but overrule or flatten them.
- Some information found through various sources is integrated into the essay. · Suggests different perspectives into/ways of looking at topic and suggests one (writer's own) as central.

Evidence from response to questions about the process of writing the essay

- Reveals an awareness of the need to find current information.
- Reveals an awareness that other sources may provide additional information to either confirm or question point of view or bias.
- Reveals an awareness that some information and information sources may present a one-sided view and may express opinions rather than facts and that some information sources may be designed to trigger emotions, conjure stereotypes, or promote support for a particular viewpoint or group.
- Reveals an awareness of the need to decide whether or not to accept a particular point of view.

Chapter 28: Past Lives: An Exercise in Historical Research with an Annotated Bibliography Requirement

Clay Williams and Anita Ondrusek

Institution Description

Hunter College is located in New York City. The library serves 15,556 undergraduates, 513 graduate students, and 608 full-time and 695 part-time faculty.

Project Participants

A historical novel is rich in its details about the lifestyles of its characters and the times in which the story is set. Some authors in this genre employ research assistants to supply them with these details; others conduct their own research. As a prelude to conducting research on a fictitious historical character, undergraduate students in an American history honors class first read passages from a historical novel by Ann Macmillan and then, interviewed her about her research methods via e-mail.

Project Description

Following these experiences, the professor and two librarians teamed together to guide students through the historical research process through lectures, demonstrations, readings, field trips, consultations, and dissemination of handouts illustrating citation and bibliographic entry styles.

Planning for Assessment

The process was a progression from setting goals to matching those goals to the ACRL *Information Literacy Competency Standards for Higher Education*, a process planned jointly by the librarians and the course professor. As a preinstructional diagnostic, the librarians asked the students to complete a First Contact Survey at the first class meeting. (The survey is provided at end of the chapter.) The responses were used to assign partners. In terms of assessment of student progress, the professor regularly devoted class time to eliciting feedback from students, and the librarians then used the professor's reports to adjust their instruction (our formative evaluation). The culminating course requirement, an annotated bibliography of resources that would assist an author in bringing a fictional character to life, was used to assess overall student learning. (A summative evaluation is provided at the end of the chapter.) Overall, the course professor evaluated the quality of the character profiles.

Developing the Assessment Instrument

The goals of the project were:

1. Students will be able to:
   - Identify historical resources and differentiate among the intended uses of these resources
   - Use historical records to place an event or person into a historical context
   - Match their varying research needs to appropriate investigative methods
   - Locate historical resources in their college library and in adjunct special collections
   - Construct and implement online search strategies when needed
   - Evaluate their historical findings in terms of relevance, validity, reliability, and accuracy
   - Develop effective research record-keeping practices
   - Construct citations that document their research sources using a standard, scholarly style
   - Synthesize research findings into an original product
2. From an affective view, students will:
   - Recognize the value of preserving the historical record and, by extension, realize the importance of maintaining historical materials collections
   - Acept that libraries and librarians are necessary entities in the research process
   - Apreciate the value of collaboration among peers to achieve an academic goal

Performance indicators and outcomes from the ACRL standards were matched to our project goals, and these became our objectives. The examples below are extracted from our full report (located on the Web at http://library.hunter.cuny.edu/clwillia/ACRL).

Objective 1: Students will be able to identify historical resources and differentiate among the intended uses of these resources.

Related Standards: Standard One

Performance Indicator 2: Identifying a variety of types and formats of potential sources for information.

Outcome 1.2.e: Differentiating between primary and secondary sources and recognizing their use and importance [specific to history as a] discipline.

Outcome 1.2.f : Realizing that information may need to be constructed with raw data from primary sources.

Objective 5: Students will be able to locate historical resources in their college library and in adjunct special collections.

Related Standards: Standard Two

Performance Indicator 3: Retrieving information online or in person in a variety of formats.

Outcome 2.3.b: Using various classification schemes and/or other systems to locate information resources within the library or to identify specific sites for physical exploration.

Outcome 2.3.c: Using specialists (in-person services) as information location advisers.

Performance Indicator 5: Managing information and its sources.

Outcome 2.5.c: Determining the availability of a source and locating it.

Objective 8: Students will be able to construct citations that document their research sources using a standard, scholarly style.

Related Standards: Standard Two

Performance Indicator 5: [Documenting/citing] sources of new information.

Outcome 2.5.c: Differentiating between the types of sources cited and [applying] the correct syntax for each citation type.

Objective 9: Students will be able to synthesize research findings into an original product.

Related Standards: Standard One

Performance Indicator 4: Using information effectively to accomplish a specific purpose, either individually or as a group.

Performance Indicator 2

Outcome 1.2.e: Recognizing that existing information can be combined with original thought, experimentation, and/or analysis to produce new information.

The History 151 Research Presentation from fall semester is available at http://library.hunter.cuny.edu/clwillia/pastlives/.

References

Gratch, Bonnie. 1985. Toward a methodology for evaluating research paper bibliographies. *Research Strategies* 3(4): 170–77.

Young, Virginia E., and Linda C. Ackerson. 1995. Evaluation of student research paper bibliographies: Refining evaluation criteria. *Research Strategies* 13(2): 80–93.

First Contact Survey

1. Contact information. (Name and Email Address)

2. What <u>home</u> computer access do you have, or expect to have, during this school year?
   A. MY OWN COMPUTER
   B. A COMPUTER SHARED WITH OTHERS
   C. NO HOME COMPUTER
   D. OTHER: ________________________________

3. Your e-mail or Internet access is, or will be, through:
   A. MY HOME INTERNET CONNECTION
   B. COLLEGE AND LIBRARY COMPUTER LABS
   C. BOTH A and B
   D. I DON'T HAVE E-MAIL YET

4. Which of the statements below describe the computer activities that apply to your use of computers? <u>Circle all that apply</u>:
   A. I send and receive E-MAIL.
   B. I use WORD PROCESSING to type class papers.
   C. I have created POWERPOINT shows.
   D. The INTERNET has helped me find information for projects and reports.

5. In the library (school, college, public, or any library), I have used the computer: <u>Circle all that apply</u>:
   A. To look up BOOKS by author or title
   B. To do SUBJECT searches
   C. To find MAGAZINE ARTICLES
   D. To find NEWSPAPER ARTICLES

6. College libraries have special research sources, many of which you will need to locate and use for assignments. Fill in the circle under the description that fits your knowledge about that library source.

<u>SOURCESDESCRIPTIONS</u>	Have used these	Heard of these	Never heard this source	Not sure of use
A. Encyclopedias				
B. Reference Books				
C. Periodicals				
D. Reserve Collection				
E. Archives				
F. Open Stacks				
G. Closed Stacks				
H. Indexes				
I. Abstracts				
J. Online Public Catalog				

K. Research Databases
L. Maps or Atlases
M. Bibliographies
N. Picture files
O. Statistical records
P. Almanacs
Q. Full-text documents
R. Primary Sources

7. To give us a little background on your school writing experiences, identify from the list below what you have written for past class assignments. Circle all that apply::

A. BOOK REPORT(S)
B. SHORT TERM PAPER(S) (1 to 5 typed pages)
C. LONG TERM PAPER(S) (6 or more typed pages)
D. ENGLISH COMPOSITION(S)
E. ESSAY(S)
F. SPEECH(ES)
G. PLAY(S)
H. POEM(S)
I. AUTOBIOGRAPHY or BIOGRAPHY (Personal histories)
J. SCIENCE EXPERIMENT or SCIENCE PROJECT REPORT(S)
K. PRESENTATION(S) (Giving a talk based on notes)
L. POSTER(S) or ART WORK (Accompanied by written descriptions)

8. In your previous research or report-writing assignments, how did you keep track of information you found? Circle all that apply:

A. KEPT NOTE CARDS
B. USED A NOTEBOOK
C. SAVED NOTES ON MY COMPUTER
D. PHOTOCOPIED and SAVED PAGES (from books, magazines, etc.)
E. KEPT COMPUTER PRINT-OUTS
F. USED HIGHLIGHTING or UNDERLINING TO MARK IMPORTANT TEXT
G. JOTTED NOTES ON SCRAP PAPER
H. KEPT NOTES IN A TABLET
I. E-MAILED INFORMATION TO MYSELF
J. MEMORIZED STUFF I READ OR DISCOVERED
K. OTHER: ____

9. <This question asked specifically about prior history courses.>

10a. Have you ever worked on an assignment with a partner or in a small group?

YES NO

10b. If YES, how would you rate that experience? Circle one number. If you feel somewhere in the middle of the extremes, circle a 2, 3, or 4.

1	2	3	4	5
A. I LEARNED SO MUCH MORE				I WOULD HAVE LEARNED MORE BY MYSELF

10c. If NO, how do you feel about the prospect of working with a classmate on an assignment?

1	2	3	4	5
B. IT SOUNDS EXCITING				I THINK I'LL HATE IT

Illus. 2: Bibliography rating sheet
Dr. McCauley's History 151 fall 2001
<Students' names and date>

Criteria	Points	Score
1. The appropriateness of the material cited as sources of information. (appropriateness=reputation of source, age, author, authority). Instructor		
2. Creativity (imaginative use of resources) Instructor		
3. Evaluation (Useful for research to the author) Instructor		
4. Inclusion of one or more primary sources (census, maps, diaries correspondence, autobiographies, etc). Librarian	2 point/source	
5. Inclusion of secondary sources. (historical encyclopedias, history texts, articles) Librarian	1 point/source	
6. Investigation of more than one media type. (print, sound, film, web). Librarian.	1 point/source	
7. Investigation beyond Hunter College's collections. Librarian	Up to 3 points	
8. Searching of online database(s) or catalog(s). Librarian.	1 point	
9. Chicago Style was the format specified by instructor. Style applied in a consistently acceptable format used in the cited literature section. Librarian Two scores assigned, one for print resources, one for media.	Inconsistent format, incomplete information- 0 pts; consistent format, incomplete information-1 pt; inconsistent format, complete information-1 pt; consistent format, complete information-2 pts; acceptable, consistent format, complete information-3 pts.	
10. Organization of document. (Will author be able to match the citations to the included material?) Librarian		

Chapter 29: Ethnography and Information Literacy: An Assessment Project

Steve Witt and Rebecca Gearhart

Institution Description

Illinois Wesleyan University is an independent, undergraduate university founded in 1850 and located in Bloomington, Illinois. The student population is 2,015, with students from thirty-two different states and thirty different countries. The university is organized around a College of Liberal Arts, a College of Fine Arts, and a School of Nursing. The College of Liberal Arts offers thirty-nine majors and three preprofessional programs: medical technology, predental, and preengineering. The College of Fine Arts includes the schools of art, music, and theatre arts, and an interdisciplinary major in music and theatre. The School of Nursing offers a four-year program and confers a bachelor's of science in nursing degree. The university strives to provide a liberal education of high quality, fostering values and skills that will sustain students over a lifetime of learning. The university is currently going through reaccreditation, so the area of assessment is of great interest to many campus constituents.

The library supports the university's mission through a model of integrating information literacy (IL) skills into the disciplines through partnerships with library and teaching faculty. Instead of teaching an IL course, IL skills are taught using a developmental approach through curriculum-based instruction and collaboration with departments and their faculty. The library is currently in the process of updating its teaching program to include outcomes assessment and further engage departmental curricula.

Project Participants

The assessment project began in the fall of 2001 with the librarian and a member of the educational studies department working together to develop and pilot a set assignments and their accompanying assessment instruments to be used in the freshman experience class, Gateway 100. Several library sessions were planned around an assignment, which used a pilot rubric to assess student performance. In the fall of 2002, this assignment and assessment tool will be reviewed and implemented in the same Gateway course.

Using a similar methodology of assignment and instrument development, the librarian then began working with an upper-level anthropology course in the spring of 2002.

The bulk of the project was spent in designing and implementing an assessment tool for an upper-level anthropology course, Gender in Cross-Cultural Perspective. Professor Gearhart has been on the faculty of IWU for three years. As an anthropology instructor, she is one of the few anthropologists who teaches undergraduate students the methodology for original ethnographic research. Each student in Anthropology 352 is required to do original ethnographic research on a topic of his o her choice that relates to the theme of the course.

In the spring of 2002, fourteen students enrolled in the course and participated in the project. They ranged in status from freshman to senior. All but two of the students had received previous library instruction, though instruction varied to a great extent.

Project Description

The decision to integrate an ethnographic research project into an upper-level anthropology courses is based on two pedagogical theories: (1) The best way to teach students the importance of cross-cultural communication, a primary goal of anthropology itself, is to require them to apply basic anthropological methods (interviewing and participant-observation) in forming relationships with members of different societies; and (2) the best way to expose students to anthropological scholarship is to require them to situate their own ethnographic research within anthropological discourse and to evaluate secondary source materials according to how well they help them gain insight into the community they are studying.

One of the drawbacks of integrating an ethnographic research project into a semester-long course is that it sends students a mixed message about how professional anthropologists do their work. Ethnographic field work among a single society is typically conducted over an extensive time period of a year or more.

Professor Gearhart continuously emphasizes this point to her students and challenges them to spend as much time with their ethnographic subjects as possible so that their final research paper is distinguishable from a paper that a journalism student might produce. For Professor Gearhart, the fact that students leave her classes and ultimately the university with cross-cultural experience and the confidence to interact with members of other societies seems to outweigh the possible misconceptions students might have of the objectives of the field of anthropology itself.

Planning the Assessment

Consistent with the library's teaching mission of collaborating with teaching faculty to integrate IL instruction into individual courses, the project's aim was to take the integration of instruction to a higher level by integrating the overall grading of assignments through the creation of qualitative assessment tools to measure student outcomes and improve student learning. With this overall objective in mind, two subgoals of the project were established. The first was to modify an assignment and create a grading rubric to be employed by the teaching faculty and addresses one or several outcomes from the *ACRL Information Literacy Standards*. The second goal was to qualitatively assess the process of research the students followed as it relates to the IL outcomes.

For this project, the assignment and grading rubric were integrated into the course's curriculum as part of a professor's existing assignment to measure student performance. The professor then used the grading rubric to evaluate, score, and provide feedback on each student's project as it progressed toward completion. Because the focus was on assessing and improving learning outcomes within a specific course, a pretest/posttest model was not followed to measure overall effect of instruction or growth within a particular area. By creating an assessment tool that would be implemented by the teaching faculty, the librarian hoped to move IL instruction away from the library's domain to allow shared ownership of pedagogical responsibilities and true collaboration among librarian, teacher, and student.

The first stage of actually developing the measurement tools was to modify the structure and evaluation of the course's ethnographic research assignment, which requires each student to keep a detailed ethnographic journal. To begin this process, the outcomes of the original assignment were compared with the ACRL IL competency standards. Because ethnographic research requires an extensive amount of work with primary and secondary source materials, human observation and interviews, and the synthesis of these materials to create original data on the topic, the realization that a successful assignment requires outcomes in almost all five of the IL standards was overwhelming. Realizing that it would be impossible to attempt to assess each of these outcomes, the next step was to choose which outcome to concentrate on in the assessment and grading. Because the ability to evaluate information and sources while incorporating the information into new knowledge and understanding of a culture is at the core of ethnographic research, the main focus was on performance indicators and outcomes from standard 3: "The information-literate student evaluates information and its sources critically and incorporates selected information into his or her knowledge base and value system."

When the outcomes were identified, the materials to support the assignment that the professor had used in the past were modified so that they offered better explanations of expectations related to the outcomes built into the assignment. In making these modifications, it was important to fully integrate IL outcomes into the assignment as processes and skills that would naturally be employed in the course of the research project. The materials to support the assignment included the instructions for conducting ethnographic research, guidelines for keeping an ethnographic journal, and grading criteria for the ethnographic journal. When the assignment was fully developed, the content of the instruction that would support the IL outcomes of the assignment were planned.

The Assessment Instrument

A brief description of the modified assignment as it appeared in the course syllabi follows:

> Small student teams will select a research topic that explores a particular aspect of one of the issues we cover in the course on a deeper level, and present that research to the class as a PowerPoint presentation. Students may further expand their research on that topic or select a different topic on which to conduct their ethnographic research. This research will consist of collecting, evaluating, and referencing secondary source material, as well as collecting primary data through interviews and participant-observation of a member or members of the society on which the research focuses. Students will record their primary and secondary research findings in an ethnographic journal, which will be periodically evaluated for its anthropological content.

With the curriculum and pedagogy established, several assessment instruments that would be used to provide students with feedback while working on the project, a grading scale for the research journal, and evidence of meeting the IL outcomes were created. The assignments were to be used in two ways during the assessment. The overall research journal and its related assignments would be assessed using a predetermined grading rubric that would be shared with the students at the beginning of the project, giving a means of providing the students with feedback and using the outcomes as part of the project's grade. In addition, the journal and instructor's feedback to the students would be qualitatively assessed at the end of the semester to determine whether there was significant correlation among the various measures of student performance, overall student performance, and other outcomes not directly addressed in the grading rubric.

The first assessment tool was the Ethnographic Research Proposal, which was assigned after the students received instruction in the library. In this assignment, the students were asked to describe their topic based on their background research, assess the quality and usefulness of the sources from their preliminary research, and create a viable research hypothesis. The second assessment consisted of journal evaluations in which the professor would provide feedback to students based on criteria from the final grading rubric. The third assessment was the overall grade on the Ethnographic Journal, which scored students on quality of secondary research, evaluation of secondary sources, ethnographic methods, and ethnographic content.

When the assignment was modified and the assessment methods established, a research proposal was submitted to the campus's institutional review board. Because the librarian planned to read the professor's comments and the student research journals, both the students and their research subjects were required to sign informed consent forms.

The class spent a total of four hours in the library engaged in lecture and discussion on research and evaluation methods in the beginning of the spring semester. During these classes, students also were given time to begin their preliminary research. The Ethnographic Research Proposals were due after the library instruction, and upon their evaluation by the professor, students began working on their ethnographic research. When the process of ethnographic research began, the students met with the professor three times to get guidance and feedback before handing in the journals for final grading. At this point in the assignment, the journal evaluations were used to ensure that the methodology and resources being used were appropriate. In addition, this type of assessment provided the professor with a chance to further educate the students on the ethnographic content and research methodology.

The final process was the quantitative assessment, which entailed reading the professor's feedback to students and the research journals to get an overall idea of what seemed to be important to both the professor and the students as they recorded their research observations. After categorizing the journals and responses, the librarian read each journal a second time to code the responses, using the same scale in coding that was used in grading the journals to enable a comparison of these results.

The assessment tools were designed to provide students with the expectations of the assignment and a developmental approach to completing the project while also providing the professor with enough information to grade the projects. The research proposal and journal evaluations were created to help guide students through the process. Because the students' primary sources were human subjects, the proposals and evaluations were used to assess ways in which the ethnographic journals showed the use of secondary sources in preparation for their interviews and observations and how their perceptions or ideas changed based on their interaction with both their primary and secondary sources. The journal grading rubric was created to provide both the students and the professor with enough information about what the expectations were without being too prescriptive and negatively affect each student's ability to perform ethnographic research as his or her topic demanded. (The assessment instruments are available at the end of the chapter.)

Results

Overall Performance on IL Outcomes

Twelve of the original thirteen students completed the Ethnographic Journal assignment. The mean score on a scale that ranges from 80 to 48, was 72.54, which closely matches the mean scores on the Secondary Research Quality and Evaluation of Secondary Sources, which were 18.13 and 18.46. (See table 29-1.) This indicates that the average student in the class was successful in achieving the IL outcomes that were taught and integrated into the assignment.

Correlation between Score on IL Outcomes with Ethnographic Outcomes

The data indicate that there is a correlation between a student's ability to both perform quality research and evaluate sources and the final ethnographic content. Although the statistics (table 29-2) point to a significant correlation, there were too few students in the group (12) to make any truly meaningful assumptions based upon the data. One way to resolve this is to increase the number in the set by continuing to use the assessment instrument and comparing the combined results of several classes.

Qualitative Analysis

To better understand the research process that the students used and some common features of successful and unsuccessful Ethnographic Journals, each journal was read closely on two separate occasions. First, each journal was read to categorize responses. Through these readings, a student's ability to compare, synthesize,

Table 29-1. Descriptive Statistics

	N	Minimum	Maximum	Mean	Std. Deviation
Total Journal	24	50	80	72.54	8.782
Secondary Research	24	12	20	18.13	2.643
Evaluation Secondary	24	12	20	18.46	2.431
Valid N	24				

Table 29-2. Correlations

		Secondary Research Quality	Evaluation Secondary Source	Ethnographic Method	Ethnographic Content
Secondary Quality	Pearson	1	.843**	.709**	.778**
	Sig. (2-tailed)	.	.000	.000	.000
	N	24	24	24	24
Evaluation Secondary Sources	Pearson	.843**	1	.809**	.776**
	Sig. (2-tailed)	.000	.	.000	.000
	N	24	24	24	24
Ethnographic Methods	Pearson	.709**	.809**	1	.733**
	Sig. (2-tailed)	.000	.000	.	.000
	N	24	24	24	24
Ethnographic Content	Pearson	.778**	.776**	.733**	1
	Sig. (2-tailed)	.000	.000	.000	.
	N	24	24	24	24

**. Correlation is significant at the 0.01 level (2-tailed).

and draw on information gathered from various secondary sources when interacting with his or her primary sources and individuals from the group she or she is studying, were evident in each journal but varied to a significant degree. These two categories correspond directly with standard 3 performance indicators 3, 4, and 7.[1]

To investigate this third variable further, each journal was coded numerically on a twenty-point scale the degree to which each student preformed within the categories mentioned above. The twenty-point scale and coding rubric were used to correspond with the scale used in grading the journals.

Using a Pearson Correlation Coefficient, the results (shown in table 29-3) of this analysis were then compared to each student's outcomes in ethnographic content, ethnographic methods, and total journal score. This analysis indicates that a student's ability to compare, synthesize, and draw conclusions correlates significantly with ethnographic content, methods, and total journal score. As stated before, the small number of subjects in the set greatly affects the validity of this analysis.

Challenges

Looking back at this project, some of the biggest challenges were in the initial stages. Identifying teaching faculty with whom to collaborate and arranging a collaboration that accommodates the schedules of teaching and library faculty is not only the first, but perhaps the most difficult, hurdle. This was not a challenge because either party tends to be unwilling or disinterested but, rather, because the

Table 29-3. Correlations

		Standard 3	Ethnographic Content	Ethnographic Methods	Total Journal Grade
Standard 3	Pearson Correlation	1	.797	.733	.893
	Sig. (2-tailed)	.	.000	.000	.000
	N	24	24	24	24
Ethnographic Content	Pearson Correlation	.797	1	.733	.902
	Sig. (2-tailed)	.000	.	.000	.000
	N	24	24	24	24
Ethnographic Methods	Pearson Correlation	.733	.733	1	.883
	Sig. (2-tailed)	.000	.000	.	.000
	N	24	24	24	24
Total Journal Grade	Pearson Correlation	.893	.902	.883	1
	Sig. (2-tailed)	.000	.000	.000	.
	N	24	24	24	24

** Correlation is significant at the 0.01 level (2-tailed).

act of changing the assignments, the pedagogy, and the grading of an established course requires time for planning and forethought.

The next challenge is resisting the urge to assess too much. Again, this is something that can be addressed at the beginning of a project. Setting reasonable goals early in the project and keeping them is essential. When working with large assignments or multistaged projects, it is easy to become sidetracked by all the data that can potentially be gathered and assessed.

A final challenge and one that should also be addressed toward the beginning of a project is realizing when and how much work will be done at the different stages of the assessment. In this project, where qualitative methods were employed, it was relatively easy to develop an assignment and rubric for assessing future student outcomes compared to the time it takes to develop a test or survey instrument that will yield quantitative data. However, the process of grading, categorizing, and coding each journal was very time-consuming compared to the time it would take to tabulate scores from a qualitative tool.

With this said, one must assume that the life of a project and collaboration are not controllable factors and approach each new project with flexibility.

Conclusion

Although on a broad scale the results of the assessment will not lead to a revolutionary method of measuring student learning and didn't use techniques new to the social sciences or field of education, the act of working collaboratively with faculty colleagues to improve assignments, bringing information literacy instruction further into the classroom, and learning new methods of assessing information literacy has already begun to impact the library's instruction program in a positive manner. The faculty that worked on this project continue to have an interest in assessing information literacy outcomes in their courses. Additional faculty have also expressed interested in working with the library to improve assignments and pilot some of the methods learned in this grant project.

Note

1. Standard 3. The information-literate student evaluates information and its sources critically and incorporates selected information into his or her knowledge base and value system.

Performance Indicators:

3. The information-literate student synthesizes main ideas to construct new concepts.

4. The information-literate student compares new knowledge with prior knowledge to determine the value added, contradictions, or other unique characteristics of the information.

7. The information-literate student determines whether the initial query should be revised.

ANTH 352: Ethnographic Research Proposals

Name: ______________________________
Date: _______________

Topic Identification: Describe the topic/society that you have decided to conduct your ethnographic research on. Provide any background information you know about the topic/society, explain your interest in this topic/society, and why you selected it:

Preliminary Research: Cite the sources you have collected and provide a one- to two-sentence description of each with reference to how it might help you in your research. Give the source a rating 1 to 5, with 1 being the least useful and 5 being the most useful.

Hypothesis: Clearly state the theory upon which your research is based. You may articulate this as a statement or as a question.

Topic Identification / Hypothesis Formation: Describe the methods you used/the sources that you found most helpful in selecting a research topic and forming a hypothesis:

Ethnographic Subject(s): Name the person/people you will work with to gain more information about how this society conceptualizes gender and/or sexuality. Write down a few of the questions you will ask your subject(s) and explain how you plan to conduct participant-observation.

Questions / Concerns You Have about This Research Project:

Journal Evaluations

Journal Evaluation Criteria for First Review

Insights you have gained on the society/community you are conducting research on from readings, films, lectures, etc.

Insights you have gained on conceptions of gender/gender roles among those people.

Your assessment of the relevancy of the articles and books you have collected so far.

Your comparative analysis of the sources.

Questions generated by the sources that you would like to ask your subject(s).

Clarity of writing.

Frequency of writing. (at least 4 substantial entries per week)

Journal Evaluation Criteria for Second Review (Feb. 13th–April 3rd)

Name: ______________________________

1. Methodology you are using to conduct your ethnographic interviews (contact interview notes, informed consent for each subject, etc.):

2. Quality of your notes on what you learned from your ethnographic subjects:

3. Insights you have gained on the society/community you are focusing on by conducting ethnographic interviews:

4. Insights you have gained on conceptions of gender/gender roles among those people by conducting ethnographic interviews.

5. Assessment of the questions you asked your ethnographic subjects:

6. Assessment of the follow-up questions you would like to ask your subjects:

7. Your comparative analysis of the sources (your subject, secondary sources).

8. Clarity of writing.

9. Frequency of writing. (at least 4 substantial entries per week)

10. Overall assessment of how your ethnographic research is coming along:

Journal Evaluation Criteria for Final Review (April 4th–April 18th)

Name: ____________________________________

1. The quality of your reflections on the methodology you used to conduct your ethnographic interviews (contact interview notes, informed consent for each subject, how you negotiated your interviews, how contact meetings shaped your understanding of the subjects, changes you made based on the contact interview):

2. The extensiveness of your notes on what you learned from your ethnographic subjects in follow-up interviews with them:

3. Summaries of insights you have gained on the society/community you are focusing on:

4. Summaries of insights you have gained on conceptions of gender/gender roles among the people you are studying:

5. Assessment of the follow-up questions you asked your ethnographic subjects:

6. Your comparative analysis of the sources (your subject, secondary sources).

7. Clarity of writing.

8. Frequency of writing. (at least 4 substantial entries per week)

9. Your general conclusions about gender/gender roles in the society you studied:

10. Your assessment of how keeping an ethnographic journal fit into the course and enhanced your understanding of anthropology/gender in cross-cultural perspective:

11. Overall quality of the ethnographic research you have conducted this semester:

Ethnographic Journal Grading Criteria

Ethnographic Journal Grading Criteria (80 points):

Secondary Research (20 points): My assessment of the quality of the sources you have referred to throughout your research to gain insight on the community you are studying.

Evaluation of Secondary Sources (20 points): Your ability to make qualitative assessment of the sources based on relevance to your topic, perspective on your topic, date of publication (is the source still relevant in a contemporary context). This is evaluated by your ability to rate your sources based on the above criteria and your discussion of the aspects of various sources that you found to be most pertinent to your research and why.

Ethnographic Methods (20 points): The way in which you go about your ethnographic research will be considered (e.g., how you initially select the society under study, how you approach your subject(s) about your research, the decision-making process that led you to use specific secondary sources, the techniques you use to collect primary ethnographic data [interviewing and participant-observation], how you build rapport with your subject(s), how you address issues of confidentiality and ethics in the field).

Ethnographic Content (20 points): The quality of the personal observations you have made while conducting the research will be considered (e.g., how articulately you analyze the information you have gathered from secondary source materials [full citations of which are required throughout the journal], how you use secondary sources to verify or refute what you learn through primary research [e.g., how you compare what you are reading with what you are learning from your personal interactions with members of the society under study], how well you describe the knowledge you have gained by interacting with your subjects, how well you document questions and ideas for future interviews).

Other Considerations:

Clarity of Writing/Data Presentation: The articulateness/neatness of your journal with be considered (e.g., is the writing legible, is it adequately descriptive, does the journal follow the guidelines, is the data presented creatively [does it include another way of presenting data other than prose, for example, drawings]).

Frequency: Do journal entries demonstrate continuous engagement in secondary and primary research (e.g., persistent collection and evaluation of secondary source materials, persistent collection and evaluation of primary data [interviews, participant-observations]). The date of all journal entries must be recorded for full credit.

Appendix 1: INFORMATION LITERACY COMPETENCY STANDARDS FOR HIGHER EDUCATION

These standards were reviewed by the ACRL Standards Committee and approved by the Board of Directors of the Association of College and Research Libraries (ACRL) on January 18, 2000, at the Midwinter Meeting of the American Library Association in San Antonio, Texas.

Introduction

Information Literacy Defined

Information literacy is a set of abilities requiring individuals to "recognize when information is needed and have the ability to locate, evaluate, and use effectively the needed information."[1] Information literacy also is increasingly important in the contemporary environment of rapid technological change and proliferating information resources. Because of the escalating complexity of this environment, individuals are faced with diverse, abundant information choices--in their academic studies, in the workplace, and in their personal lives. Information is available through libraries, community resources, special interest organizations, media, and the Internet—and increasingly, information comes to individuals in unfiltered formats, raising questions about its authenticity, validity, and reliability. In addition, information is available through multiple media, including graphical, aural, and textual, and these pose new challenges for individuals in evaluating and understanding it. The uncertain quality and expanding quantity of information pose large challenges for society. The sheer abundance of information will not in itself create a more informed citizenry without a complementary cluster of abilities necessary to use information effectively.

Information literacy forms the basis for lifelong learning. It is common to all disciplines, to all learning environments, and to all levels of education. It enables learners to master content and extend their investigations, become more self-directed, and assume greater control over their own learning. An information literate individual is able to:

- Determine the extent of information needed
- Access the needed information effectively and efficiently
- Evaluate information and its sources critically
- Incorporate selected information into one's knowledge base
- Use information effectively to accomplish a specific purpose
- Understand the economic, legal, and social issues surrounding the use of information, and access and use information ethically and legally

Information Literacy and Information Technology

Information literacy is related to information technology skills, but has broader implications for the individual, the educational system, and for society. Information technology skills enable an individual to use computers, software applications, databases, and other technologies to achieve a wide variety of academic, work-related, and personal goals. Information literate individuals necessarily develop some technology skills.

Information literacy, while showing significant overlap with information technology skills, is a distinct and broader area of competence. Increasingly, information technology skills are interwoven with, and support, information literacy. A 1999 report from the National Research Council promotes the concept of "fluency" with information technology and delineates several distinctions useful in understanding relationships among information literacy, computer literacy, and broader technological competence. The report notes that "computer literacy" is concerned with rote learning of specific hardware and software applications, while "fluency with technology" focuses on understanding the underlying concepts of technology and applying problem-solving and critical thinking to using technology. The report also discusses differences between information technology fluency and information literacy as it is understood in K–12 and higher education. Among these are information literacy's focus on content, communication, analysis, information searching, and evaluation; whereas information technology "fluency" focuses on a deep understanding of technology and graduated, increasingly skilled use of it.[2]

"Fluency" with information technology may require more intellectual abilities than the rote learning of software and hardware associated with "computer literacy", but the focus is still on the technology itself. Information literacy, on the other hand, is an intellectual framework for understanding, finding, evaluating, and using information--activities which may be accomplished in part by fluency with information technology, in part by sound investigative methods, but most important, through critical discernment and reasoning. Information literacy initiates, sustains, and extends lifelong learning through abilities which may use technologies but are ultimately independent of them.

Information Literacy and Higher Education

Developing lifelong learners is central to the mission of higher education institutions. By ensuring that individuals have the intellectual abilities of reasoning and critical thinking, and by helping them construct a framework for learning how to learn, colleges and universities provide the foundation for continued growth throughout their careers, as well as in their roles as informed citizens and members of communities. Information literacy is a key component of, and contributor to, lifelong learning. Information literacy competency extends learning beyond formal classroom settings and provides practice with self-directed investigations as individuals move into internships, first professional positions, and increasing responsibilities in all arenas of life. Because information literacy augments students' competency with evaluating, managing, and using information, it is now considered by several regional and discipline-based accreditation associations as a key outcome for college students.[3]

For students not on traditional campuses, information resources are often available through networks and other channels, and distributed learning technologies permit teaching and learning to occur when the teacher and the student are not in the same place at the same time. The challenge for those promoting information literacy in distance education courses is to develop a comparable range of experiences in learning about information resources as are offered on traditional campuses. Information literacy competencies for distance learning students should be comparable to those for "on campus" students.

Incorporating information literacy across curricula, in all programs and services, and throughout the administrative life of the university, requires the collaborative efforts of faculty, librarians, and administrators. Through lectures and by leading discussions, faculty establish the context for learning. Faculty also inspire students to explore the unknown, offer guidance on how best to fulfill information needs, and monitor students' progress. Academic librarians coordinate the evaluation and selection of intellectual resources for programs and services; organize, and maintain collections and many points of access to information; and provide instruction to students and faculty who seek information. Administrators create opportunities for collaboration and staff development among faculty, librarians, and other professionals who initiate information literacy programs, lead in planning and budgeting for those programs, and provide ongoing resources to sustain them.

Information Literacy and Pedagogy

The Boyer Commission Report, Reinventing Undergraduate Education, recommends strategies that require the student to engage actively in "framing of a significant question or set of questions, the research or creative exploration to find answers, and the communications skills to convey the results..."[4] Courses structured in such a way create student-centered learning environments where inquiry is the norm, problem solving becomes the focus, and thinking critically is part of the process. Such learning environments require information literacy competencies.

Gaining skills in information literacy multiplies the opportunities for students' self-directed learning, as they become engaged in using a wide variety of information sources to expand their knowledge, ask informed questions, and sharpen their critical thinking for still further self-directed learning. Achieving competency in information literacy requires an understanding that this cluster of abilities is not extraneous to the curriculum but is woven into the curriculum's content, structure, and sequence. This curricular integration also affords many possibilities for furthering the influence and impact of such student-centered teaching methods as problem-based learning, evidence-based learning, and inquiry learning. Guided by faculty and others in problem-based approaches, students reason about course content at a deeper level than is possible through the exclusive use of lectures and textbooks. To take fullest advantage of problem-based learning, students must often use thinking skills requiring them to become skilled users of information sources in many locations and formats, thereby increasing their responsibility for their own learning.

To obtain the information they seek for their investigations, individuals have many options. One is to utilize an information retrieval system, such as may be found in a library or in databases accessible by computer from any location. Another option is to select an appropriate investigative method for observing phenomena directly. For example, physicians, archaeologists, and astronomers frequently depend upon physical examination to detect the presence of particular phenomena. In addition, mathematicians, chemists, and physicists often utilize technologies such as statistical software or simulators to create artificial conditions in which to observe and analyze the interaction of phenomena. As students progress through their undergraduate years and graduate programs, they need to have repeated opportunities for seeking, evaluating, and managing information gathered from multiple sources and discipline-specific research methods.

Use of the Standards

Information Literacy Competency Standards for Higher Education provides a framework for assessing the information literate individual. It also extends the work of the American Association of School Librarians Task Force on Information Literacy Standards, thereby providing higher education an opportunity to articulate its information literacy competencies with those of K–12 so that a continuum of expectations develops for students at all levels. The competencies presented here outline the process by which faculty, librarians and others pinpoint specific indicators that identify a student as information literate.

Students also will find the competencies useful, because they provide students with a framework for gaining control over how they interact with information in their environment. It will help to sensitize them to the need to develop a metacognitive approach to learning, making them conscious of the explicit actions required for gathering, analyzing, and using information. All students are expected to demonstrate all of the competencies described in this document, but not everyone will demonstrate them to the same level of proficiency or at the same speed.

Furthermore, some disciplines may place greater emphasis on the mastery of competencies at certain points in the process, and therefore certain competencies would receive greater weight than others in any rubric for measurement. Many of the competencies are likely to be performed recursively, in that the reflective and evaluative aspects included within each standard will require the student to return to an earlier point in the process, revise the information-seeking approach, and repeat the same steps.

To implement the standards fully, an institution should first review its mission and educational goals to determine how information literacy would improve learning and enhance the institution's effectiveness. To facilitate acceptance of the concept, faculty and staff development is also crucial.

Information Literacy and Assessment

In the following competencies, there are five standards and twenty-two performance indicators. The standards focus upon the needs of students in higher education at all levels. The standards also list a range of outcomes for assessing student progress toward information literacy. These outcomes serve as guidelines for faculty, librarians, and others in developing local methods for measuring student learning in the context of an institution's unique mission. In addition to assessing all students' basic information literacy skills, faculty and librarians should also work together to develop assessment instruments and strategies in the context of particular disciplines, as information literacy manifests itself in the specific understanding of the knowledge creation, scholarly activity, and publication processes found in those disciplines.

In implementing these standards, institutions need to recognize that different levels of thinking skills are associated with various learning outcomes—and therefore different instruments or methods are essential to assess those outcomes. For example, both "higher order" and "lower order" thinking skills, based on Bloom's

Taxonomy of Educational Objectives, are evident throughout the outcomes detailed in this document. It is strongly suggested that assessment methods appropriate to the thinking skills associated with each outcome be identified as an integral part of the institution's implementation plan.

For example, the following outcomes illustrate "higher order" and "lower order" thinking skills:

"Lower Order" thinking skill:

Outcome 2.2.2. Identifies keywords, synonyms, and related terms for the information needed.

"Higher Order" thinking skill:

Outcome 3.3.2. Extends initial synthesis, when possible, to a higher level of abstraction to construct new hypotheses that may require additional information.

Faculty, librarians, and others will find that discussing assessment methods collaboratively is a very productive exercise in planning a systematic, comprehensive information literacy program. This assessment program should reach all students, pinpoint areas for further program development, and consolidate learning goals already achieved. It also should make explicit to the institution's constituencies how information literacy contributes to producing educated students and citizens.

Notes

1. American Library Association. Presidential Committee on Information Literacy. Final Report.(Chicago: American Library Association, 1989.)

2. National Research Council.Commission on Physical Sciences, Mathematics, and Applications. Committee on Information Technology Literacy, Computer Science and Telecommunications Board. Being Fluent with Information Technology. Publication. (Washington, D.C.: National Academy Press, 1999) http://www.nap.edu/catalog/6482.html

3. Several key accrediting agencies concerned with information literacy are: The Middle States Commission on Higher Education (MSCHE), the Western Association of Schools and College (WASC), and the Southern Association of Colleges and Schools (SACS).

4. Boyer Commission on Educating Undergraduates in the Research University. Reinventing Undergraduate Education: A Blueprint for America's Research Universities. http://notes.cc.sunysb.edu/Pres/boyer.nsf/

Standards, Performance Indicators, and Outcomes

Standard One

The information literate student determines the nature and extent of the information needed.

Performance Indicators:

1.The information literate student defines and articulates the need for information.

Outcomes include:

a. Confers with instructors and participates in class discussions, peer workgroups, and electronic discussions to identify a research topic, or other information need

b. Develops a thesis statement and formulates questions based on the information need

c. Explores general information sources to increase familiarity with the topic

d. Defines or modifies the information need to achieve a manageable focus

e. Identifies key concepts and terms that describe the information need

f. Recognizes that existing information can be combined with original thought, experimentation, and/or analysis to produce new information

2. The information literate student identifies a variety of types and formats of potential sources for information.

Outcomes include:

a. Knows how information is formally and informally produced, organized, and disseminated

b. Recognizes that knowledge can be organized into disciplines that influence the way information is accessed

c. Identifies the value and differences of potential resources in a variety of formats (e.g., multimedia, database, website, data set, audio/visual, book)

d. Identifies the purpose and audience of potential resources (e.g., popular vs. scholarly, current vs. historical)

e. Differentiates between primary and secondary sources, recognizing how their use and importance vary with each discipline

f. Realizes that information may need to be constructed with raw data from primary sources

3. The information literate student considers the costs and benefits of acquiring the needed information.

Outcomes include:

a. Determines the availability of needed information and makes decisions on broadening the information seeking process beyond local resources (e.g., interlibrary loan; using resources at ther locations; obtaining images, videos, text, or sound)

b. Considers the feasibility of acquiring a new language or skill (e.g., foreign or discipline-based) in order to gather needed information and to understand its context

c. Defines a realistic overall plan and timeline to acquire the needed information

4. The information literate student reevaluates the nature and extent of the information need.

Outcomes include:

a. Reviews the initial information need to clarify, revise, or refine the question

b. Describes criteria used to make information decisions and choices

Standard Two

The information literate student accesses needed information effectively and efficiently.

Performance Indicators:

1. The information literate student selects the most appropriate investigative methods or information retrieval systems for accessing the needed information.

Outcomes include:

a. Identifies appropriate investigative methods (e.g., laboratory experiment, simulation, fieldwork)

b. Investigates benefits and applicability of various investigative methods

c. Investigates the scope, content, and organization of information retrieval systems

d. Selects efficient and effective approaches for accessing the information needed from the investigative method or information retrieval system

2. The information literate student constructs and implements effectively-designed search strategies.

Outcomes include:

a. Develops a research plan appropriate to the investigative method

b. Identifies keywords, synonyms and related terms for the information needed

c. Selects controlled vocabulary specific to the discipline or information retrieval source

d. Constructs a search strategy using appropriate commands for the information retrieval system selected (e.g., Boolean operators, truncation, and proximity for search engines; internal organizers such as indexes for books)

e. Implements the search strategy in various information retrieval systems using different user interfaces and search engines, with different command languages, protocols, and search parameters

f. Implements the search using investigative protocols appropriate to the discipline

3. The information literate student retrieves information online or in person using a variety of methods.

Outcomes include:

a. Uses various search systems to retrieve information in a variety of formats

b. Uses various classification schemes and other systems (e.g., call number systems or indexes) to locate information resources within the library or to identify specific sites for physical exploration

c. Uses specialized online or in person services available at the institution to retrieve information needed (e.g., interlibrary loan/document delivery, professional associations, institutional research offices, community resources, experts and practitioners)

d. Uses surveys, letters, interviews, and other forms of inquiry to retrieve primary information

4. The information literate student refines the search strategy if necessary.

Outcomes include:

a. Assesses the quantity, quality, and relevance of the search results to determine whether alternative information retrieval systems or investigative methods should be utilized

b. Identifies gaps in the information retrieved and determines if the search strategy should be revised

c. Repeats the search using the revised strategy as necessary

5. The information literate student extracts, records, and manages the information and its sources.

Outcomes include:

a. Selects among various technologies the most appropriate one for the task of extracting the needed information (e.g., copy/paste software functions, photocopier, scanner, audio/visual equipment, or exploratory instruments)

b. Creates a system for organizing the information

c. Differentiates between the types of sources cited and understands the elements and correct syntax of a citation for a wide range of resources

d. Records all pertinent citation information for future reference

e. Uses various technologies to manage the information selected and organized

Standard Three

The information literate student evaluates information and its sources critically and incorporates selected information into his or her knowledge base and value system.

Performance Indicators:

1. The information literate student summarizes the main ideas to be extracted from the information gathered.

Outcomes include:

a. Reads the text and selects main ideas

b. Restates textual concepts in his/her own words and selects data accurately

c. Identifies verbatim material that can be then appropriately quoted

2. The information literate student articulates and applies initial criteria for evaluating both the information and its sources.

Outcomes include:

a. Examines and compares information from various sources in order to evaluate reliability, validity, accuracy, authority, timeliness, and point of view or bias

b. Analyzes the structure and logic of supporting arguments or methods

c. Recognizes prejudice, deception, or manipulation

d. Recognizes the cultural, physical, or other context within which the information was created and understands the impact of context on interpreting the information

3. The information literate student synthesizes main ideas to construct new concepts.

Outcomes include:

a. Recognizes interrelationships among concepts and combines them into potentially useful primary statements with supporting evidence

b. Extends initial synthesis, when possible, at a higher level of abstraction to construct new hypotheses that may require additional information

c. Utilizes computer and other technologies (e.g. spreadsheets, databases, multimedia, and audio or visual equipment) for studying the interaction of ideas and other phenomena

4. The information literate student compares new knowledge with prior knowledge to determine the value added, contradictions, or other unique characteristics of the information.

Outcomes include:

a. Determines whether information satisfies the research or other information need

b. Uses consciously selected criteria to determine whether the information contradicts or verifies information used from other sources

c. Draws conclusions based upon information gathered

d. Tests theories with discipline-appropriate techniques (e.g., simulators, experiments)

e. Determines probable accuracy by questioning the source of the data, the limitations of the information gathering tools or strategies, and the reasonableness of the conclusions

f. Integrates new information with previous information or knowledge
g. Selects information that provides evidence for the topic

5. The information literate student determines whether the new knowledge has an impact on the individual's value system and takes steps to reconcile differences.

Outcomes include:
a. Investigates differing viewpoints encountered in the literature
b. Determines whether to incorporate or reject viewpoints encountered

6. The information literate student validates understanding and interpretation of the information through discourse with other individuals, subject-area experts, and/or practitioners.

Outcomes include:
a. Participates in classroom and other discussions
b. Participates in class-sponsored electronic communication forums designed to encourage discourse on the topic (e.g., email, bulletin boards, chat rooms)
c. Seeks expert opinion through a variety of mechanisms (e.g., interviews, email, listservs)

7. The information literate student determines whether the initial query should be revised.

Outcomes include:
a. Determines if original information need has been satisfied or if additional information is needed
b. Reviews search strategy and incorporates additional concepts as necessary
c. Reviews information retrieval sources used and expands to include others as needed

Standard Four

The information literate student, individually or as a member of a group, uses information effectively to accomplish a specific purpose.

Performance Indicators:

1. The information literate student applies new and prior information to the planning and creation of a particular product or performance.

Outcomes include:
a. Organizes the content in a manner that supports the purposes and format of the product or performance (e.g. outlines, drafts, storyboards)
b. Articulates knowledge and skills transferred from prior experiences to planning and creating the product or performance
c. Integrates the new and prior information, including quotations and

paraphrasings, in a manner that supports the purposes of the product or performance

d. Manipulates digital text, images, and data, as needed, transferring them from their original locations and formats to a new context

2. The information literate student revises the development process for the product or performance.

Outcomes include:

a. Maintains a journal or log of activities related to the information seeking, evaluating, and communicating process

b. Reflects on past successes, failures, and alternative strategies

3. The information literate student communicates the product or performance effectively to others.

Outcomes include:

a. Chooses a communication medium and format that best supports the purposes of the product or performance and the intended audience

b. Uses a range of information technology applications in creating the product or performance

c. Incorporates principles of design and communication

d. Communicates clearly and with a style that supports the purposes of the intended audience

Standard Five

The information literate student understands many of the economic, legal, and social issues surrounding the use of information and accesses and uses information ethically and legally.

Performance Indicators:

1. The information literate student understands many of the ethical, legal and socioeconomic issues surrounding information and information technology.

Outcomes include:

a. Identifies and discusses issues related to privacy and security in both the print and electronic environments

b. Identifies and discusses issues related to free vs. fee-based access to information

c. Identifies and discusses issues related to censorship and freedom of speech

d. Demonstrates an understanding of intellectual property, copyright, and fair use of copyrighted material

2. The information literate student follows laws, regulations, institutional policies, and etiquette related to the access and use of information resources.

Outcomes include:

a. Participates in electronic discussions following accepted practices (e.g. "Netiquette")

b. Uses approved passwords and other forms of ID for access to information resources

c. Complies with institutional policies on access to information resources

d. Preserves the integrity of information resources, equipment, systems and facilities

e. Legally obtains, stores, and disseminates text, data, images, or sounds

f. Demonstrates an understanding of what constitutes plagiarism and does not represent work attributable to others as his/her own

g. Demonstrates an understanding of institutional policies related to human subjects research

3. The information literate student acknowledges the use of information sources in communicating the product or performance.

Outcomes include:

a. Selects an appropriate documentation style and uses it consistently to cite sources

b. Posts permission granted notices, as needed, for copyrighted material

About the Authors

Alison Armstrong is the head of training and educational services for university libraries at the University of Cincinnati (UC). She is responsible for a wide-range of instructional and management activities and has been actively involved with new initiatives related to the first year experience, student technology resources and information literacy. Prior to working at UC, she was co-chair of the Reference and Instruction Team at the University of Nevada Las Vegas. Her M.L.S. and B.A. (English) are from the University of Wisconsin-Madison. She is a recent past-president of ALA's Library Instruction Roundtable (LIRT). Her most recent presentation (May 2003) with her colleague Jane Carlin, was to the Academic Library Association of Ohio (ALAO), entitled "What's the Problem: Enriching Library Instruction Through Problem-Based Learning."

Elizabeth (Beth) Fuseler Avery is the director of library services at Western State College of Colorado. Before joining Western State she was library director at Lamar University, and head of sciences and technology at Colorado State University. She has developed and taught for-credit library instruction classes. She is the 1994 recipient of ALA, Association for Library Collections & Technical Services, Blackwell North American Scholarship Award with Joel Rutstein and Anna DeMiller for their article in *Advances in Librarianship*, "Ownership versus access: Shifting perspectives for Libraries." She holds an M.L.S. from Drexel University and a A.B. in education from the College of William and Mary. Her professional interests include bibliographic instruction, digital reference services, mentoring and staff development and training. With Terry Dahlin and Deborah Carver she edited *Staff Development: A Practical Guide*. 3rd ed. ALA Editions, 2001.

Michael Barrett is the chair of the Reference and Instructional Services Department, Oviatt Library; California State University, Northridge. He also serves as History and Sociology library specialist. He holds a bachelor's from the University of California, Los Angeles, and a masters in Library science from the University of Southern California.

Lori Buchanan is the instructional services librarian at Austin Peay State University in Clarksville, Tennessee, where she facilitates the Library's Instructional Services Team and assists with virtual and face-to-face reference. She received a B.A. in English from the University of North Carolina at Chapel Hill and a masters in library science from Indiana University, Bloomington. She participated in the ACRL Institute for Information Literacy Immersion 2000 Program, and was the 2002 recipient of Tennessee's James E. Ward Library Instruction Award. In 2002, she co-authored "Integrating Information Literacy into the Virtual University: A Course Model" which appeared in Teaching and Assessing Information Skills in the Twenty-first Century: A Global Perspective, *Library Trends* 51(2), edited by Hannelore Rader.

Barbara Burd is head of information literacy programs at Colgate University, Hamilton, New York. Before coming to Colgate, she served as the business librarian at Regent University, where she collaborated with business faculty for this project. She received her undergraduate degree from Pennsylvania State University, her M.L.S. from SUNY-Albany and her Ph.D. in Organizational Leadership from Regent University. Her research interests included information literacy and assessment, and work values and person-organization fit of librarians. She is a member of the advisory panel for ACRL's Characteristics of Best Practices of Information Literacy.

Bennett Cherry is assistant professor of organizational behavior and human resources at California State University, San Marcos. He received his Ph.D. in Management at the University of Arizona. He has an undergraduate degree in Industrial/Organizational Psychology and a Masters in Management. He has published extensively in the area of service relationships in business. He co-presented Reflections on collaboration: Learning outcomes and information literacy assessment in the business curriculum at the LOEX of the West 2002 Conference. He is faculty fellow of the CSUSM Teaching and Learning with Technology Roundtable. His affiliations include the Academy of Management.

Cynthia Comer is head of reference and instruction at the Oberlin College Library in Ohio. Over the past several years, she has been active in the library's various information literacy initiatives, including planning and teaching faculty workshops, working individually with faculty to incorporate information literacy into courses, collaborating with faculty who teach in the college's first year seminar program, and serving as a project team member for a consortially-developed information literacy web tutorial. She has been involved recently with the library's unique program to recruit undergraduate students from diverse backgrounds into librarianship, helping design and teach the curriculum as well as developing projects for student participants. Previously, she was Reference Librarian at Oberlin and at North Georgia College. She earned her B.A. and M.L.S. from Emory University in Atlanta, Georgia. Professional interests include collaboration in digital reference services, assessing student learning outcomes, and designing effective library orientation for new students.

Jennifer Dorner is humanities and social sciences librarian and assistant professor at Portland State University. Throughout her career, she has taught information skills to undergraduate and graduate students, faculty members, staff, K–12 teachers, and members of the community. Currently, she teaches in the Masters of Education Program at City University. Her work has appeared *Nurse Educator, Computers in Nursing, Reference Services Review*, and the *Journal of Academic Librarianship*. Formerly the editor of *Public Services Quarterly*, she is currently co-editor of *Research Strategies*. Jennifer received her M.L.S. from the University of Washington and is currently completing an M.A. in History from Ball State University.

Cathy Eckman is a reference librarian at Midlands Technical College (MTC) and manages the library's health sciences and law collections. She is currently working with faculty, department heads, and administrators to integrate information literacy instruction into the MTC Arts and Sciences Division curriculum. Before joining MTC in 1995, Cathy served as coordinator of library instruction at the University of South Carolina, Columbia. Cathy received a B.A. in anthropology and an M.L.S. from Indiana University, as well as a Graduate Study Certificate in women's studies from the University of South Carolina.

Janet Feldmann is associate librarian and director of library and media resources for Indiana University Purdue University Columbus. She holds an undergraduate degree from the University of Arizona and a masters degree in library science from the University of Denver. She has long been involved with distance education, serving as chair of several committees for the Distance Education Section of ACRL. Her current research is focused primarily on the integration of library instruction into the curriculum.

Ann Manning Fiegen is associate business and economics librarian at California State University, San Marcos. She has previously served in science and technical services positions in academic libraries. She received her M.L.S. from the University of Arizona and a B.A. in Political Science. Her research and publications are in the areas of information literacy in business, performance measures and process improvement. She is a member of RUSA/BRASS and served as one of the consultants on information literacy to ACRL.

Dana Franks is a reference and instruction librarian at Highline Community College in Des Moines, Washington. Dana received her M.S.L.S. from Columbia University and her B.A. from the University of Vermont. She is an alumnus of the Institute for Information Literacy's *Immersion* program. Since attending, she has led her department in developing a program of outcomes-based information literacy instruction at the college. Dana serves on her colleges Standards, Outcomes and Competencies Committee that, in the spring of 2003, adopted a campus-wide information literacy outcome which she drafted.

Marcia Freyman is information services librarian and coordinator of bibliographic instruction at Lexington Community College in Lexington, Kentucky. She has served in the area of public services at this institution for ten years. She received her undergraduate degree in Art History from SUNY Buffalo, her M.A. in Art History from the George Washington University, and her M.S.L.S. from the University of Kentucky.

Nancy Gauss, public services librarian, directs the library's information literacy program at Western State College and serves as the college archivist. She represents the library on Western's Academic Assessment Committee, the Center for Teaching Excellence advisory board, and the Faculty Senate. Like all Western librarians, she performs general reference duties and loves helping the undergraduate students succeed. Prior to coming to Western in 1990, she was Head of the Archives and Records Management Department at the Georgia Institute of Technology. She holds an M.A. in Librarianship and Information Management from the University of Denver and is a member of ALA, the Society of American Archivists, and the Academy of Certified Archivists.

Rebecca Gearhart is an assistant professor of anthropology at Illinois Wesleyan University. Dr. Gearhart received a Ph.D. in anthropology from the University of Florida in 1998. She takes an interdisciplinary approach (visual anthropology, history, and performance studies) to her research on non-western music and dance. Her area of interest is East Africa, where she has frequently lived over the past fifteen years, primarily among the Swahili people of the Kenya coast.

Bonnie Gratch-Lindauer is the coordinator of library instructional services for City College of San Francisco. She has held public services and administrative positions in all types of academic libraries in New York, Ohio and California since 1978. She has served on many ACRL committees, including the Information Literacy Standards Task Force that drafted the Information Literacy Competencies for Higher Education and currently is a member of ACRL's Institute for Information Literacy's Executive Committee. She has authored or co-authored numerous publications, and is the 1999 recipient of the K.G. Saur Award for the best *College & Research Libraries* article. She is currently a lead team member of the Bay Area Community Colleges Information Competency Assessment Project, a collaborative project to develop and field-test a two-part information literacy challenge out exam. Undergraduate degree from California State University-San Francisco; M.L.S. from Syracuse University and M.P.A. from State University of NY-Brockport.

Gregory Heald is the head of instructional services at the University of Northern Colorado. Additionally, as chair of the UNC Libraries Curriculum Committee, he coordinates the implementation of a campus wide "Information Literacy Framework". He has spoken at numerous state and national conventions on information literacy and student achievement. His research is currently focused on the relationship between information literacy and the retention of under-represented populations in higher education. He holds degrees from St. John's College and the University of Rhode Island.

Elizabeth O. Hutchins is a reference-instruction librarian at St. Olaf College and coordinator of library instruction. She has served as a teacher, librarian, and administrator in K-12 schools and institutions of higher education in the United States and Asia. She received her undergraduate degree from Wellesley College and holds master's degrees in divinity from Harvard University and in library science from Simmons College Graduate School of Library and Information Science. Professional areas of interest include teaching and learning styles, pedagogy, curriculum development, and faculty collaboration.

Andy Kivel is department chair and information technology librarian at Diablo Valley College. He has promoted information literacy issues as a member of the Counseling and Library Faculty Issues Committee of the Academic Senate for California Community Colleges and the Chancellor's Office Library and Learning Resource Programs Advisory Committee. Before joining the college faculty he was the research director at the DataCenter, a non-profit research center in Oakland, California. He received his undergraduate degree from the University of Massachusetts and his master's in library science from the University of California, Berkeley.

Ken Kempcke is a reference librarian and instruction coordinator at the Montana State University (MSU)-Bozeman Libraries. He holds an M.A. in American Studies from Purdue University, and an M.A. in Library and Information Science from Indiana University. Ken worked for three years as a social science reference librarian at Texas A&M University before joining the MSU faculty in 1997. His current research focuses on the teaching of information literacy, and he has contributed articles dealing with librarianship and the social sciences to several journals and reference publications.

Lorrie A. Knight is an associate professor at the University of the Pacific where she serves as reference/instruction librarian. Lorrie previously worked as a reference librarian at Connecticut College and Louisiana State University. She is the author of a number of publications, the most recent being "The Role of Assessment in Library User Education" in Reference Services Review. Lorrie has a B.A. in Political Science from the University of Texas, Austin, and an M.L.I.S. from Louisiana State University.

Barbara Kobritz received her M.L.S. from Syracuse University in 1995 and worked for two years as a trainer for NYSERNet before becoming the instructional services librarian for TC3. She is a graduate of the Institute for Information Literacy's Immersion Program and the recipient of the 2001 Ebsco Community College Learning Resources Achievement Award for Program Development for her faculty training workshop, "Detectives in the Classroom." In 2001 she also received the State University of New York Chancellor's/Trustees' Award for Excellence in Librarianship.

Patrick McCarthy holds the position of coordinator of instruction at Colorado State University Libraries. He has developed and delivered ACRL Information Literacy Competency Standards courses for graduate and undergraduate instruction. In addition, he has designed methods to assess information literacy competency at both the secondary and higher education levels. He has a master's degree in library science from the University of Wisconsin Milwaukee and is in the process of completing a doctorate at Colorado State University.

Anita Ondrusek has been a librarian and media specialist in settings serving children, health professionals, and college students. She currently is the science/reference librarian at Hunter College, City University of New York. She received her undergraduate degree from Millersville University, holds master's degrees in education from Elmira College and in library and information science from Pratt Institute, and received her Ph.D. in instructional systems from the Pennsylvania State College. Her research interests center upon end-user learning and behavior.

Robert Schroeder is a reference librarian at Spokane Falls Community College in Washington. He has also worked as a reference librarian in a corporate library and at the University of Detroit Mercy. He received his undergraduate degree from Oakland University in Rochester Michigan, a master's degree in accounting from Walsh College in Troy Michigan, and his M.L.I.S. from Wayne State University in Detroit. He is co-author of *Internet Research–Illustrated* (2002) a Thomson Course Technology publication.

Risë L. Smith is public services librarian/professor at Karl E. Mundt Library, Dakota State University in Madison, South Dakota. Her responsibilities include: teaching information literacy; providing reference services; designing, creating content, and managing development of the library's web pages; and supervising circulation, interlibrary loan and media services. She holds master's degrees in anthropology from the University of Michigan and in library science from San Jose State University. Risë attended Track II of Immersion '00, the second Institute for Information Literacy Immersion Program. She completed her third year on the Best Practices Advisory Panel of the ACRL Institute for Information Literacy in 2003.

Gabriela Sonntag is the coordinator for the Information Literacy Program at the California State University in San Marcos (CSUSM). She received her undergraduate degree from the University of Arizona and holds an M.L.S. from the University of Texas at Austin. She participated in the California State University information competency assessment project, was the leader of a team of CSUSM librarians serving as Consultants for Information Literacy for the Association of College and Research Libraries, and was the project manager for the ACRL/IMLS Assessing Student Learning Outcomes grant.

Ann Viles is coordinator of reference and instruction at Appalachian State University in Boone, North Carolina. Before coming to Appalachian, she served as music librarian at the Curtis Institute of Music, the University of Tennessee, and the University of Memphis. She received her undergraduate degree and a master's degree in music from the University of Tennessee. She also holds a Ph.D. in musicology from Bryn Mawr College and an M.L.S. from the University of North Carolina, Chapel Hill. She was the editor of "Fast Facts" in *C&RL News* from June 2000 to July 2003.

Marjorie Warmkessel, coordinator of public services at Millersville University of Pennsylvania, is responsible for coordinating the library instruction program and for providing collection development and library instruction for academic programs in the humanities. She is also director of the university's Center for Academic Excellence. She received a B.A. in classics from Goucher College, an M.S. in L.S. from the University of North Carolina at Chapel Hill, and an M.A. and Ph.D. in Comparative Literature from Rutgers University.

Clay Williams is currently coordinator of library instruction at Hunter College. Most recently, he was in the same position at Ferris State University in Michigan. He holds a B.A. in classics from Grinnell College, an M.A. in history from University of Idaho, and an M.S. in library and information science from University of Illinois, Urbana-Champaign. He is currently a member-at-large for the ACRL

Instruction Section. He is author of "The Guide for Colored Travelers: A Reflection of the Urban League," *Journal of American & Comparative Cultures*, fall, 2001, and recently co-authored an article with Madeline Ford on library instruction in sociology that was published in *Public Services Quarterly*.

Steve Witt is an assistant professor and information services librarian at Illinois Wesleyan University's Ames Library, where he is currently coordinating the campus information literacy program and serving as liaison to the psychology, mathematics, and computer science departments. He has taught and worked professionally as a librarian for the past eight years in corporate and academic positions in the U.S. and Japan. Professor Witt earned an M.S. in library and information science from the university and holds B.A. degrees from the University of Illinois and Eastern Illinois University.